CAMDEN COUNTY LIBRARY
203 LAUREL ROAD
VOORHEES, NJ 08043

0500000707377 3

D0885209

DAREDEVIL BY MARK WAID VOL. 6. Contains material originally published in magazine form as DAREDEVIL #28-30 and INDESTRUCTIBLE HULK #9-10. First printing 2014. ISBN# 978-0-7851-6679-5. Published by MARVEL WORLDWIDE, INC., a subsidiary of MARVEL ENTERTAINMENT, LLC. OFFICE OF PUBLICATION: 135 West 50th Street, New York, NY 10020. Copyright © 2013 and 2014 Marvel Characters, Inc. All rights reserved. All characters featured in this issue and the distinctive names and likenesses thereof, and all related indicia are trademarks of Marvel Characters, Inc. No similarity between any of the names, characters, persons, and/or institutions in this magazine with those of any living or dead person or institution is intended, and any such similarity which may exist is purely coincidental. **Printed in the U.S.A.** ALAN FINE, EVP - Office of the President, Marvel Worldwide, Inc. and EVP & CMO Marvel Characters B.V.; DAN BUCKLEY, Publisher & President - Print, Animation & Digital Divisions; JOE QUESADA, Chief Creative Officer; TOM BREVOORT, SVP of Publishing; DAVID BOGART, SVP of Operations & Procurement, Publishing; C.B. CEBULSKI, SVP of Creator & Content Development; DAVID GABRIEL, SVP Print, Sales & Marketing; JIM O'KEEFE, VP of Operations & Logistics; DAN CARR, Executive Director of Publishing Technology; SUSAN CRESPI, Editorial Operations Manager; ALEX MORALES, Publishing Operations Manager; STAN LEE, Chairman Emeritus. For information regarding advertising in Marvel Comics or on Marvel.com, please contact Niza Disla, Director of Marvel Partnerships, at ndisla@marvel.com. For Marvel subscription inquiries, please call 800-217-9158. **Manufactured between 6/27/2014 and 8/4/2014 by R.R. DONNELLEY, INC., SALEM, VA, USA.**

10 9 8 7 6 5 4 3 2 1

SEP 2 5 2014

WRITER
MARK WAID

DAREDEVIL #28-29
PENCILER & COLORIST
JAVIER RODRIGUEZ
INKER
ALVARO LOPEZ

DAREDEVIL #30
ARTIST
CHRIS SAMNEE
COLOR ARTIST
JAVIER RODRIGUEZ

LETTERER
VC'S JOE CARAMAGNA
COVER ARTISTS
CHRIS SAMNEE & **JAVIER RODRIGUEZ**
ASSISTANT EDITOR
ELLIE PYLE
EDITOR
STEPHEN WACKER
SPECIAL THANKS TO **TOM PEYER**

INDESTRUCTIBLE HULK #9-10
ARTIST
MATTEO SCALERA
COLOR ARTIST
VAL STAPLES

LETTERER
CHRIS ELIOPOULOS
COVER ARTIST
PAOLO RIVERA
ASSISTANT EDITOR
JON MOISAN
EDITOR
MARK PANICCIA

COLLECTION EDITOR & DESIGN *CORY LEVINE*
ASSISTANT EDITOR *SARAH BRUNSTAD*
ASSOCIATE MANAGING EDITOR *ALEX STARBUCK*
EDITORS, SPECIAL PROJECTS *JENNIFER GRÜNWALD* & *MARK D. BEAZLEY*
SENIOR EDITOR, SPECIAL PROJECTS *JEFF YOUNGQUIST*
SVP PRINT, SALES & MARKETING *DAVID GABRIEL*

EDITOR IN CHIEF *AXEL ALONSO*
CHIEF CREATIVE OFFICER *JOE QUESADA*
PUBLISHER *DAN BUCKLEY*
EXECUTIVE PRODUCER *ALAN FINE*

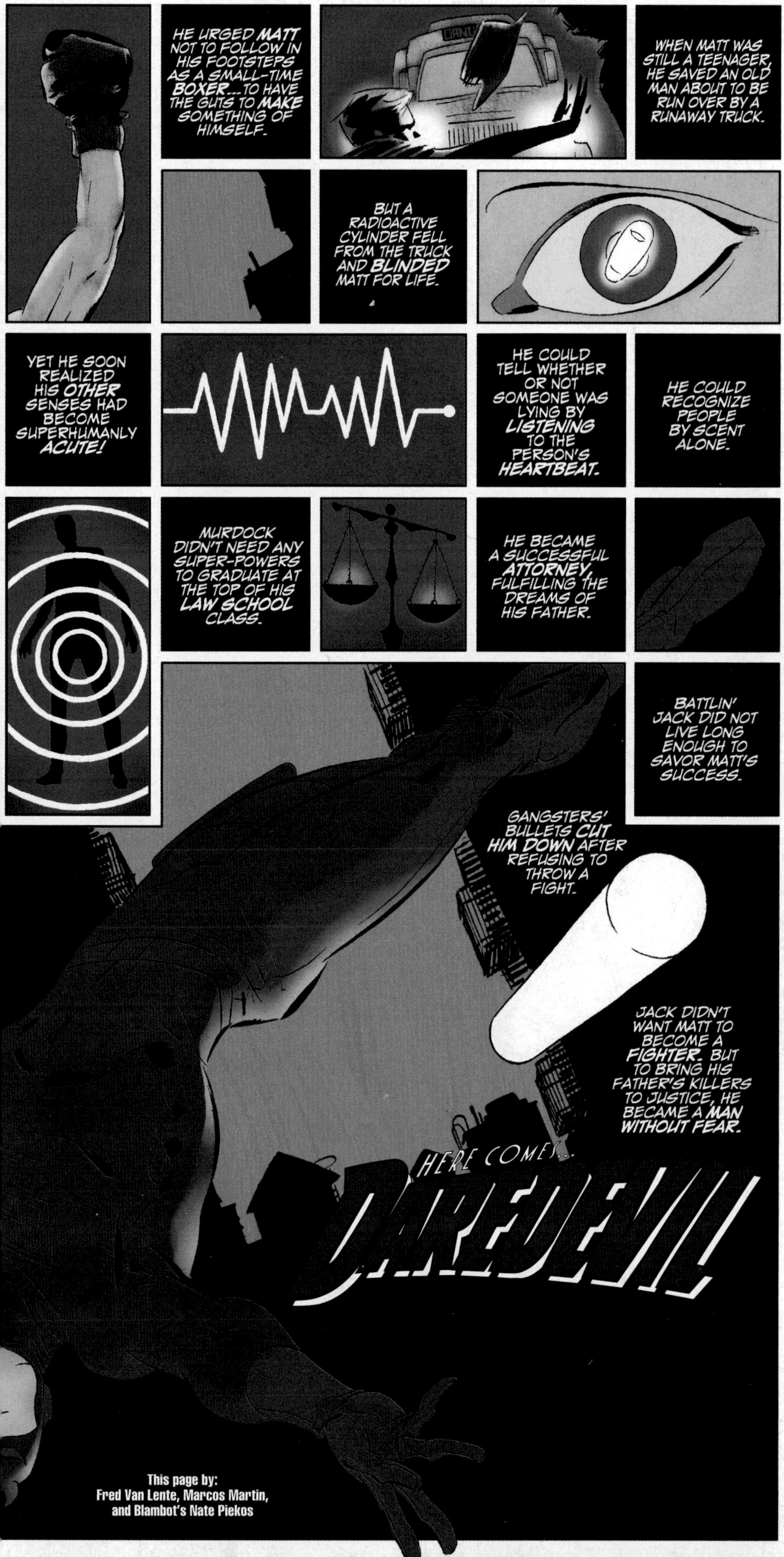

HE URGED MATT NOT TO FOLLOW IN HIS FOOTSTEPS AS A SMALL-TIME BOXER... TO HAVE THE GUTS TO MAKE SOMETHING OF HIMSELF.
WHEN MATT WAS STILL A TEENAGER, HE SAVED AN OLD MAN ABOUT TO BE RUN OVER BY A RUNAWAY TRUCK.
BUT A RADIOACTIVE CYLINDER FELL FROM THE TRUCK AND BLINDED MATT FOR LIFE.
YET HE SOON REALIZED HIS OTHER SENSES HAD BECOME SUPERHUMANLY ACUTE!
HE COULD TELL WHETHER OR NOT SOMEONE WAS LYING BY LISTENING TO THE PERSON'S HEARTBEAT.
HE COULD RECOGNIZE PEOPLE BY SCENT ALONE.
MURDOCK DIDN'T NEED ANY SUPER-POWERS TO GRADUATE AT THE TOP OF HIS LAW SCHOOL CLASS.
HE BECAME A SUCCESSFUL ATTORNEY, FULFILLING THE DREAMS OF HIS FATHER.
BATTLIN' JACK DID NOT LIVE LONG ENOUGH TO SAVOR MATT'S SUCCESS.
GANGSTERS' BULLETS CUT HIM DOWN AFTER REFUSING TO THROW A FIGHT.
JACK DIDN'T WANT MATT TO BECOME A FIGHTER. BUT TO BRING HIS FATHER'S KILLERS TO JUSTICE, HE BECAME A MAN WITHOUT FEAR.
HERE COMES...
DAREDEVIL!

This page by:
Fred Van Lente, Marcos Martin,
and Blambot's Nate Piekos

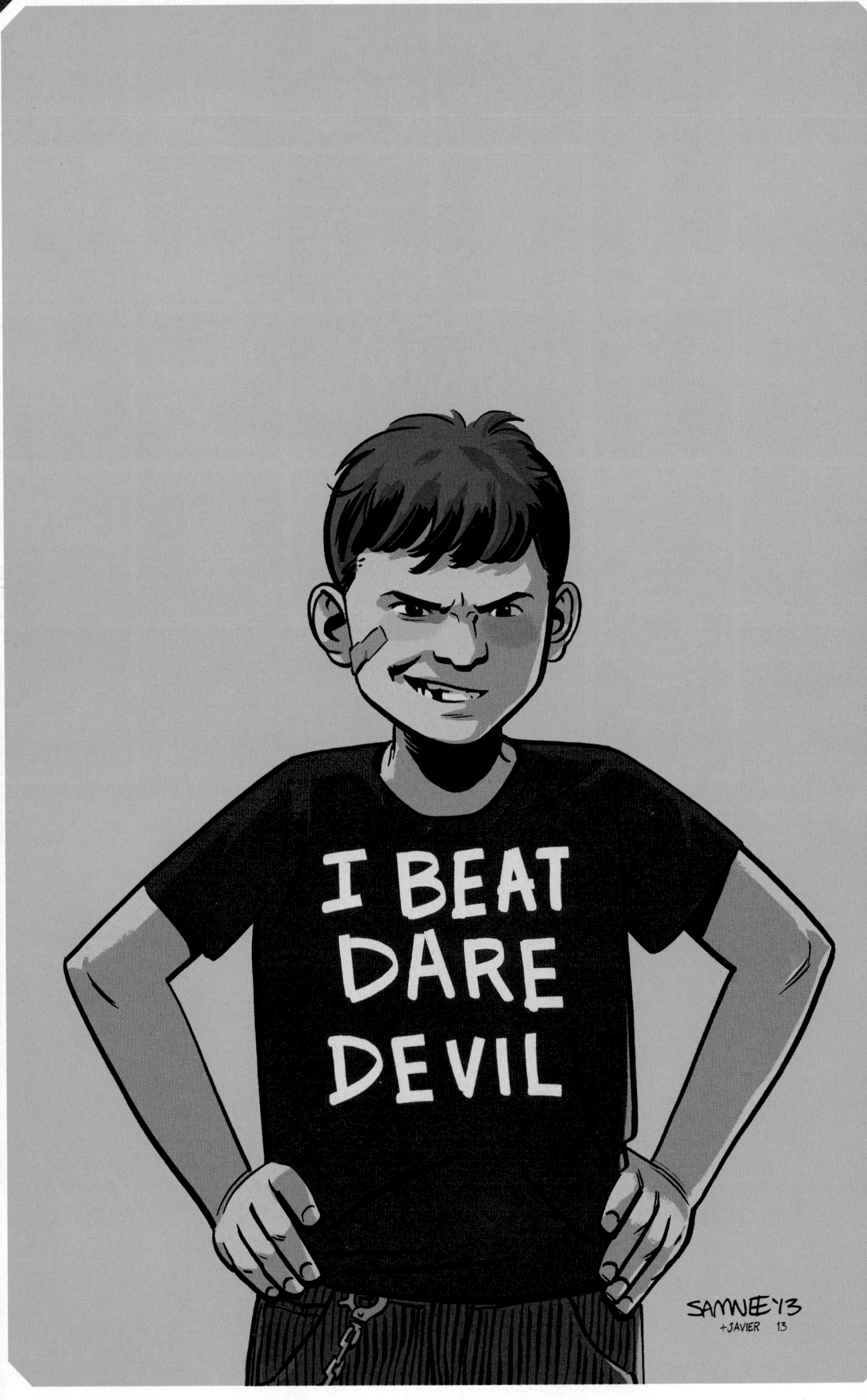
I BEAT DARE DEVIL
SAMNEE '13
+JAVIER 13

DAREDEVIL #28

INAL

DAILY BUGLE

NEW YORK'S FINEST DAILY NEWSPAPER

SINCE 1897
$1.00 (in NYC)
$1.50 (outside city)

ISIDE: SPIDER-SLAYER TO BE EXECUTED ABOARD THE RAFT! WHERE ARE THE FANTASTIC FOUR? NEW NOVA! NEW WARRIOR?

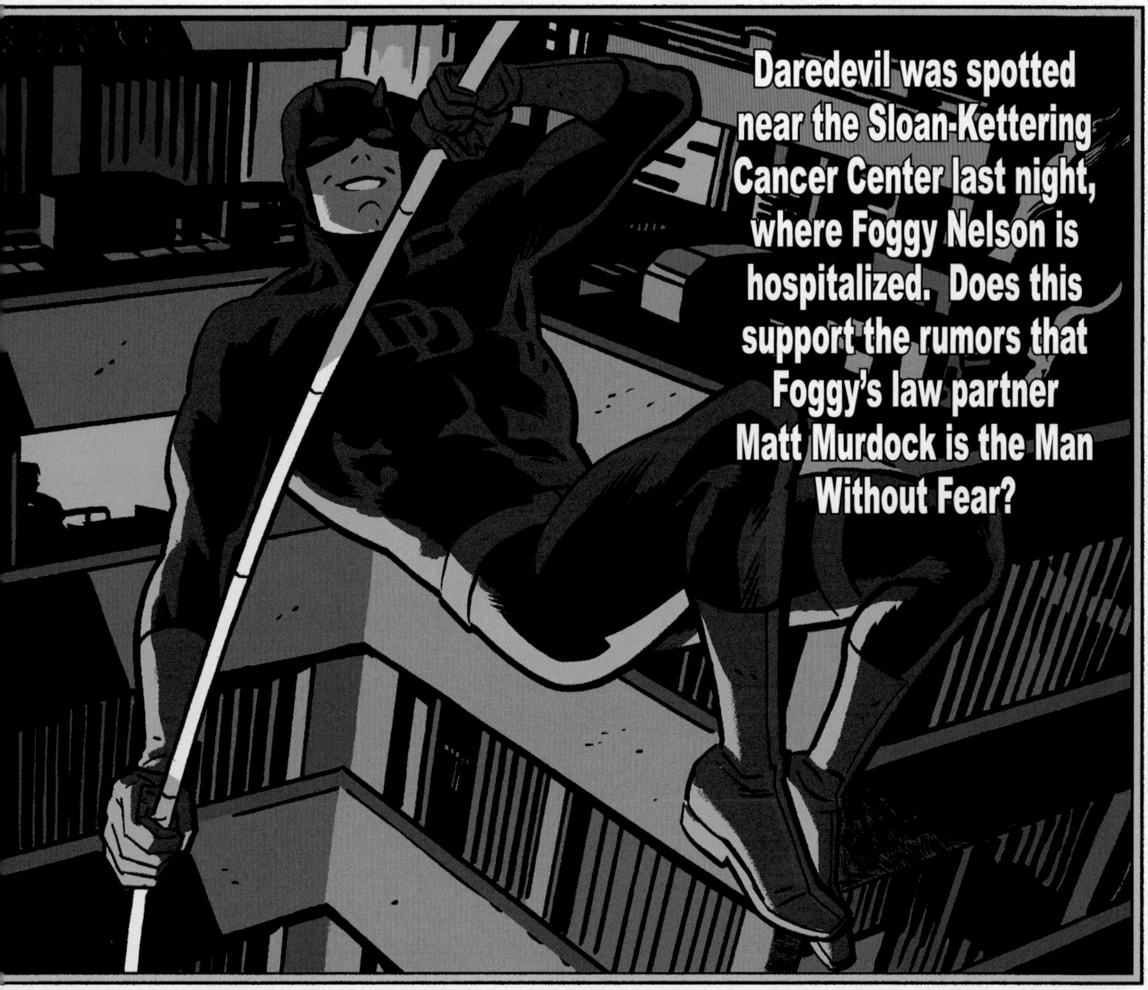
Daredevil was spotted near the Sloan-Kettering Cancer Center last night, where Foggy Nelson is hospitalized. Does this support the rumors that Foggy's law partner Matt Murdock is the Man Without Fear?

HELP WANTED

he Law Firm of Nelson and Murdock seeks an experienced trial lawyer to emporarily handle Mr. Nelson's caseload while he is out for treatment. Min. 5 Years xperience required. Public defense background a plus. Must have excellent and erifiable references. Those interested in working with Daredevil need not apply.

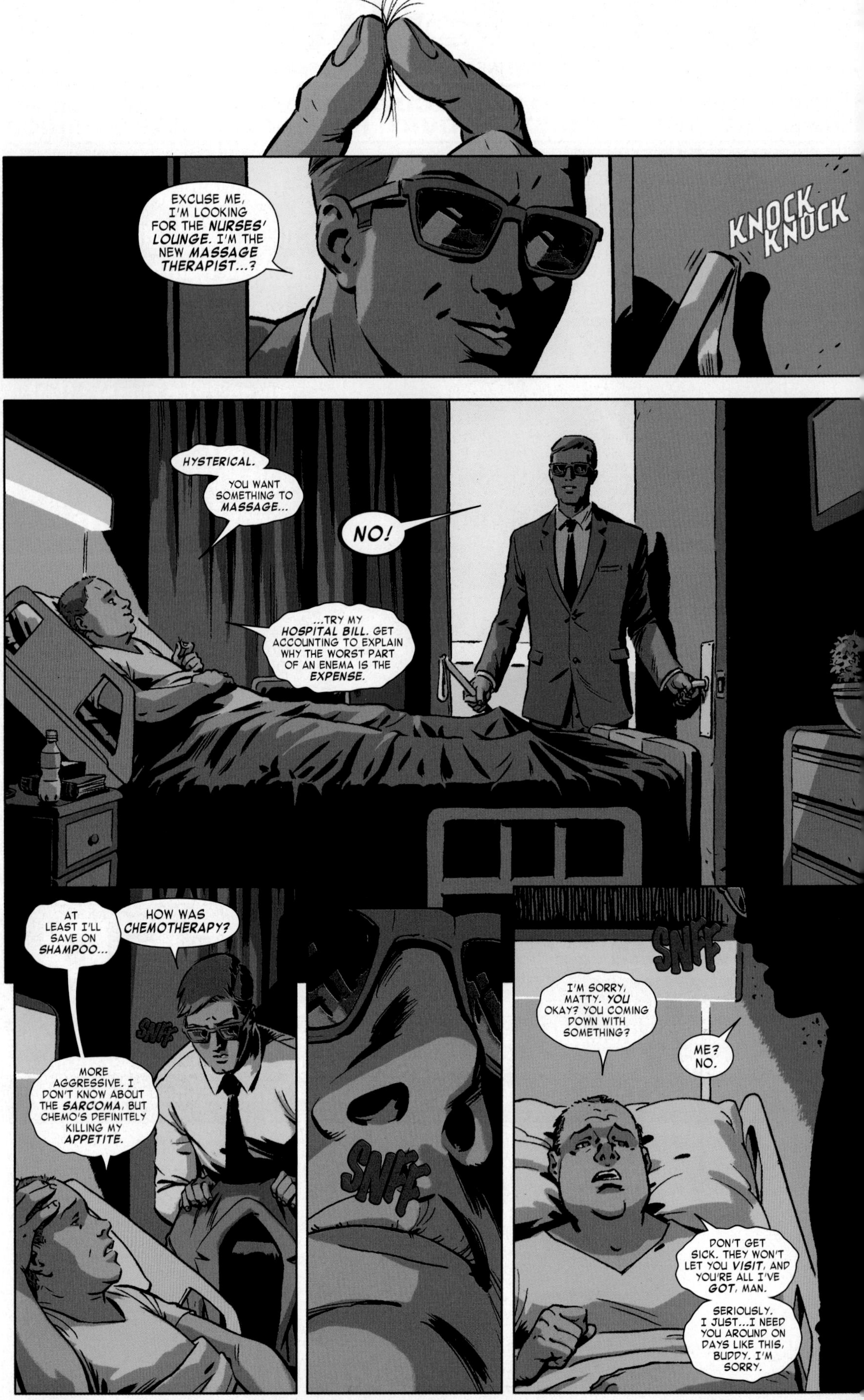

EXCUSE ME, I'M LOOKING FOR THE NURSES' LOUNGE. I'M THE NEW MASSAGE THERAPIST...?
KNOCK KNOCK
HYSTERICAL.
YOU WANT SOMETHING TO MASSAGE...
NO!
...TRY MY HOSPITAL BILL. GET ACCOUNTING TO EXPLAIN WHY THE WORST PART OF AN ENEMA IS THE EXPENSE.
HOW WAS CHEMOTHERAPY?
AT LEAST I'LL SAVE ON SHAMPOO...
SNFF
MORE AGGRESSIVE. I DON'T KNOW ABOUT THE SARCOMA, BUT CHEMO'S DEFINITELY KILLING MY APPETITE.
SNFF
SNFF
I'M SORRY, MATTY. YOU OKAY? YOU COMING DOWN WITH SOMETHING?
ME? NO.
DON'T GET SICK. THEY WON'T LET YOU VISIT, AND YOU'RE ALL I'VE GOT, MAN.
SERIOUSLY. I JUST...I NEED YOU AROUND ON DAYS LIKE THIS, BUDDY. I'M SORRY.

YOU'D DO THE SAME FOR *ME*?

OF COURSE.

THEN STOP APOLOGIZING. I'M--

YOU'RE NOT LEAVING?

--JUST GOING TO THE *LITTLE BOY'S ROOM.* ALL GOOD.

hhhHURRGGHH

hkkkuukk-kk-k

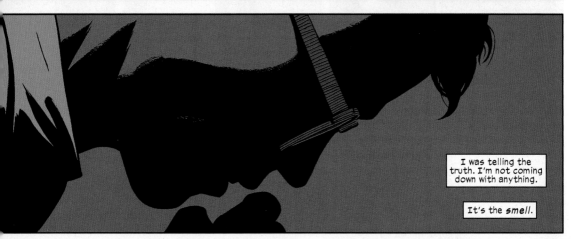

I was telling the truth. I'm not coming down with anything.

It's the *smell*.

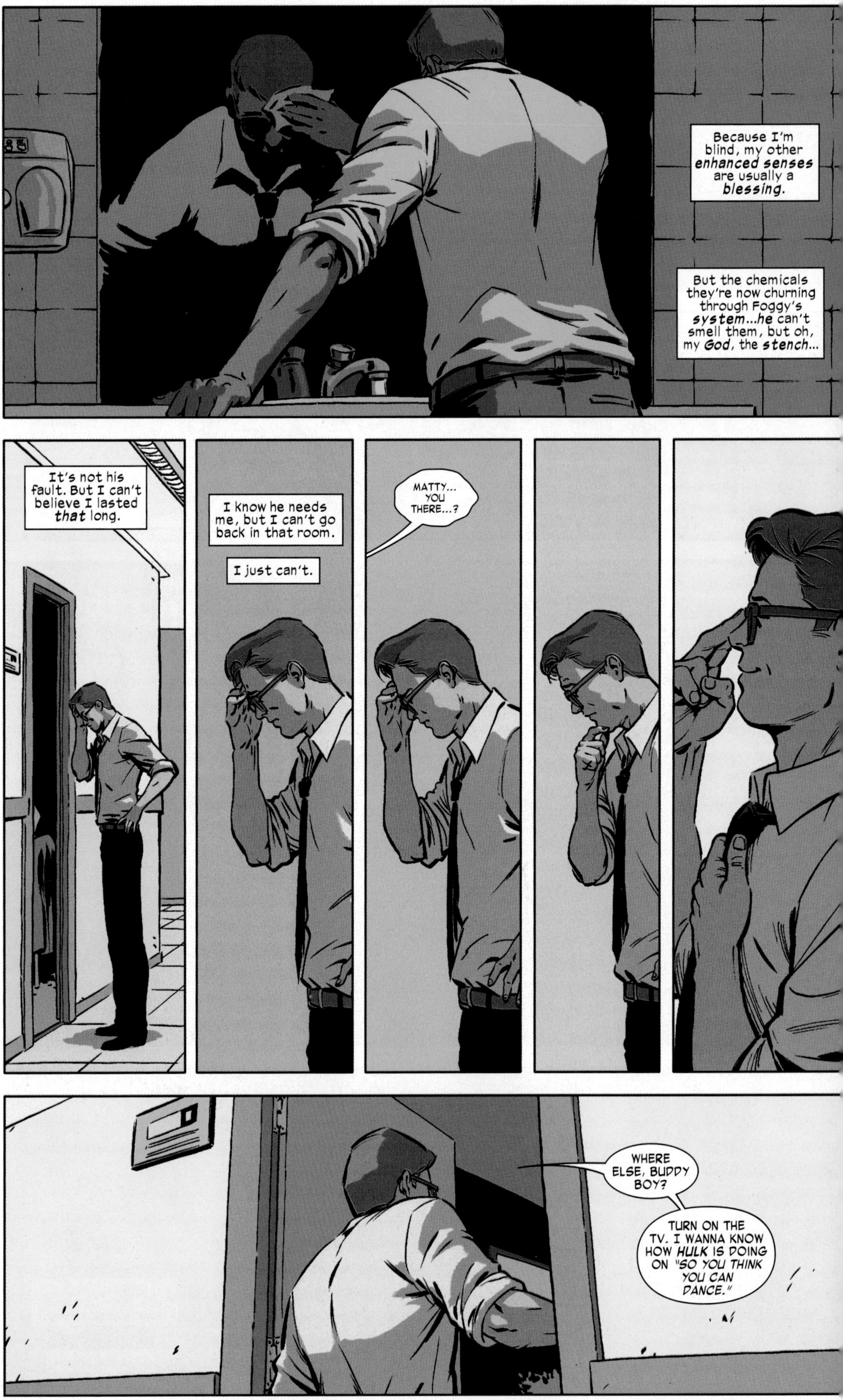

Because I'm blind, my other enhanced senses are usually a blessing.
But the chemicals they're now churning through Foggy's system...he can't smell them, but oh, my God, the stench...
It's not his fault. But I can't believe I lasted that long.
I know he needs me, but I can't go back in that room.
I just can't.
MATTY... YOU THERE...?
WHERE ELSE, BUDDY BOY?
TURN ON THE TV. I WANNA KNOW HOW HULK IS DOING ON "SO YOU THINK YOU CAN DANCE."

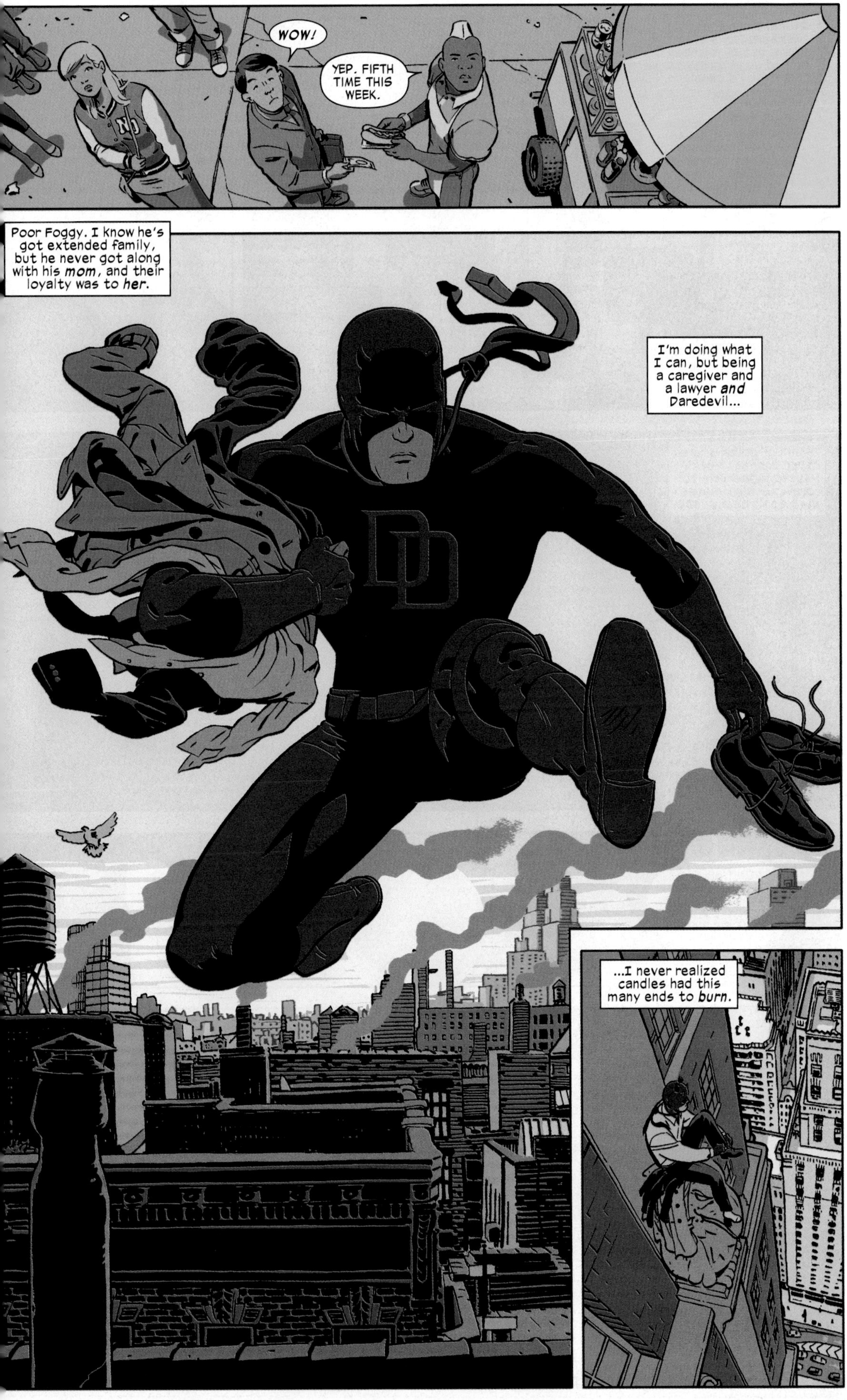
WOW!
YEP. FIFTH TIME THIS WEEK.
Poor Foggy. I know he's got extended family, but he never got along with his *mom*, and their loyalty was to *her*.
I'm doing what I can, but being a caregiver and a lawyer *and* Daredevil...
...I never realized candles had this many ends to *burn*.

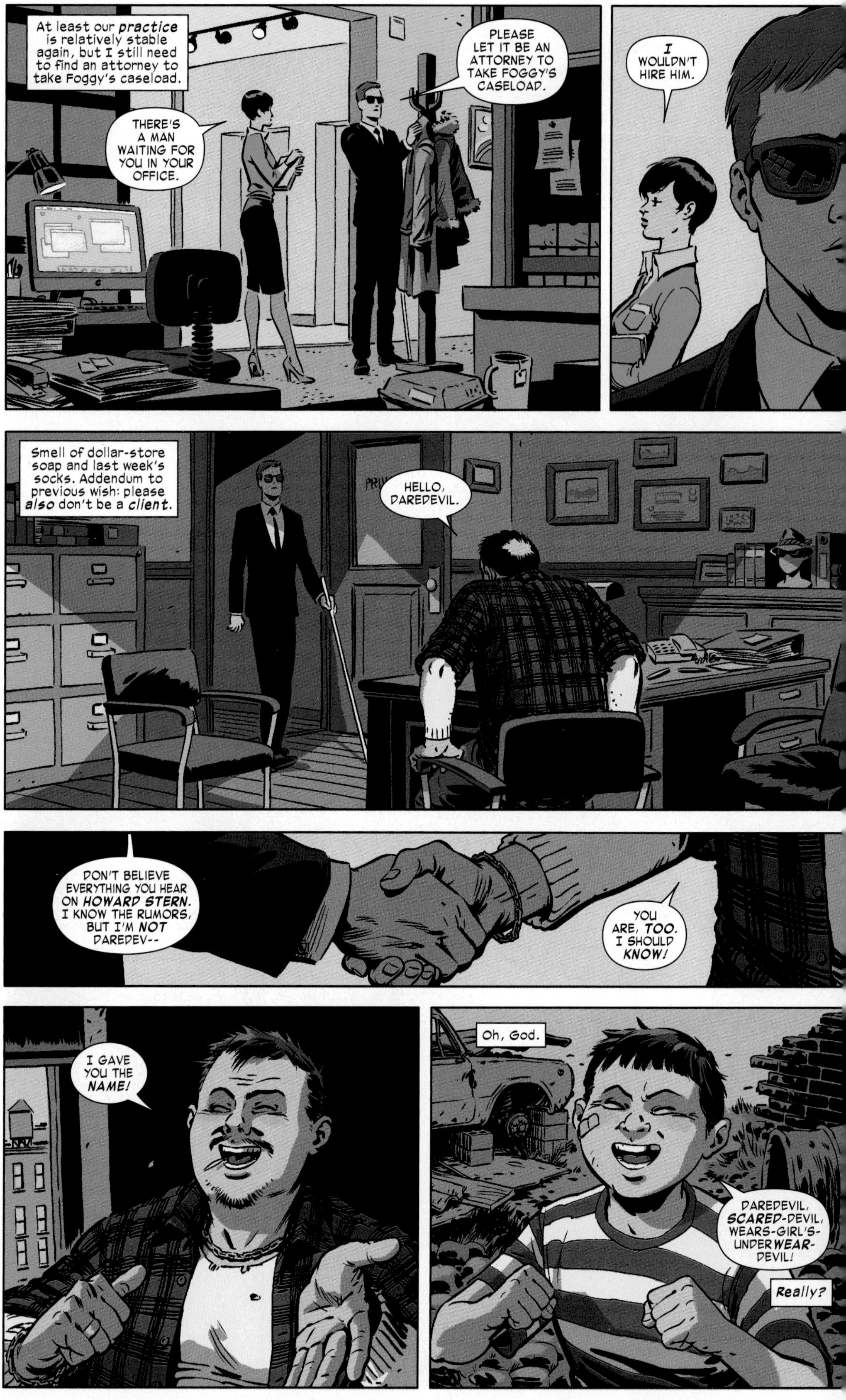

At least our *practice* is relatively stable again, but I still need to find an attorney to take Foggy's caseload.
THERE'S A MAN WAITING FOR YOU IN YOUR OFFICE.
PLEASE LET IT BE AN ATTORNEY TO TAKE FOGGY'S CASELOAD.
I WOULDN'T HIRE HIM.
Smell of dollar-store soap and last week's socks. Addendum to previous wish: please *also* don't be a *client*.
HELLO, DAREDEVIL.
DON'T BELIEVE EVERYTHING YOU HEAR ON *HOWARD STERN*. I KNOW THE RUMORS, BUT I'M *NOT* DAREDEV--
YOU ARE, *TOO*. I SHOULD *KNOW!*
I GAVE YOU THE *NAME!*
Oh, God.
DAREDEVIL, *SCARED*-DEVIL, WEARS-GIRL'S-UNDER*WEAR*-DEVIL!
Really?

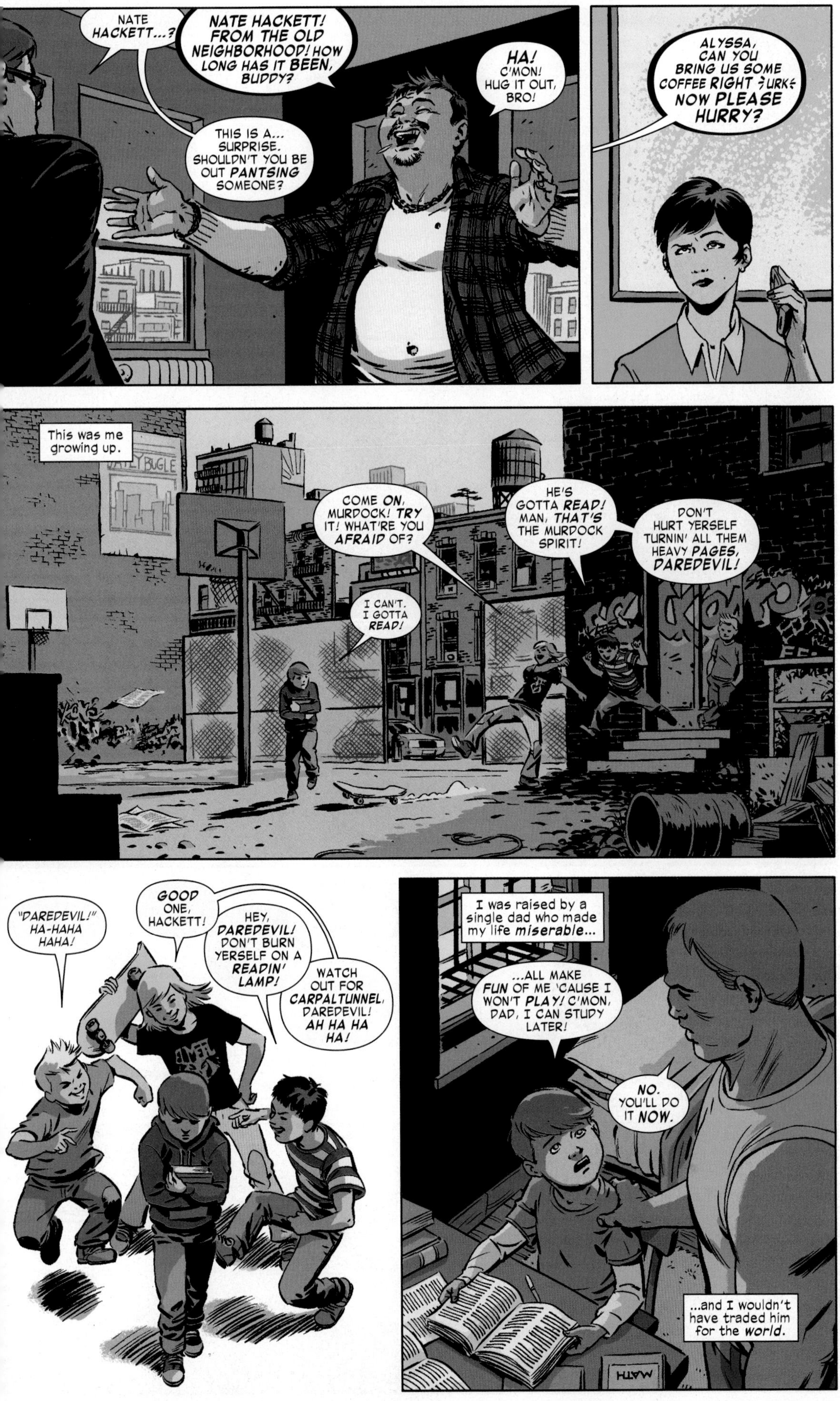
NATE HACKETT...?
NATE HACKETT! FROM THE OLD NEIGHBORHOOD! HOW LONG HAS IT BEEN, BUDDY?
THIS IS A... SURPRISE. SHOULDN'T YOU BE OUT PANTSING SOMEONE?
HA! C'MON! HUG IT OUT, BRO!
ALYSSA, CAN YOU BRING US SOME COFFEE RIGHT -URK- NOW PLEASE HURRY?
This was me growing up.
COME ON, MURDOCK! TRY IT! WHAT'RE YOU AFRAID OF?
I CAN'T. I GOTTA READ!
HE'S GOTTA READ! MAN, THAT'S THE MURDOCK SPIRIT!
DON'T HURT YERSELF TURNIN' ALL THEM HEAVY PAGES, DAREDEVIL!
"DAREDEVIL!" HA-HAHA HAHA!
GOOD ONE, HACKETT!
HEY, DAREDEVIL! DON'T BURN YERSELF ON A READIN' LAMP!
WATCH OUT FOR CARPALTUNNEL, DAREDEVIL! AH HA HA HA!
I was raised by a single dad who made my life miserable...
...ALL MAKE FUN OF ME 'CAUSE I WON'T PLAY! C'MON, DAD, I CAN STUDY LATER!
NO. YOU'LL DO IT NOW.
...and I wouldn't have traded him for the world.

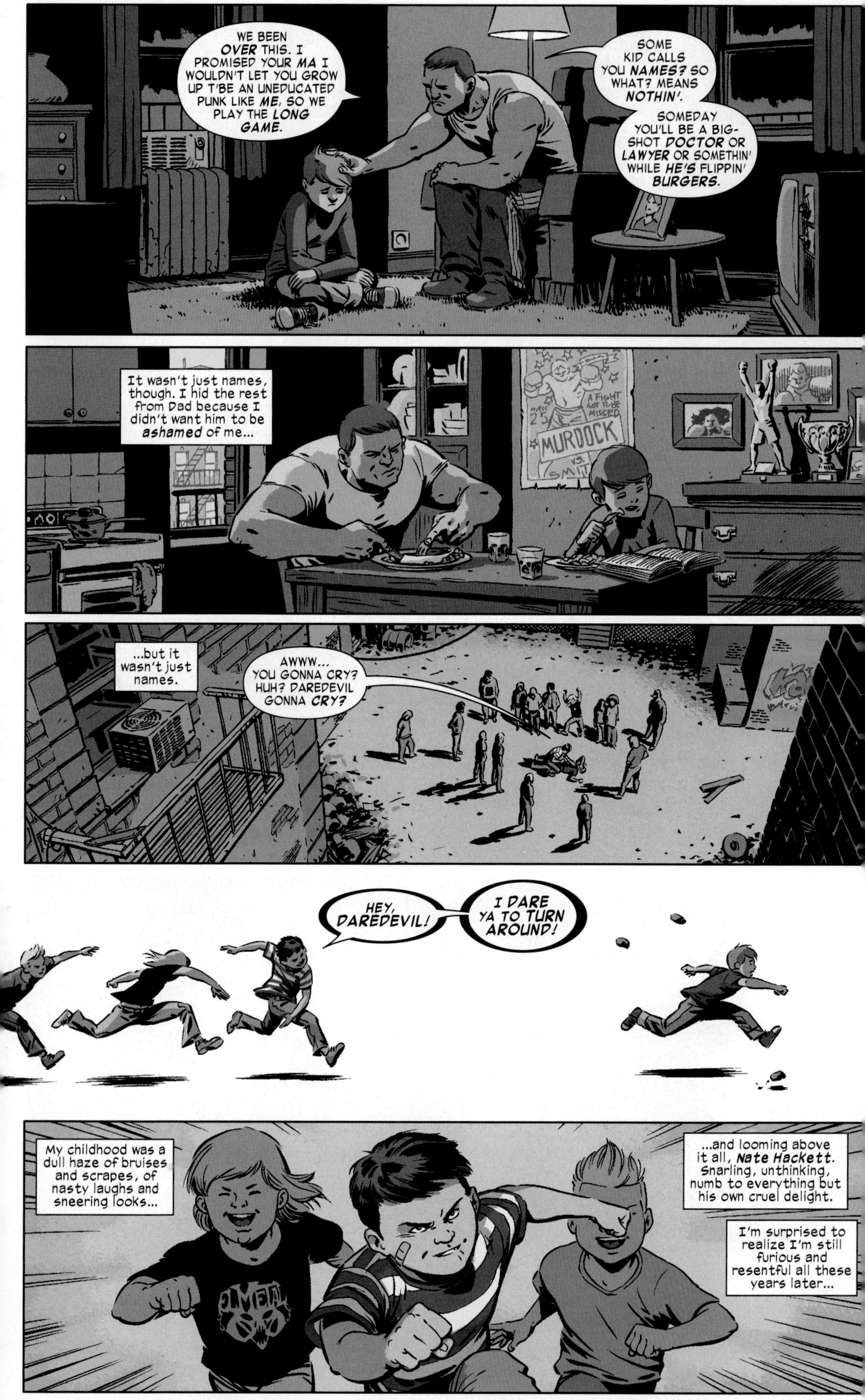

WE BEEN OVER THIS. I PROMISED YOUR MA I WOULDN'T LET YOU GROW UP T'BE AN UNEDUCATED PUNK LIKE ME, SO WE PLAY THE LONG GAME.
SOME KID CALLS YOU NAMES? SO WHAT? MEANS NOTHIN'.
SOMEDAY YOU'LL BE A BIG-SHOT DOCTOR OR LAWYER OR SOMETHIN' WHILE HE'S FLIPPIN' BURGERS.
It wasn't just names, though. I hid the rest from Dad because I didn't want him to be ashamed of me...
A FIGHT NOT TO BE MISSED
MURDOCK VS. SMIT
...but it wasn't just names.
AWWW... YOU GONNA CRY? HUH? DAREDEVIL GONNA CRY?
HEY, DAREDEVIL!
I DARE YA TO TURN AROUND!
My childhood was a dull haze of bruises and scrapes, of nasty laughs and sneering looks...
...and looming above it all, Nate Hackett. Snarling, unthinking, numb to everything but his own cruel delight.
I'm surprised to realize I'm still furious and resentful all these years later...

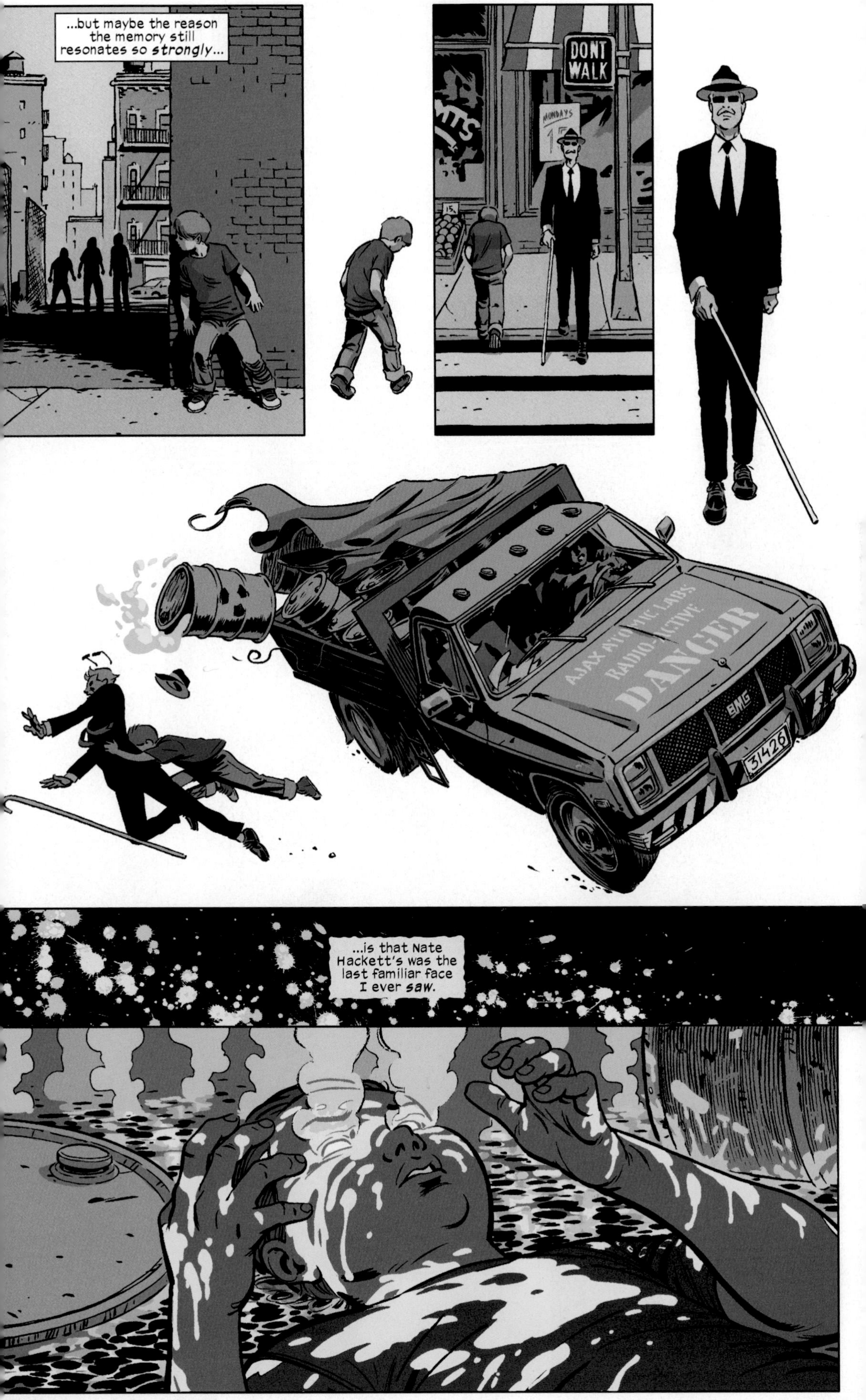
...but maybe the reason the memory still resonates so *strongly*...
DONT WALK
MONDAYS
AJAX ATOMIC LABS
RADIO-ACTIVE
DANGER
31426
...is that Nate Hackett's was the last familiar face I ever *saw*.

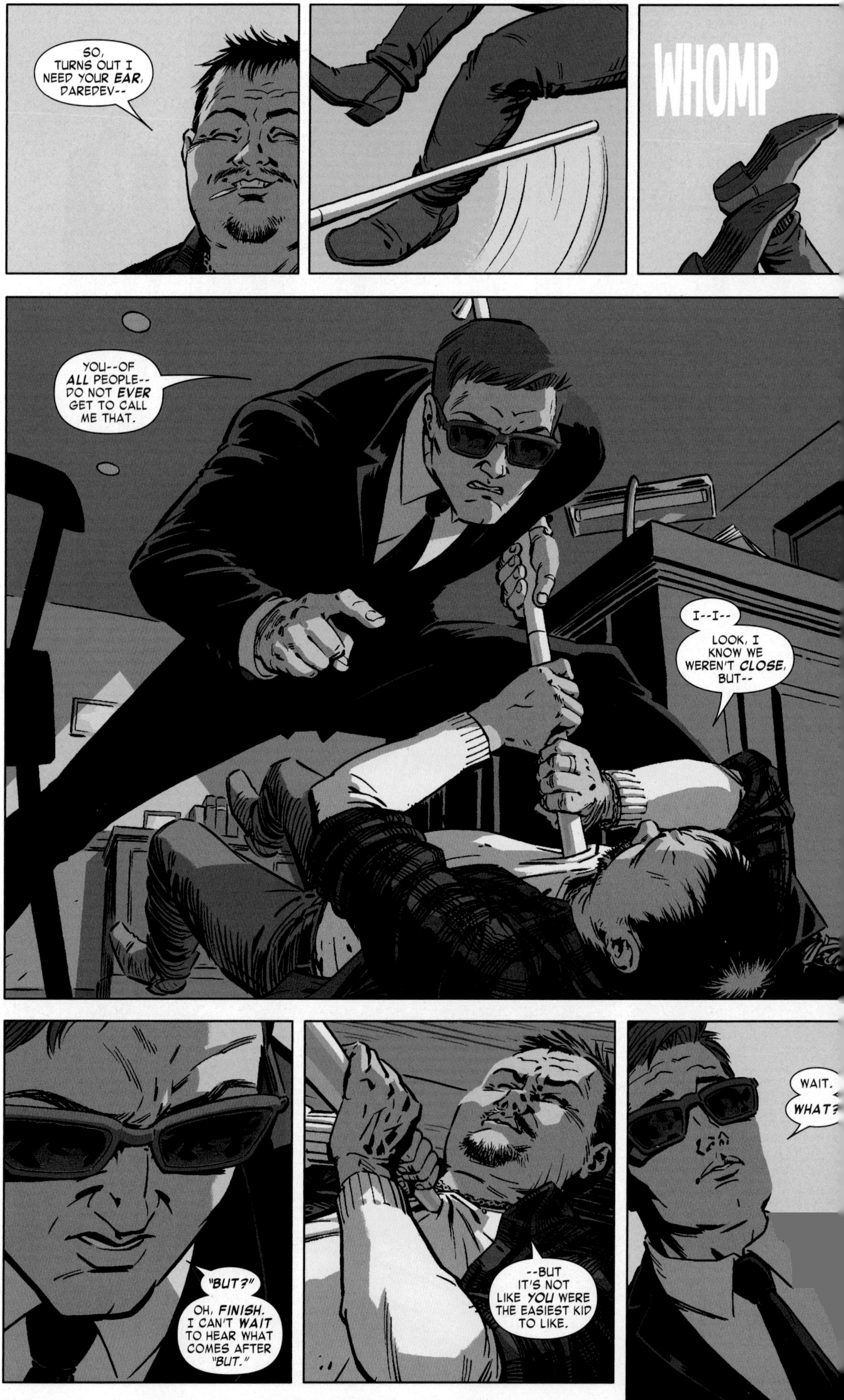

SO, TURNS OUT I NEED YOUR *EAR*, DAREDEV--
WHOMP
YOU--OF *ALL* PEOPLE--DO NOT *EVER* GET TO CALL ME THAT.
I--I--
LOOK, I KNOW WE WEREN'T *CLOSE*, BUT--
"BUT?"
OH, *FINISH*. I CAN'T *WAIT* TO HEAR WHAT COMES AFTER "BUT."
--BUT IT'S NOT LIKE *YOU* WERE THE EASIEST KID TO LIKE.
WAIT.
WHAT?

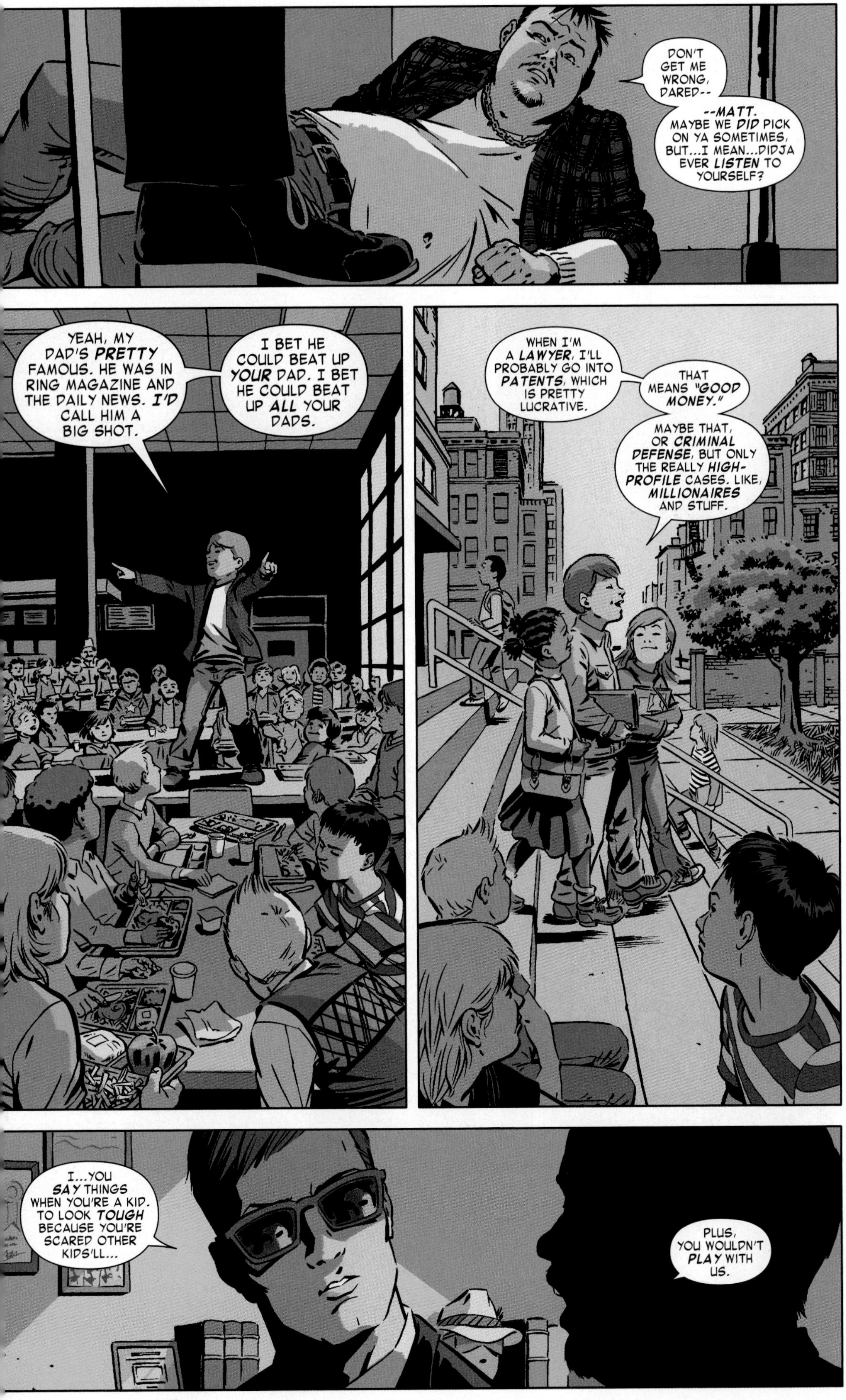
DON'T GET ME WRONG, DARED--
--MATT. MAYBE WE DID PICK ON YA SOMETIMES, BUT...I MEAN...DIDJA EVER LISTEN TO YOURSELF?
YEAH, MY DAD'S PRETTY FAMOUS. HE WAS IN RING MAGAZINE AND THE DAILY NEWS. I'D CALL HIM A BIG SHOT.
I BET HE COULD BEAT UP YOUR DAD. I BET HE COULD BEAT UP ALL YOUR DADS.
WHEN I'M A LAWYER, I'LL PROBABLY GO INTO PATENTS, WHICH IS PRETTY LUCRATIVE.
THAT MEANS "GOOD MONEY."
MAYBE THAT, OR CRIMINAL DEFENSE, BUT ONLY THE REALLY HIGH-PROFILE CASES. LIKE, MILLIONAIRES AND STUFF.
I...YOU SAY THINGS WHEN YOU'RE A KID. TO LOOK TOUGH BECAUSE YOU'RE SCARED OTHER KIDS'LL...
PLUS, YOU WOULDN'T PLAY WITH US.

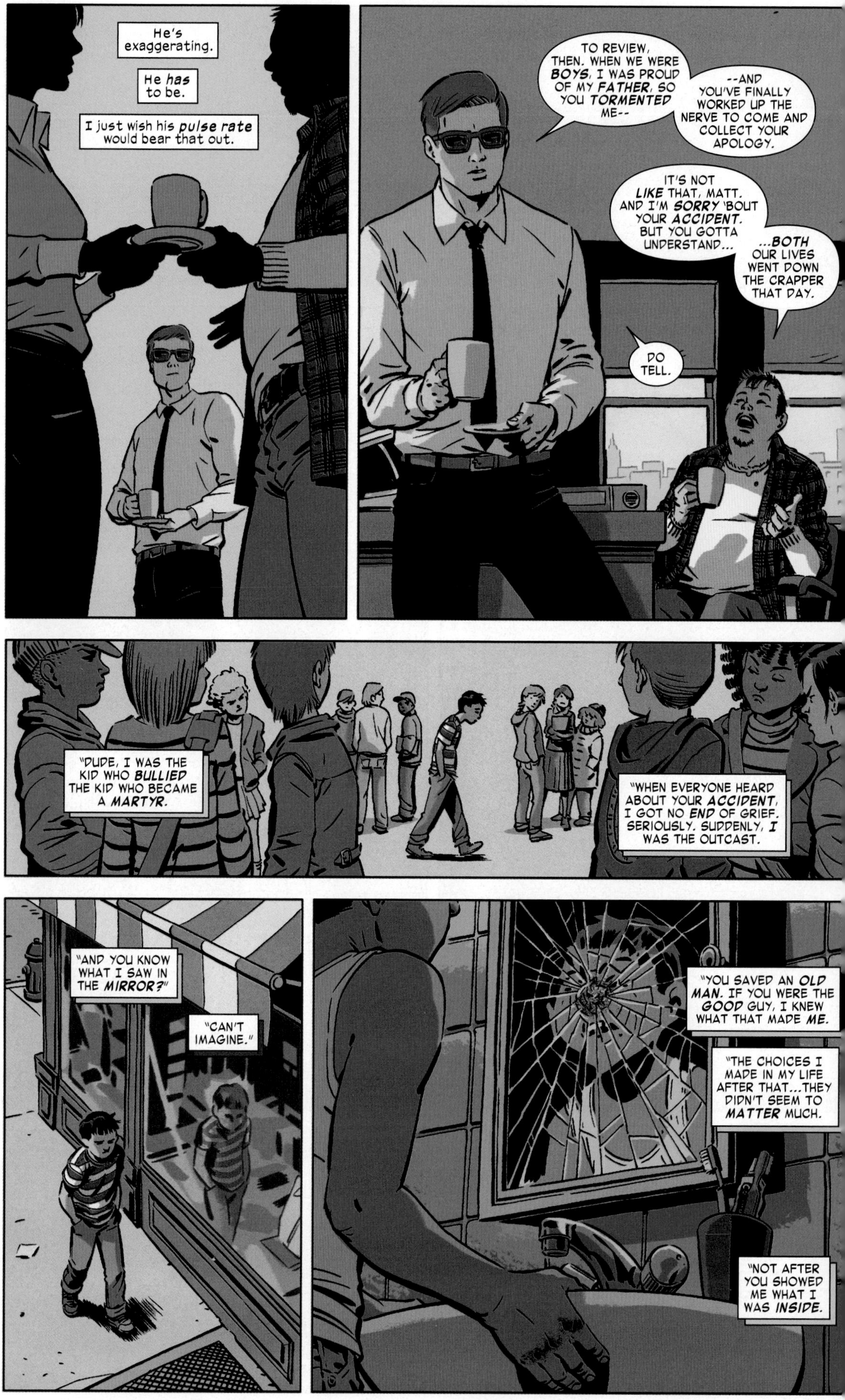
He's exaggerating.
He *has* to be.
I just wish his *pulse rate* would bear that out.
TO REVIEW, THEN. WHEN WE WERE *BOYS*, I WAS PROUD OF MY *FATHER*, SO YOU *TORMENTED* ME--
--AND YOU'VE FINALLY WORKED UP THE NERVE TO COME AND COLLECT YOUR APOLOGY.
IT'S NOT *LIKE* THAT, MATT. AND I'M *SORRY* 'BOUT YOUR *ACCIDENT*. BUT YOU GOTTA UNDERSTAND...
...*BOTH* OUR LIVES WENT DOWN THE CRAPPER THAT DAY.
DO TELL.
"DUDE, I WAS THE KID WHO *BULLIED* THE KID WHO BECAME A *MARTYR*.
"WHEN EVERYONE HEARD ABOUT YOUR *ACCIDENT*, I GOT NO *END* OF GRIEF. SERIOUSLY. SUDDENLY, *I* WAS THE OUTCAST.
"AND YOU KNOW WHAT I SAW IN THE *MIRROR?*"
"CAN'T IMAGINE."
"YOU SAVED AN *OLD MAN*. IF YOU WERE THE *GOOD* GUY, I KNEW WHAT THAT MADE *ME*.
"THE CHOICES I MADE IN MY LIFE AFTER THAT...THEY DIDN'T SEEM TO *MATTER* MUCH.
"NOT AFTER YOU SHOWED ME WHAT I WAS *INSIDE*.

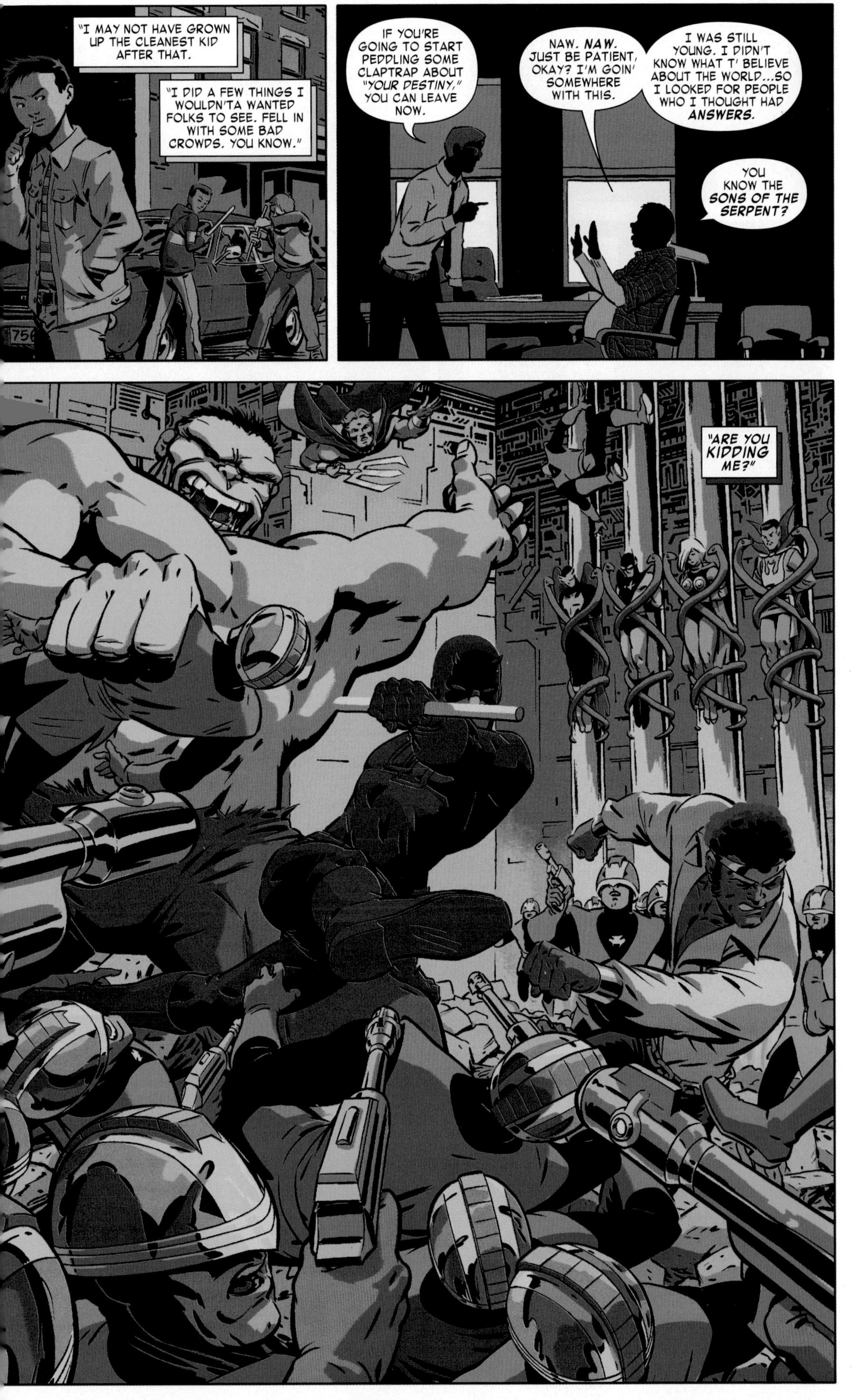
"I MAY NOT HAVE GROWN UP THE CLEANEST KID AFTER THAT.
"I DID A FEW THINGS I WOULDN'TA WANTED FOLKS TO SEE. FELL IN WITH SOME BAD CROWDS. YOU KNOW."
IF YOU'RE GOING TO START PEDDLING SOME CLAPTRAP ABOUT "YOUR DESTINY," YOU CAN LEAVE NOW.
NAW. NAW. JUST BE PATIENT, OKAY? I'M GOIN' SOMEWHERE WITH THIS.
I WAS STILL YOUNG. I DIDN'T KNOW WHAT T' BELIEVE ABOUT THE WORLD...SO I LOOKED FOR PEOPLE WHO I THOUGHT HAD ANSWERS.
YOU KNOW THE SONS OF THE SERPENT?
"ARE YOU KIDDING ME?"

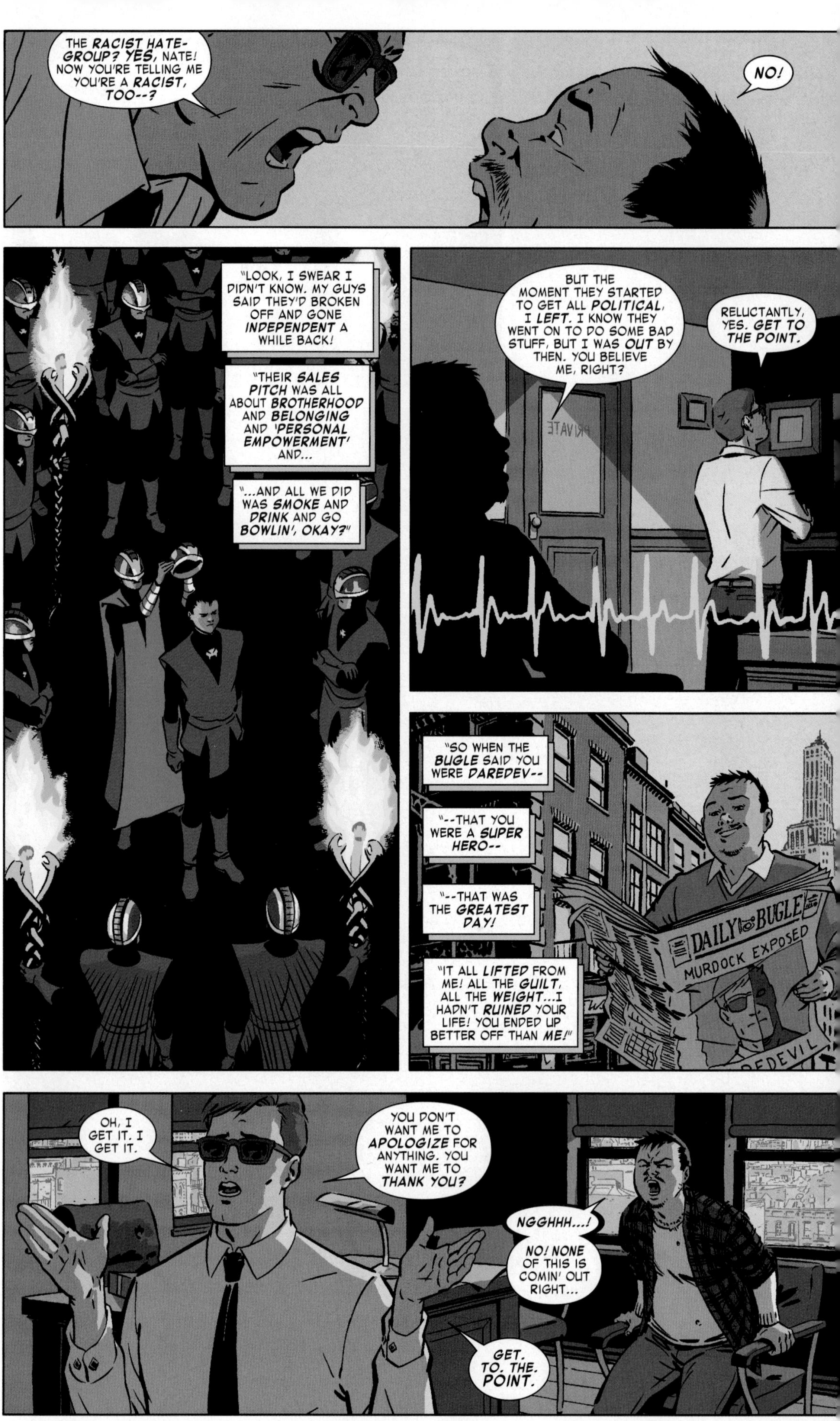
THE RACIST HATE-GROUP? YES, NATE! NOW YOU'RE TELLING ME YOU'RE A RACIST, TOO--?
NO!
"LOOK, I SWEAR I DIDN'T KNOW. MY GUYS SAID THEY'D BROKEN OFF AND GONE INDEPENDENT A WHILE BACK!
"THEIR SALES PITCH WAS ALL ABOUT BROTHERHOOD AND BELONGING AND 'PERSONAL EMPOWERMENT' AND...
"...AND ALL WE DID WAS SMOKE AND DRINK AND GO BOWLIN', OKAY?"
BUT THE MOMENT THEY STARTED TO GET ALL POLITICAL, I LEFT. I KNOW THEY WENT ON TO DO SOME BAD STUFF, BUT I WAS OUT BY THEN. YOU BELIEVE ME, RIGHT?
PRIVATE
RELUCTANTLY, YES. GET TO THE POINT.
"SO WHEN THE BUGLE SAID YOU WERE DAREDEV--
"--THAT YOU WERE A SUPER HERO--
"--THAT WAS THE GREATEST DAY!
"IT ALL LIFTED FROM ME! ALL THE GUILT, ALL THE WEIGHT...I HADN'T RUINED YOUR LIFE! YOU ENDED UP BETTER OFF THAN ME!"
DAILY BUGLE
MURDOCK EXPOSED
OH, I GET IT. I GET IT.
YOU DON'T WANT ME TO APOLOGIZE FOR ANYTHING. YOU WANT ME TO THANK YOU?
NGGHHH...!
NO! NONE OF THIS IS COMIN' OUT RIGHT...
GET. TO. THE. POINT.

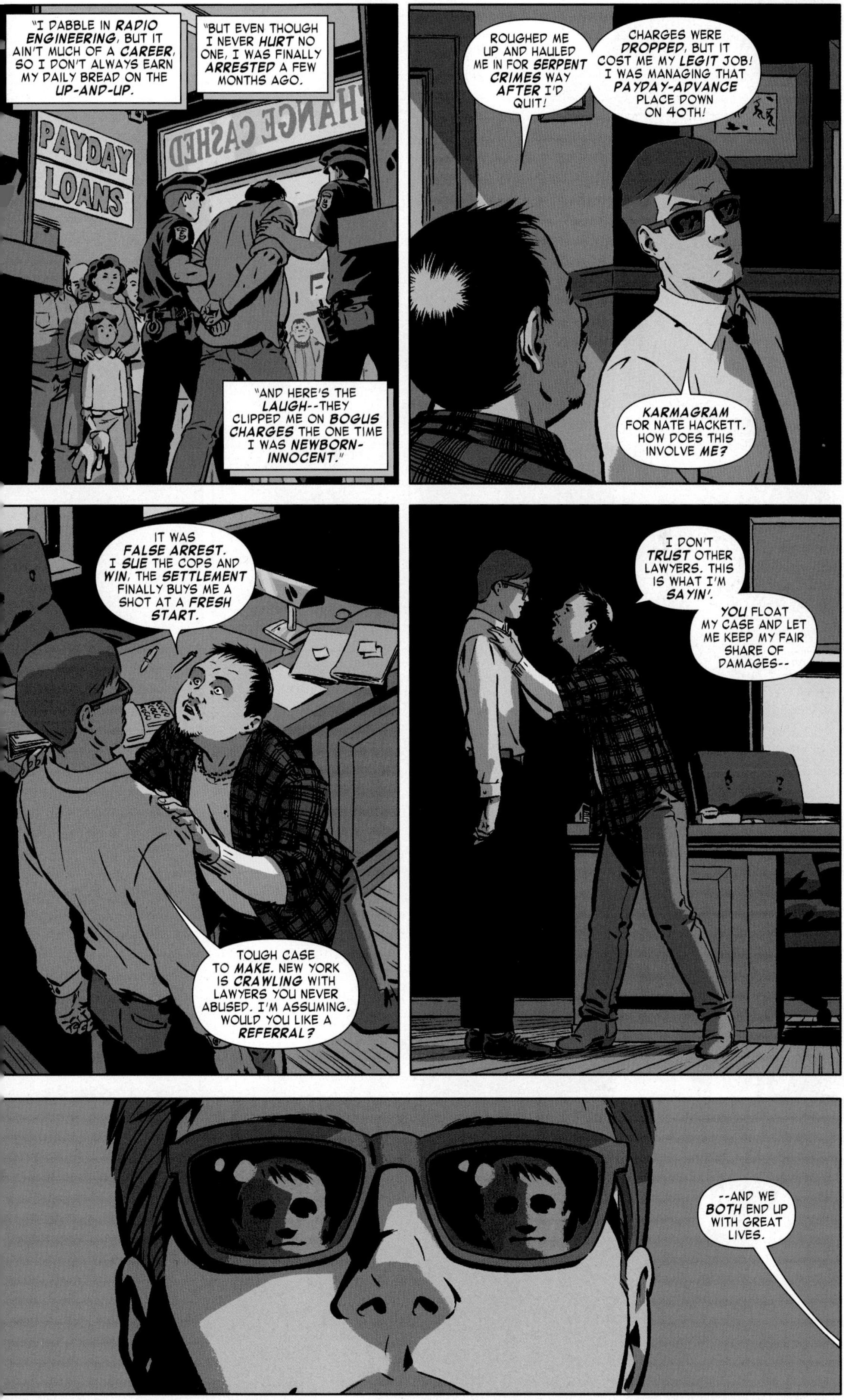
"I DABBLE IN RADIO ENGINEERING, BUT IT AIN'T MUCH OF A CAREER, SO I DON'T ALWAYS EARN MY DAILY BREAD ON THE UP-AND-UP.
"BUT EVEN THOUGH I NEVER HURT NO ONE, I WAS FINALLY ARRESTED A FEW MONTHS AGO.
PAYDAY LOANS
HANGE CASHED
"AND HERE'S THE LAUGH--THEY CLIPPED ME ON BOGUS CHARGES THE ONE TIME I WAS NEWBORN-INNOCENT."
ROUGHED ME UP AND HAULED ME IN FOR SERPENT CRIMES WAY AFTER I'D QUIT!
CHARGES WERE DROPPED, BUT IT COST ME MY LEGIT JOB! I WAS MANAGING THAT PAYDAY-ADVANCE PLACE DOWN ON 40TH!
KARMAGRAM FOR NATE HACKETT. HOW DOES THIS INVOLVE ME?
IT WAS FALSE ARREST. I SUE THE COPS AND WIN, THE SETTLEMENT FINALLY BUYS ME A SHOT AT A FRESH START.
TOUGH CASE TO MAKE. NEW YORK IS CRAWLING WITH LAWYERS YOU NEVER ABUSED. I'M ASSUMING. WOULD YOU LIKE A REFERRAL?
I DON'T TRUST OTHER LAWYERS. THIS IS WHAT I'M SAYIN'.
YOU FLOAT MY CASE AND LET ME KEEP MY FAIR SHARE OF DAMAGES--
--AND WE BOTH END UP WITH GREAT LIVES.

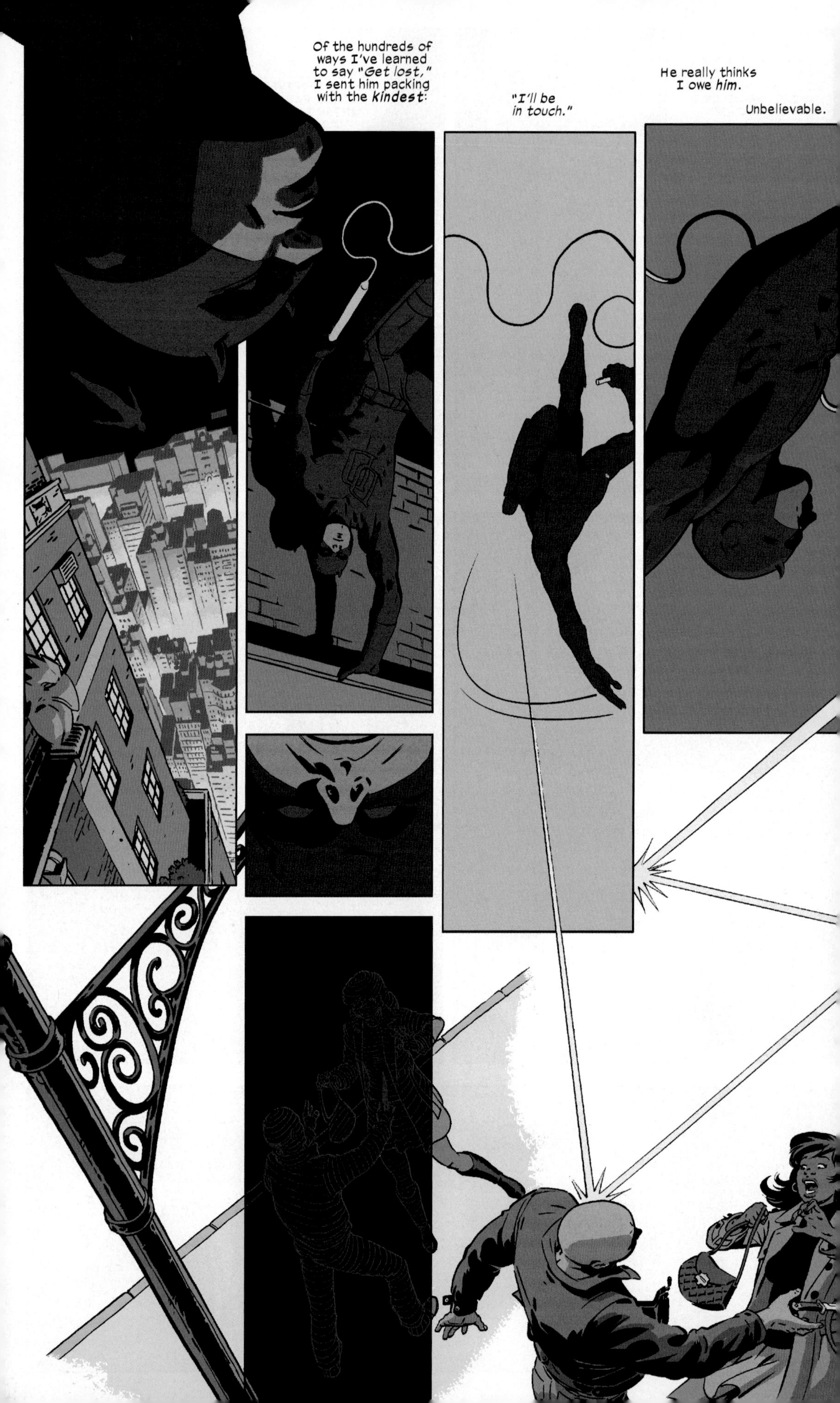
Of the hundreds of ways I've learned to say "*Get lost,*" I sent him packing with the ***kindest***:
"*I'll be in touch.*"
He really thinks I owe *him*.
Unbelievable.

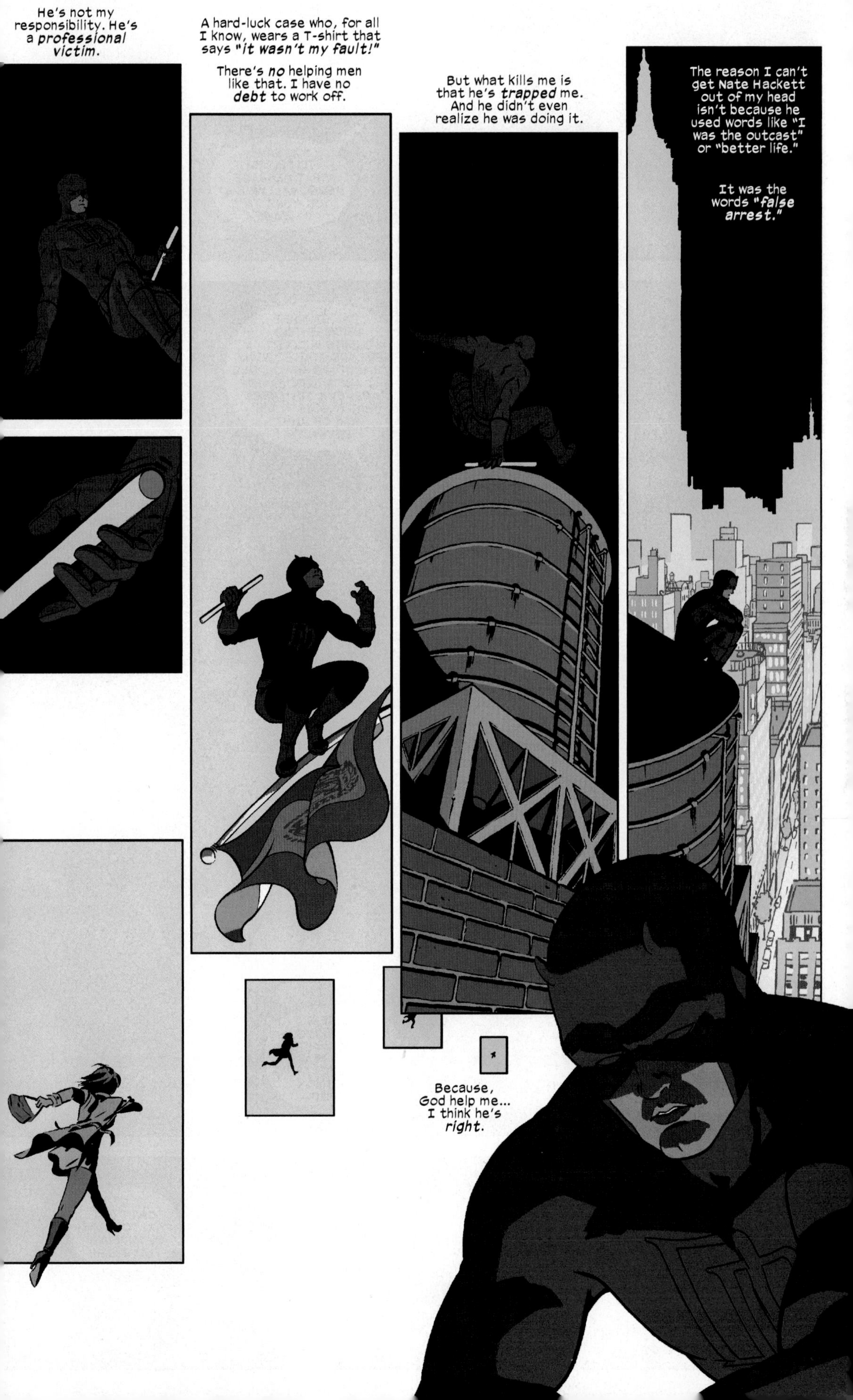
He's not my responsibility. He's a *professional victim.*
A hard-luck case who, for all I know, wears a T-shirt that says "*it wasn't my fault!*"
There's *no* helping men like that. I have no *debt* to work off.
But what kills me is that he's *trapped* me. And he didn't even realize he was doing it.
The reason I can't get Nate Hackett out of my head isn't because he used words like "I was the outcast" or "better life."
It was the words "*false arrest.*"
Because, God help me... I think he's *right.*

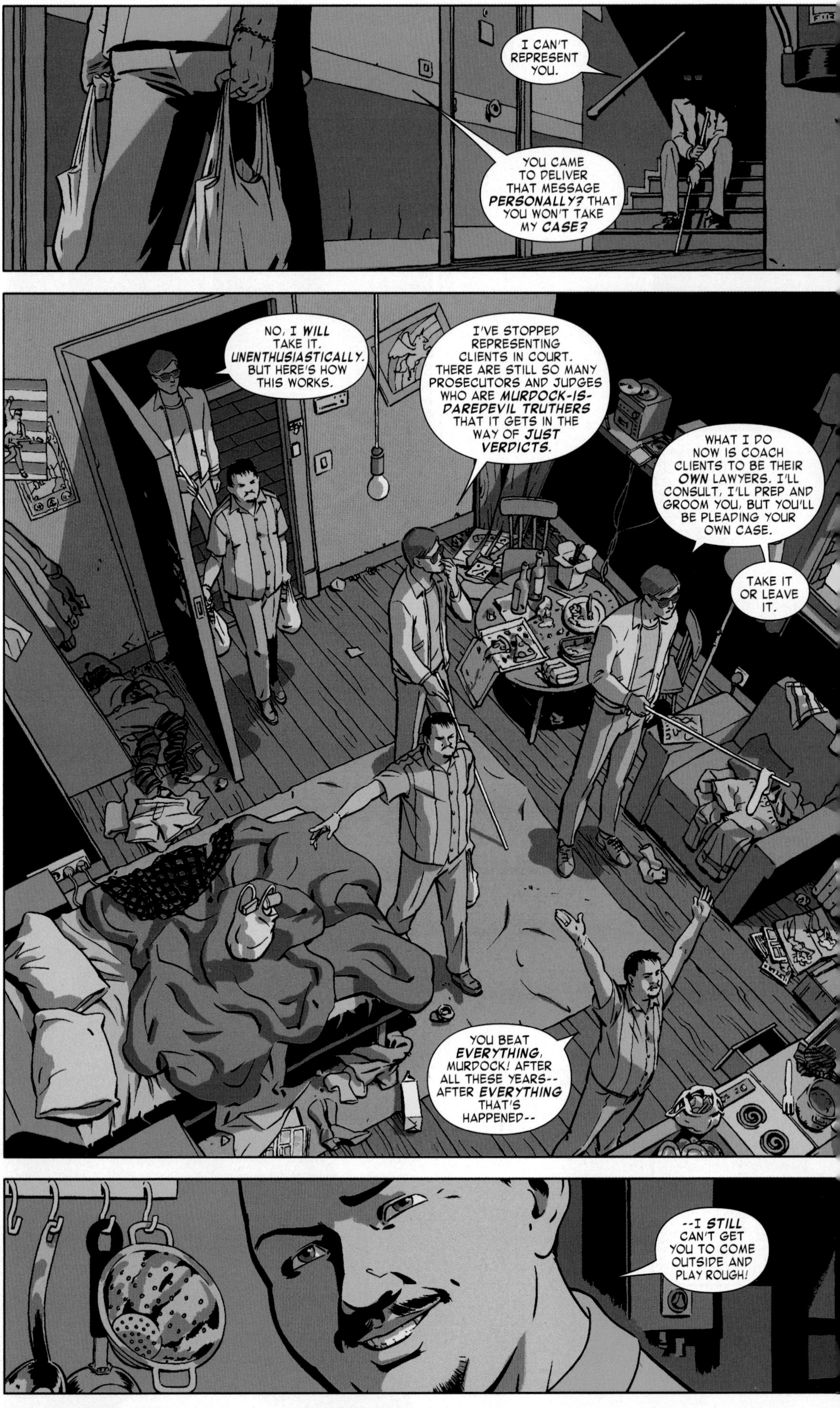
I CAN'T REPRESENT YOU.
YOU CAME TO DELIVER THAT MESSAGE PERSONALLY? THAT YOU WON'T TAKE MY CASE?
NO, I WILL TAKE IT. UNENTHUSIASTICALLY. BUT HERE'S HOW THIS WORKS.
I'VE STOPPED REPRESENTING CLIENTS IN COURT. THERE ARE STILL SO MANY PROSECUTORS AND JUDGES WHO ARE MURDOCK-IS-DAREDEVIL TRUTHERS THAT IT GETS IN THE WAY OF JUST VERDICTS.
WHAT I DO NOW IS COACH CLIENTS TO BE THEIR OWN LAWYERS. I'LL CONSULT, I'LL PREP AND GROOM YOU, BUT YOU'LL BE PLEADING YOUR OWN CASE.
TAKE IT OR LEAVE IT.
YOU BEAT EVERYTHING, MURDOCK! AFTER ALL THESE YEARS-- AFTER EVERYTHING THAT'S HAPPENED--
--I STILL CAN'T GET YOU TO COME OUTSIDE AND PLAY ROUGH!

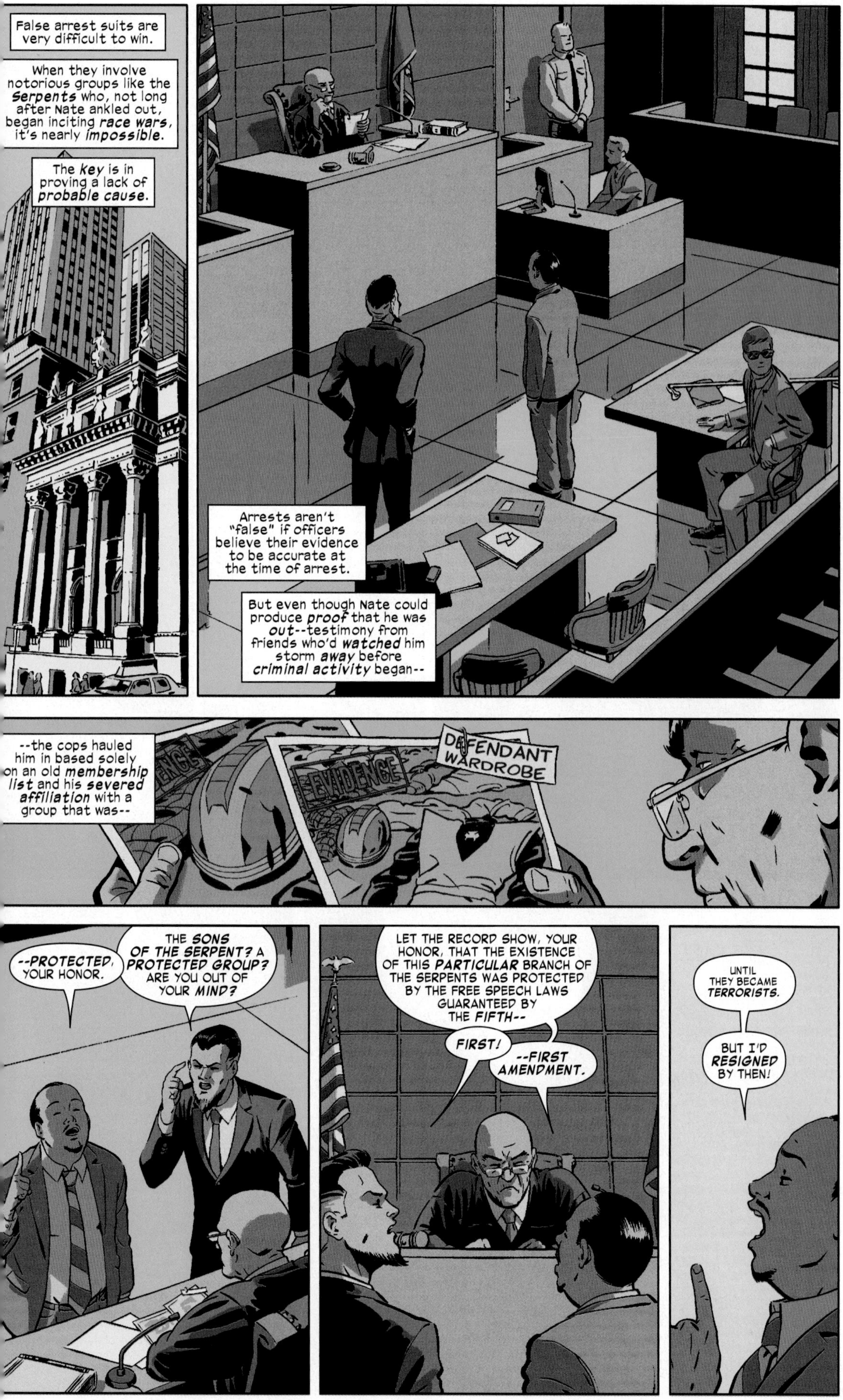

False arrest suits are very difficult to win.
When they involve notorious groups like the *Serpents* who, not long after Nate ankled out, began inciting *race wars*, it's nearly *impossible*.
The *key* is in proving a lack of *probable cause*.
Arrests aren't "false" if officers believe their evidence to be accurate at the time of arrest.
But even though Nate could produce *proof* that he was *out*--testimony from friends who'd *watched* him storm *away* before *criminal activity* began--
--the cops hauled him in based solely on an old *membership list* and his *severed affiliation* with a group that was--
EVIDENCE
DEFENDANT WARDROBE
--PROTECTED, YOUR HONOR.
THE *SONS OF THE SERPENT?* A *PROTECTED GROUP?* ARE YOU OUT OF YOUR *MIND?*
LET THE RECORD SHOW, YOUR HONOR, THAT THE EXISTENCE OF THIS *PARTICULAR* BRANCH OF THE SERPENTS WAS PROTECTED BY THE FREE SPEECH LAWS GUARANTEED BY THE *FIFTH*--
FIRST!
--*FIRST AMENDMENT.*
UNTIL THEY BECAME *TERRORISTS.*
BUT I'D *RESIGNED* BY THEN!

AS YOU *KNOW*, NO ONE *"RESIGNS"* FROM THE *SERPENTS*, YOUR HONOR!

I DID! AND THE COPS *KNEW* THAT, AND I COULD *PROVE* IT, AND WHEN I WAS A *MEMBER*, NOT ONLY WAS THAT BRANCH *LEGAL*--

--BUT ACCORDING TO THE NCAA--

NAACP!

--WAIT--*NAACP* VERSUS *ALABAMA* CASE, JUST OBTAINING *MY NAME* AS A *FORMER* MEMBER WAS A VIOLATION OF THE *FIFTH*--

Fourteenth!

FOURTEENTH!

--FOURTEENTH AMENDMENT!

I HAD A *LEGAL RIGHT* TO BE A SERPENT WITHOUT *PERSECUTION* AT THE *TIME*.

"AND PROBABLE CAUSE DOES NOT EXIST IF AN INDIVIDUAL HAS A CLEARLY ESTABLISHED LEGAL RIGHT TO ENGAGE IN THE ACTIVITY THAT... THAT..."

...HANG ON...

"...THAT PROMPTED THE ARREST!"

CASE CLOSED!

THAT'S FOR *ME* TO DECIDE, MR. HACKETT. TELL ME...WHY *DID* YOU LEAVE THE SERPENTS?

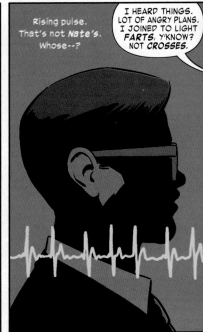

Rising pulse. That's not *Nate's*. Whose--?

I HEARD THINGS. LOT OF ANGRY PLANS. I JOINED TO LIGHT *FARTS*, Y'KNOW? NOT *CROSSES*.

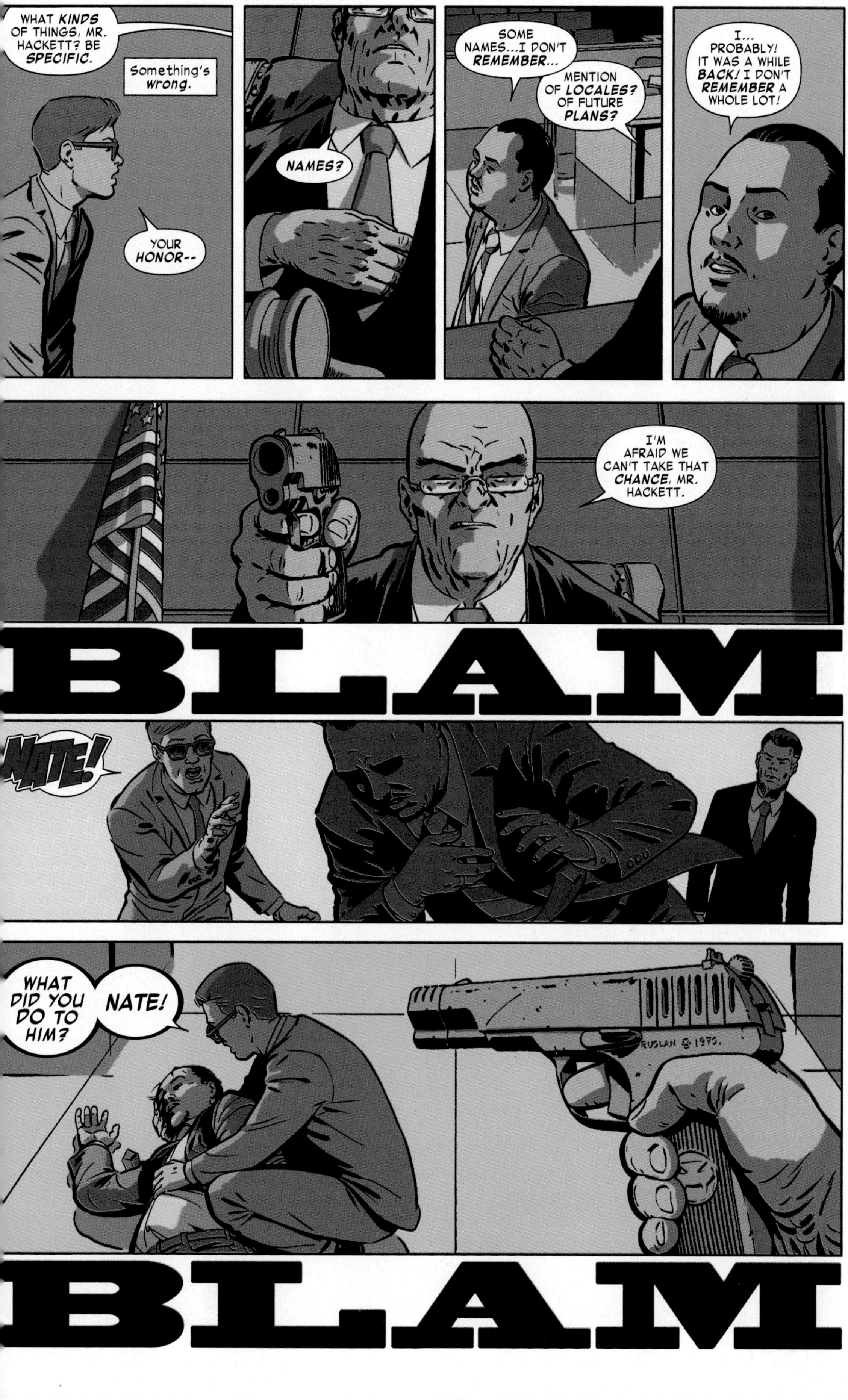

WHAT KINDS OF THINGS, MR. HACKETT? BE SPECIFIC.
Something's wrong.
YOUR HONOR--
NAMES?
SOME NAMES...I DON'T REMEMBER...
MENTION OF LOCALES? OF FUTURE PLANS?
I... PROBABLY! IT WAS A WHILE BACK! I DON'T REMEMBER A WHOLE LOT!
I'M AFRAID WE CAN'T TAKE THAT CHANCE, MR. HACKETT.
BLAM
NATE!
WHAT DID YOU DO TO HIM?
NATE!
RUSLAN 1975.
BLAM

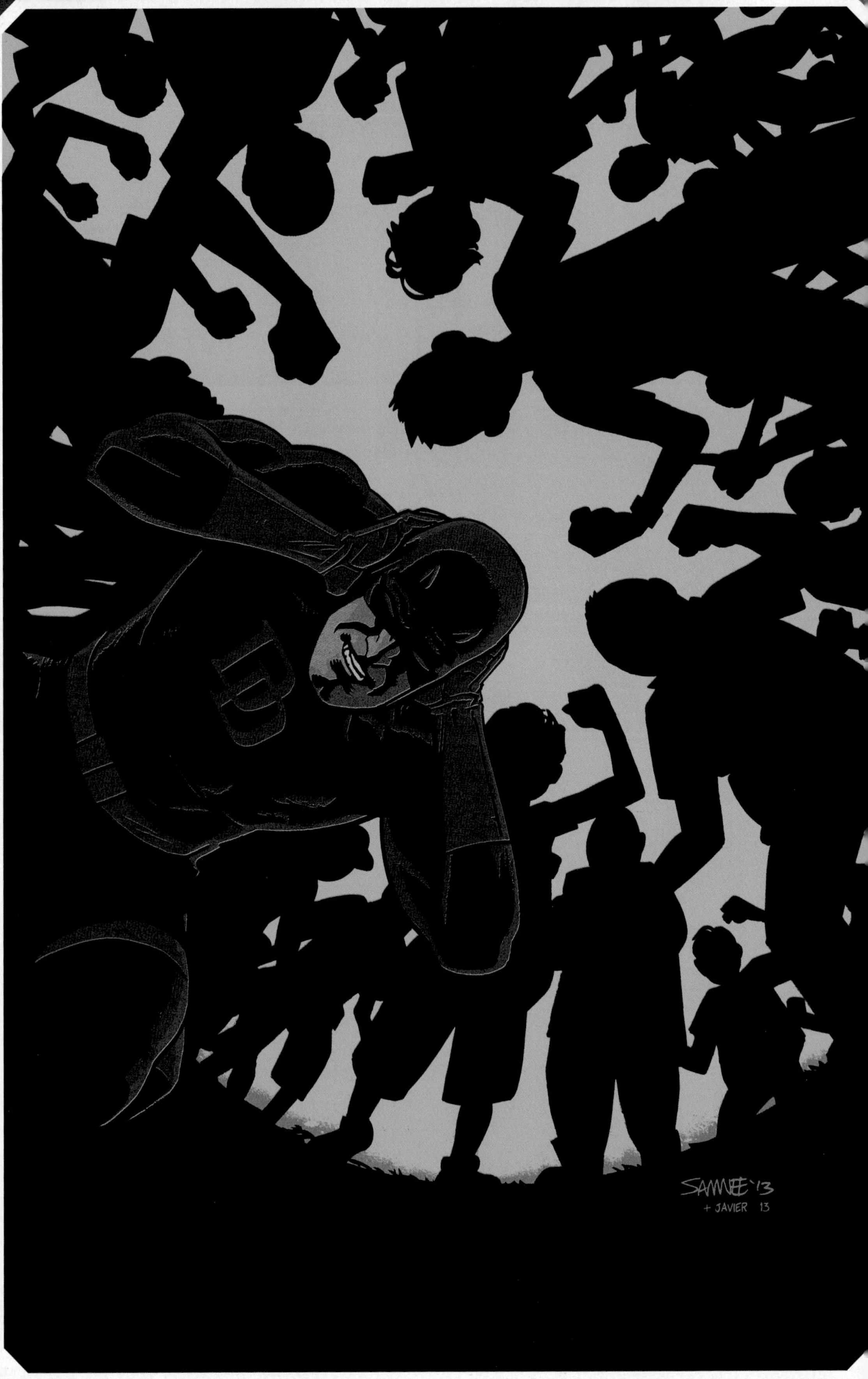
SAMNEE '13
+ JAVIER 13

DAREDEVIL #29

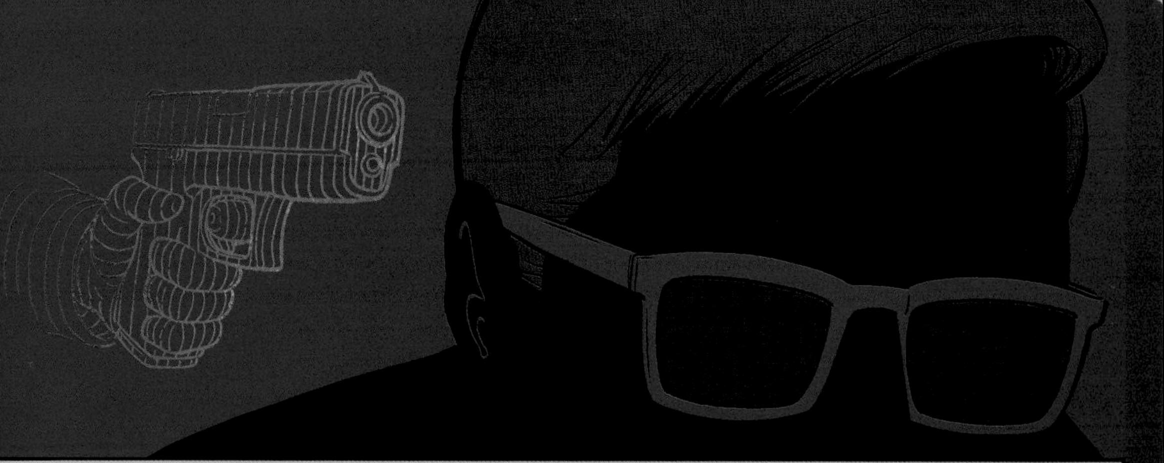

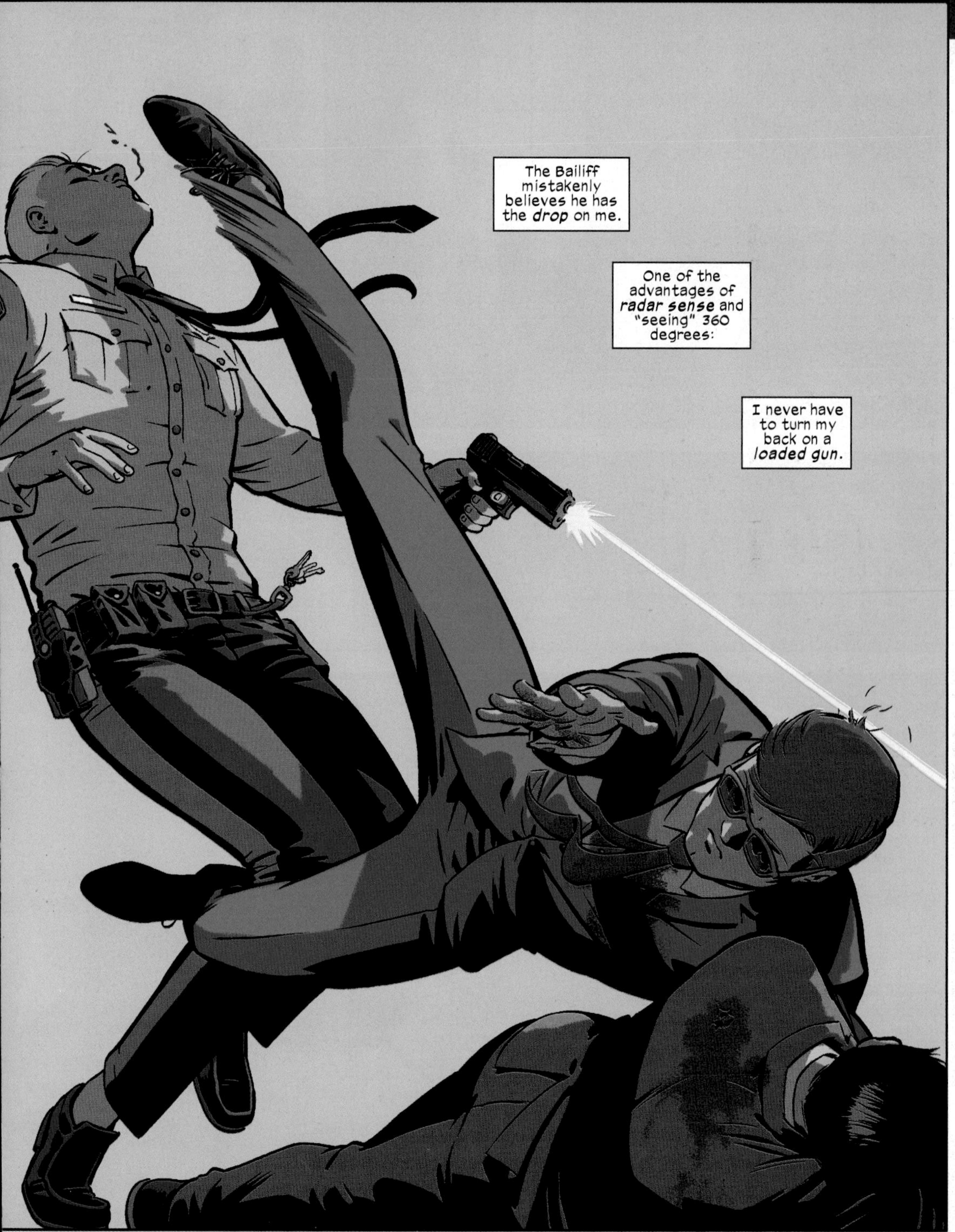

The Bailiff mistakenly believes he has the *drop* on me.
One of the advantages of *radar sense* and "seeing" 360 degrees:
I never have to turn my back on a *loaded gun*.

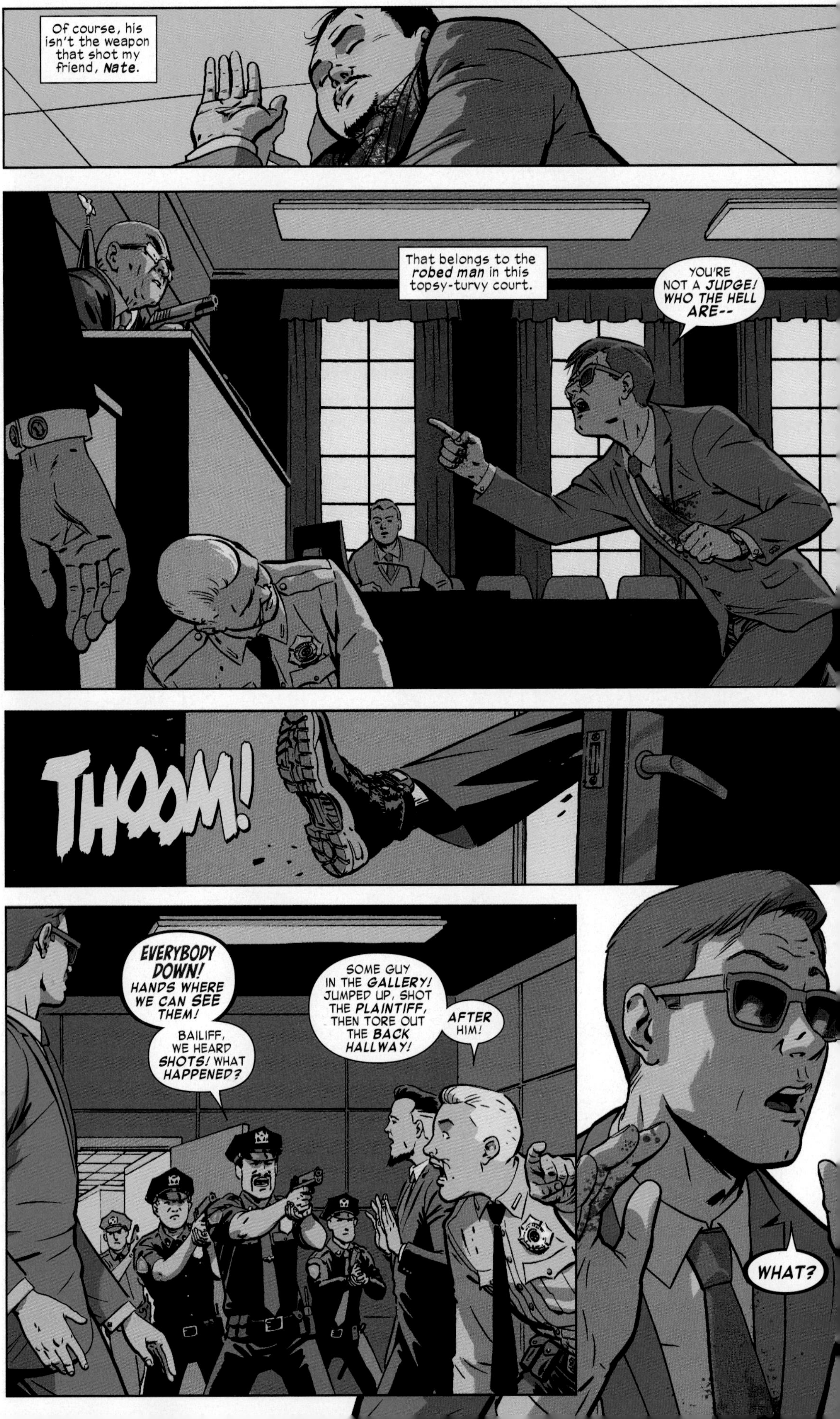

Of course, his isn't the weapon that shot my friend, Nate.
That belongs to the robed man in this topsy-turvy court.
YOU'RE NOT A JUDGE! WHO THE HELL ARE--
THOOM!
EVERYBODY DOWN! HANDS WHERE WE CAN SEE THEM!
BAILIFF, WE HEARD SHOTS! WHAT HAPPENED?
SOME GUY IN THE GALLERY! JUMPED UP, SHOT THE PLAINTIFF, THEN TORE OUT THE BACK HALLWAY!
AFTER HIM!
WHAT?

THAT'S A *LIE!*

SIR, ARE YOU HURT?

NO, BUT MY FRIEND

WE'LL *ATTEND* TO HIM, SIR! WILL SOMEONE HELP THIS MAN *OUT OF OUR WAY?*

GET YOUR HANDS OFF ME! THERE *IS* NO *FLEEING GUNMAN!* IT WAS THE JUDGE!

HE'S *CONFUSED*, OFFICER! WE *ALL* ARE! IT WAS SO *SHOCKING--!*

TELL ME HOW A *STRANGER* GOT A *LOADED GUN* INTO MY *COURTROOM!*

THERE WAS NO STRANGER!

REALLY.

GO AHEAD, BLIND MAN. TELL THE POLICE WHAT *YOU* "SAW."

More than you *think*, ratbag, but who's going to *listen?*

Everyone *else* present was an *eyewitness*: the judge, the bailiff, a prosecutor and a court reporter--all of them *lying*.

All of them either members *of*, or on the take *from*, the white supremacists called the *Sons of the Serpent*--

--so afraid Nate *knows* something that they rigged a *hit* in broad daylight.

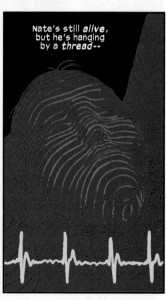

Nate's still *alive*, but he's hanging by a *thread--*

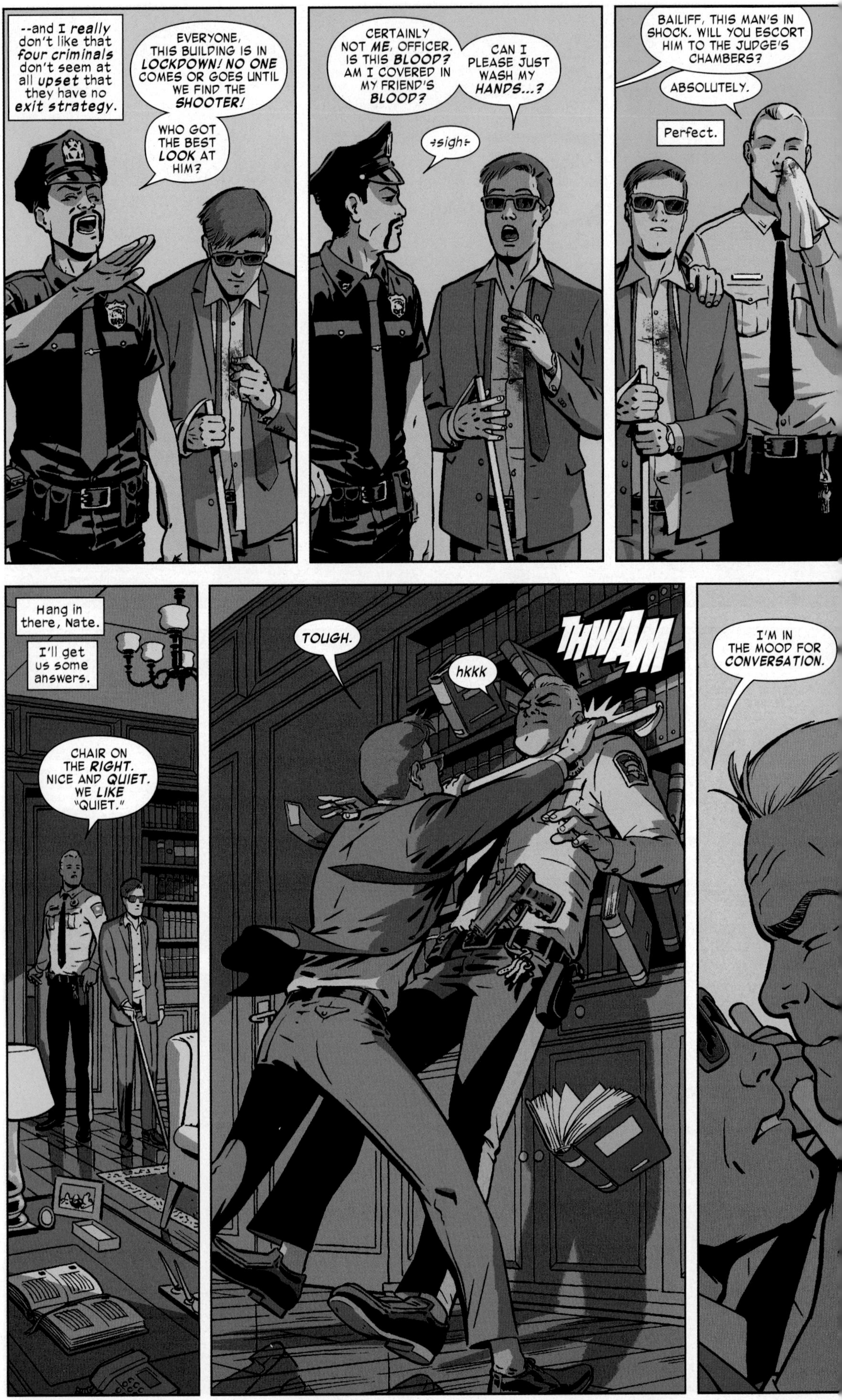
--and I really don't like that four criminals don't seem at all upset that they have no exit strategy.
EVERYONE, THIS BUILDING IS IN LOCKDOWN! NO ONE COMES OR GOES UNTIL WE FIND THE SHOOTER!
WHO GOT THE BEST LOOK AT HIM?
CERTAINLY NOT ME, OFFICER. IS THIS BLOOD? AM I COVERED IN MY FRIEND'S BLOOD?
CAN I PLEASE JUST WASH MY HANDS...?
-sigh-
BAILIFF, THIS MAN'S IN SHOCK. WILL YOU ESCORT HIM TO THE JUDGE'S CHAMBERS?
ABSOLUTELY.
Perfect.
Hang in there, Nate.
I'll get us some answers.
CHAIR ON THE RIGHT. NICE AND QUIET. WE LIKE "QUIET."
TOUGH.
hkkk
THWAM
I'M IN THE MOOD FOR CONVERSATION.

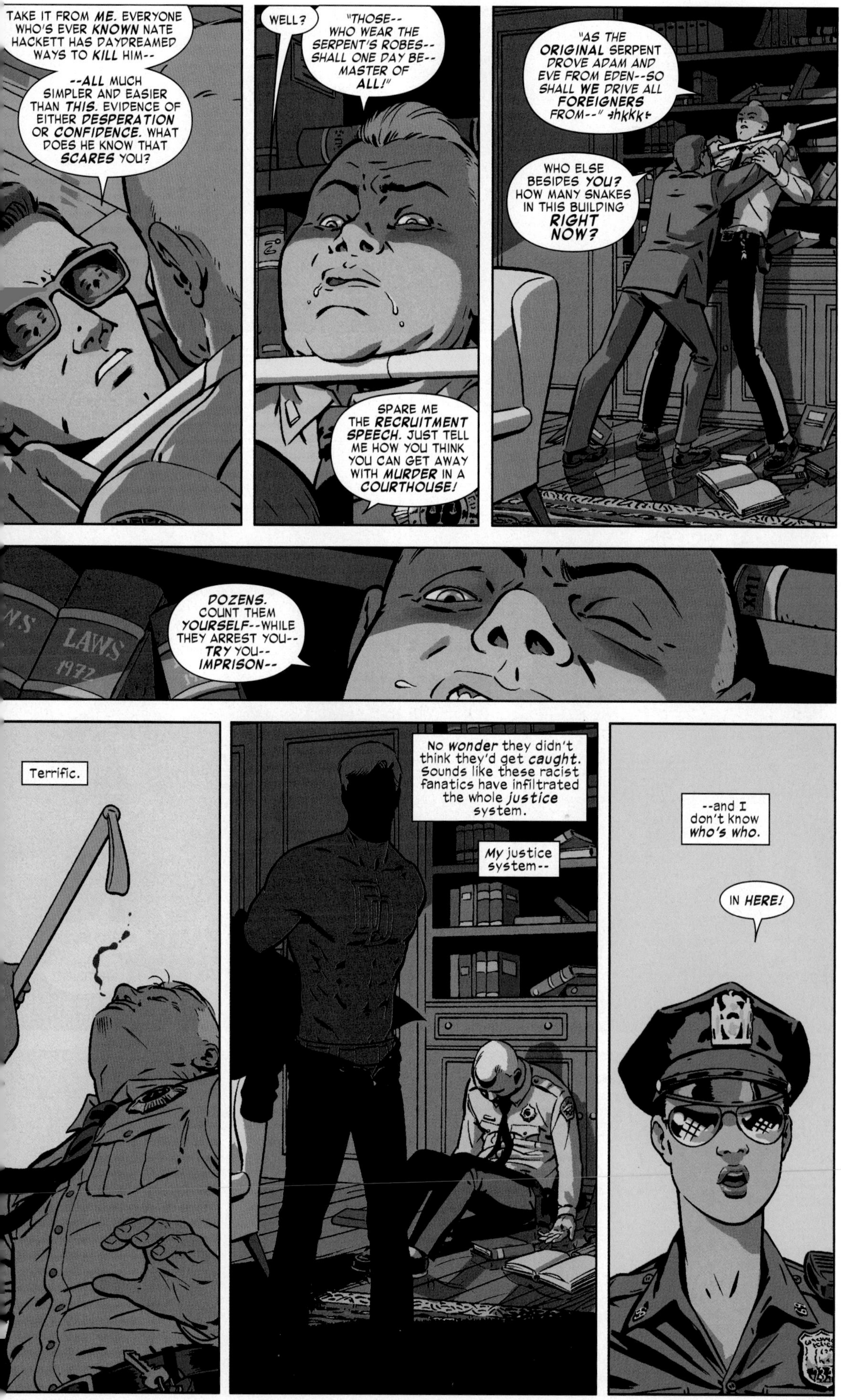
TAKE IT FROM ME. EVERYONE WHO'S EVER KNOWN NATE HACKETT HAS DAYDREAMED WAYS TO KILL HIM--
--ALL MUCH SIMPLER AND EASIER THAN THIS. EVIDENCE OF EITHER DESPERATION OR CONFIDENCE. WHAT DOES HE KNOW THAT SCARES YOU?
WELL?
"THOSE-- WHO WEAR THE SERPENT'S ROBES-- SHALL ONE DAY BE-- MASTER OF ALL!"
SPARE ME THE RECRUITMENT SPEECH. JUST TELL ME HOW YOU THINK YOU CAN GET AWAY WITH MURDER IN A COURTHOUSE!
"AS THE ORIGINAL SERPENT DROVE ADAM AND EVE FROM EDEN--SO SHALL WE DRIVE ALL FOREIGNERS FROM--" ghkkk
WHO ELSE BESIDES YOU? HOW MANY SNAKES IN THIS BUILDING RIGHT NOW?
DOZENS. COUNT THEM YOURSELF--WHILE THEY ARREST YOU-- TRY YOU-- IMPRISON--
LAWS 1972
Terrific.
No wonder they didn't think they'd get caught. Sounds like these racist fanatics have infiltrated the whole justice system.
My justice system--
--and I don't know who's who.
IN HERE!

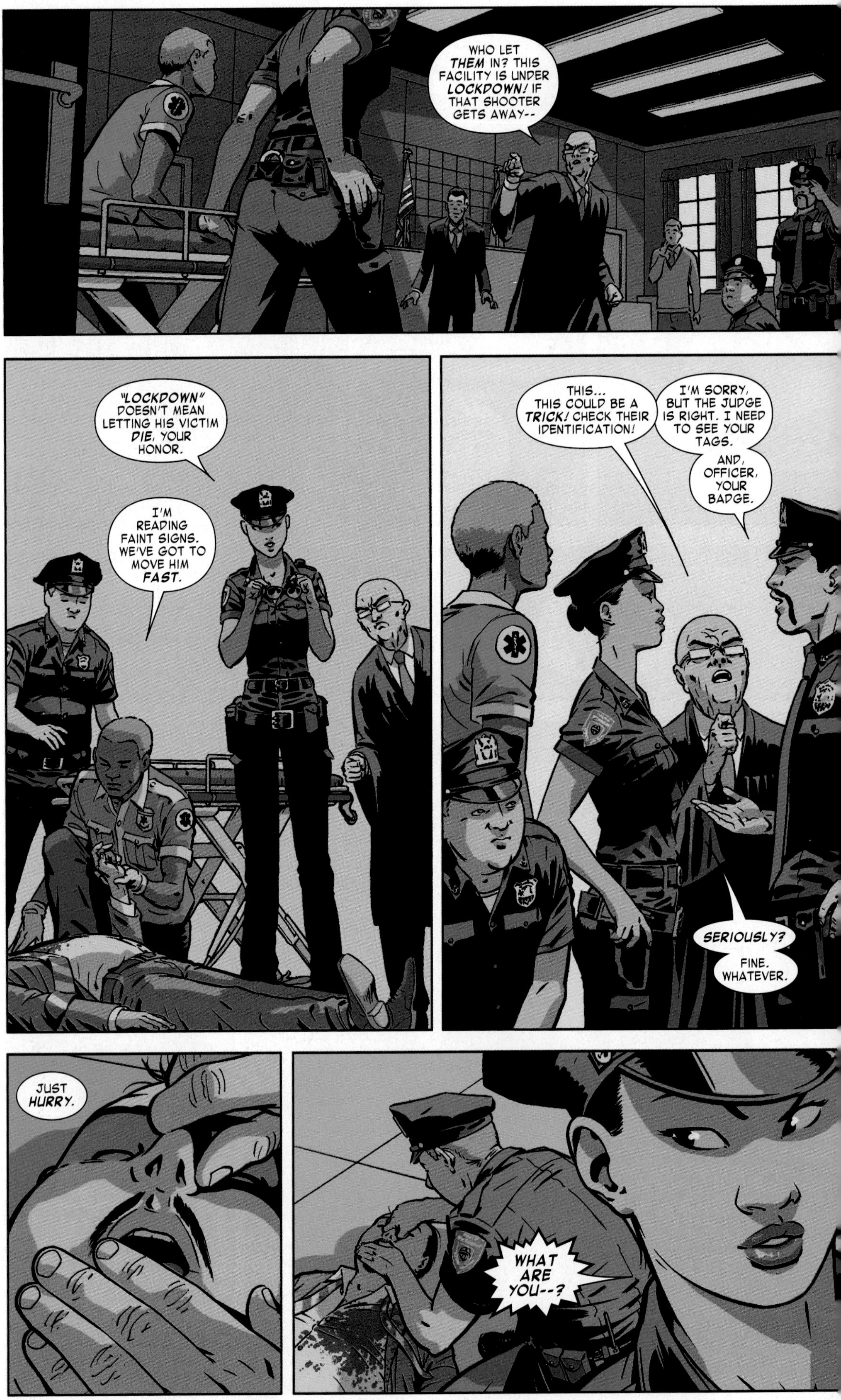
WHO LET THEM IN? THIS FACILITY IS UNDER LOCKDOWN! IF THAT SHOOTER GETS AWAY--
"LOCKDOWN" DOESN'T MEAN LETTING HIS VICTIM DIE, YOUR HONOR.
I'M READING FAINT SIGNS. WE'VE GOT TO MOVE HIM FAST.
THIS... THIS COULD BE A TRICK! CHECK THEIR IDENTIFICATION!
I'M SORRY, BUT THE JUDGE IS RIGHT. I NEED TO SEE YOUR TAGS.
AND, OFFICER, YOUR BADGE.
SERIOUSLY?
FINE. WHATEVER.
JUST HURRY.
WHAT ARE YOU--?

KRAK

AAAH!

WHO **ELSE** WANTS TO TAKE A CRACK AT HIM?

DAREDEVIL? WHAT'S GOING ON HERE?

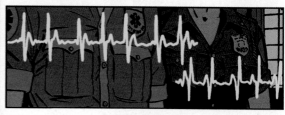

I SAVED YOUR PATIENT'S **LIFE.** THAT *"OFFICER"* WAS **SMOTHERING** HIM.

HE'S TELLING THE **TRUTH.** I **SAW** IT.

AND **YOU** SEEM MIGHTY **NERVOUS.**

WELL, **YEAH!** SO YOU'RE **BOTH** SONS OF THE SERPENT?

DO I **LOOK** LIKE A WHITE SUPREMACIST?

Ouch. What am I, *blind?*

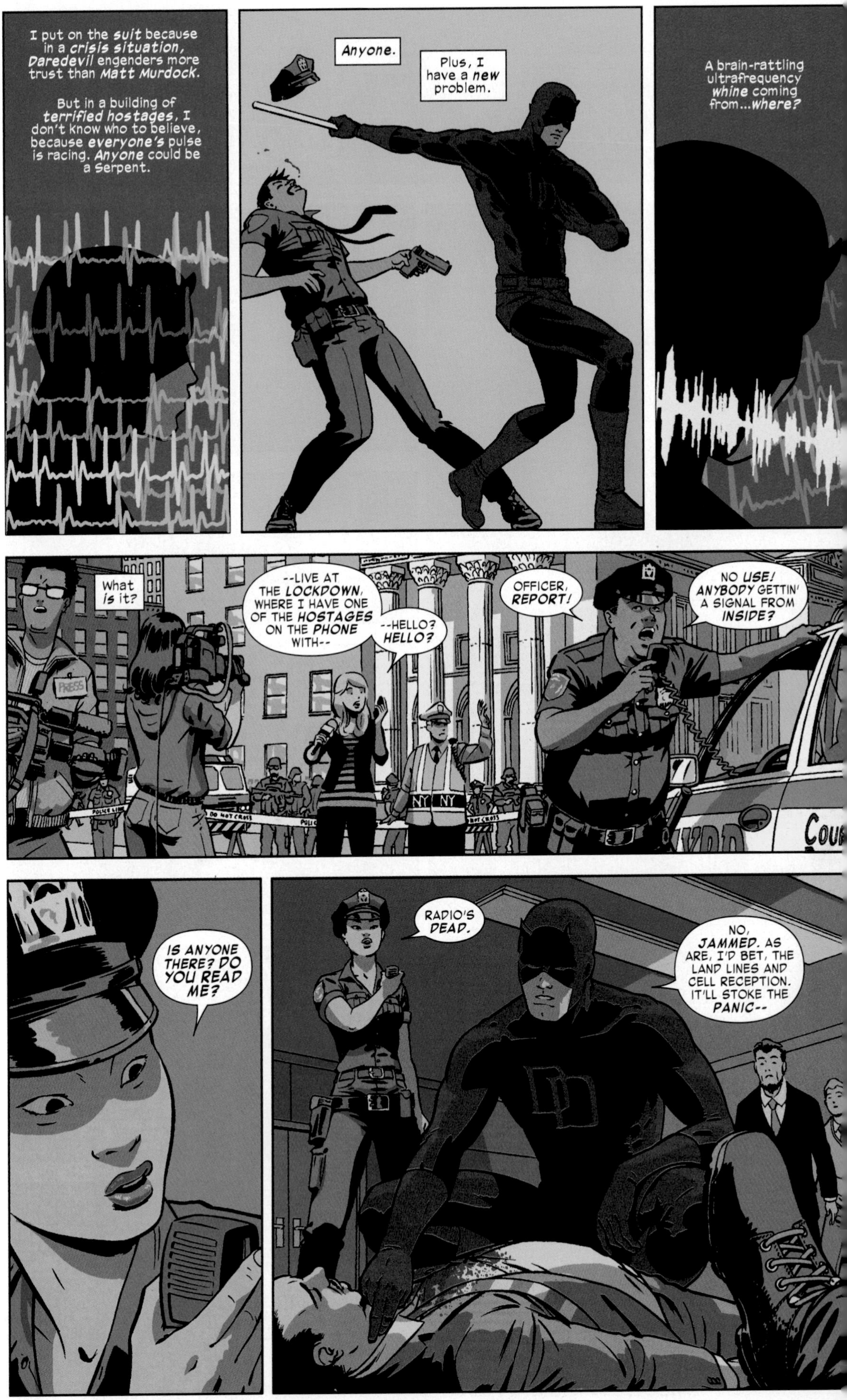

I put on the suit because in a crisis situation, Daredevil engenders more trust than Matt Murdock.
But in a building of terrified hostages, I don't know who to believe, because everyone's pulse is racing. Anyone could be a Serpent.
Anyone.
Plus, I have a new problem.
A brain-rattling ultrafrequency whine coming from...where?
What is it?
--LIVE AT THE LOCKDOWN, WHERE I HAVE ONE OF THE HOSTAGES ON THE PHONE WITH--
--HELLO? HELLO?
OFFICER, REPORT!
NO USE! ANYBODY GETTIN' A SIGNAL FROM INSIDE?
PRESS
POLICE LINE
DO NOT CROSS
NY NY
IS ANYONE THERE? DO YOU READ ME?
RADIO'S DEAD.
NO, JAMMED. AS ARE, I'D BET, THE LAND LINES AND CELL RECEPTION. IT'LL STOKE THE PANIC--

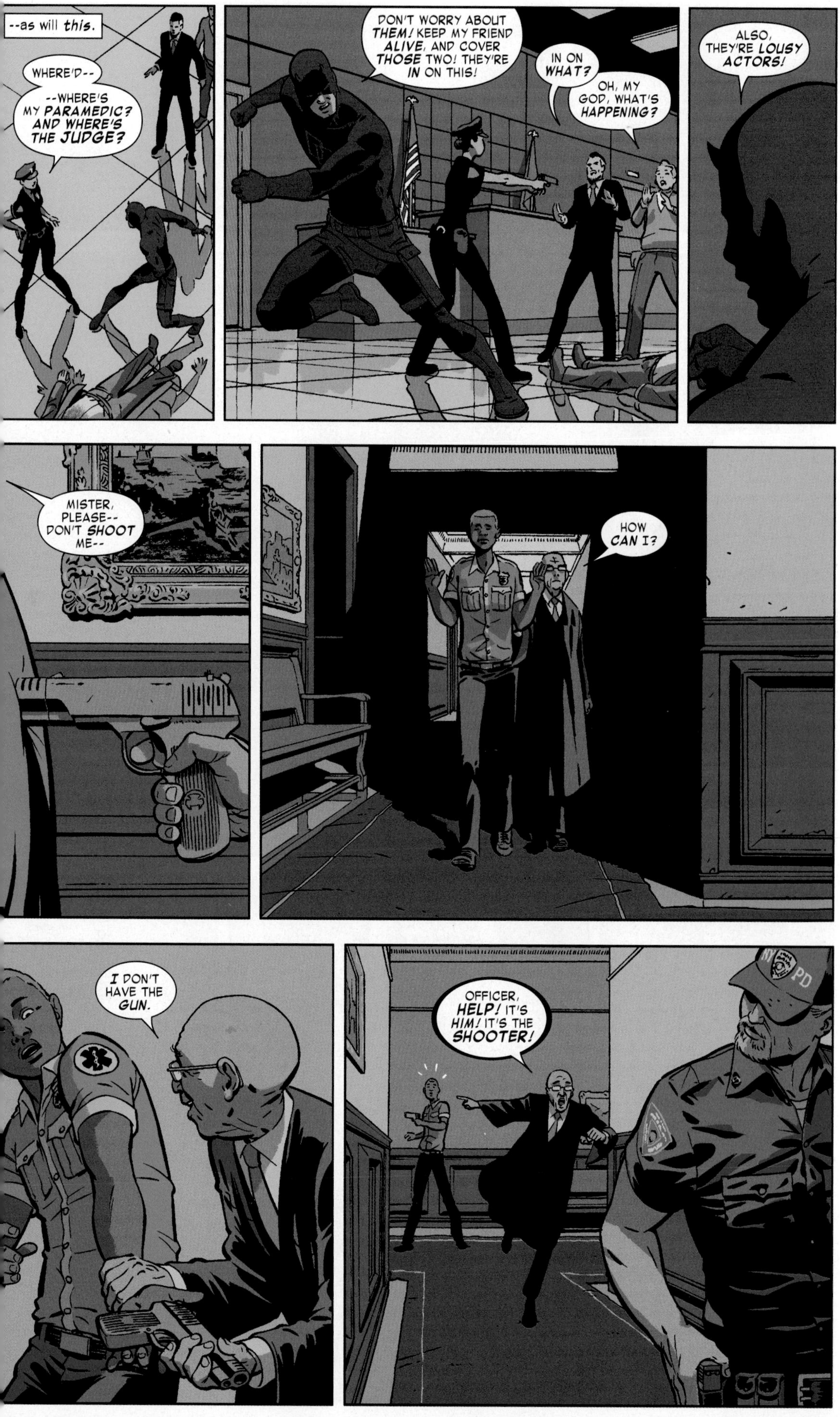

--as will this.
WHERE'D--
--WHERE'S MY PARAMEDIC? AND WHERE'S THE JUDGE?
DON'T WORRY ABOUT THEM! KEEP MY FRIEND ALIVE, AND COVER THOSE TWO! THEY'RE IN ON THIS!
IN ON WHAT?
OH, MY GOD, WHAT'S HAPPENING?
ALSO, THEY'RE LOUSY ACTORS!
MISTER, PLEASE-- DON'T SHOOT ME--
HOW CAN I?
I DON'T HAVE THE GUN.
OFFICER, HELP! IT'S HIM! IT'S THE SHOOTER!
NYPD

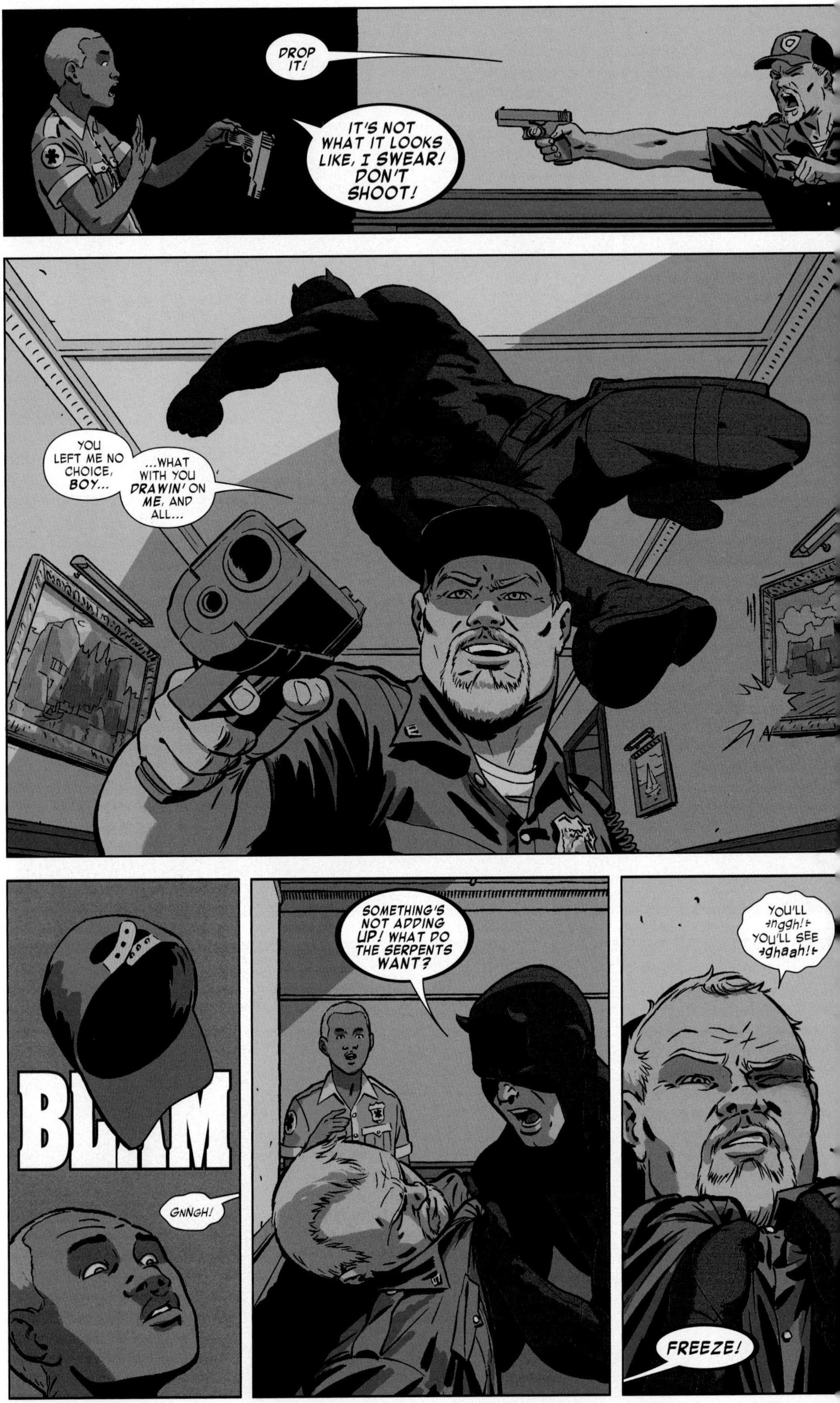
DROP IT!
IT'S NOT WHAT IT LOOKS LIKE, I SWEAR! DON'T SHOOT!
YOU LEFT ME NO CHOICE, BOY...
...WHAT WITH YOU DRAWIN' ON ME, AND ALL...
BLAM
GNNGH!
SOMETHING'S NOT ADDING UP! WHAT DO THE SERPENTS WANT?
YOU'LL ngh! YOU'LL SEE ghaah!
FREEZE!

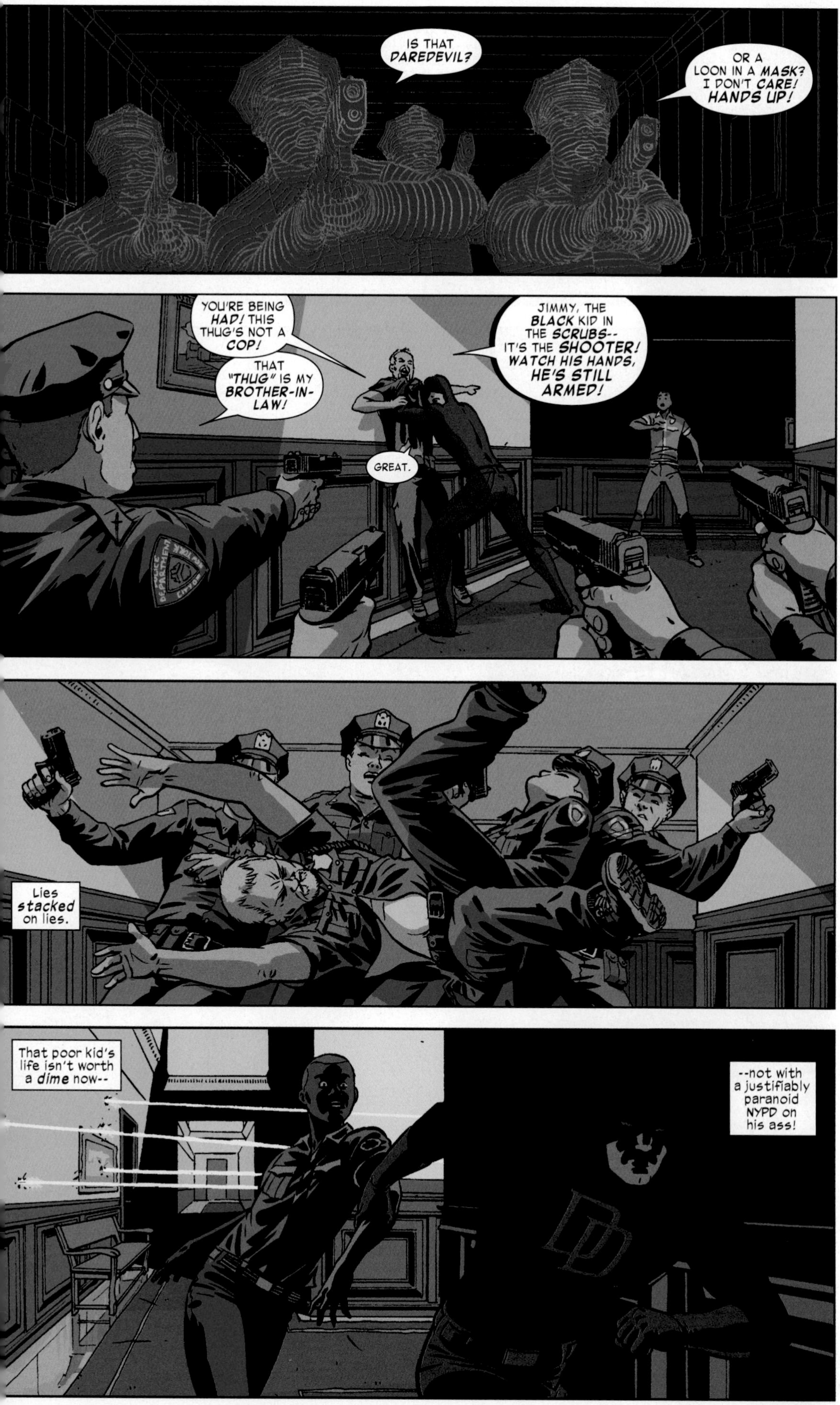

IS THAT DAREDEVIL?
OR A LOON IN A MASK? I DON'T CARE! HANDS UP!
YOU'RE BEING HAD! THIS THUG'S NOT A COP!
THAT "THUG" IS MY BROTHER-IN-LAW!
JIMMY, THE BLACK KID IN THE SCRUBS-- IT'S THE SHOOTER! WATCH HIS HANDS, HE'S STILL ARMED!
GREAT.
Lies stacked on lies.
That poor kid's life isn't worth a dime now--
--not with a justifiably paranoid NYPD on his ass!

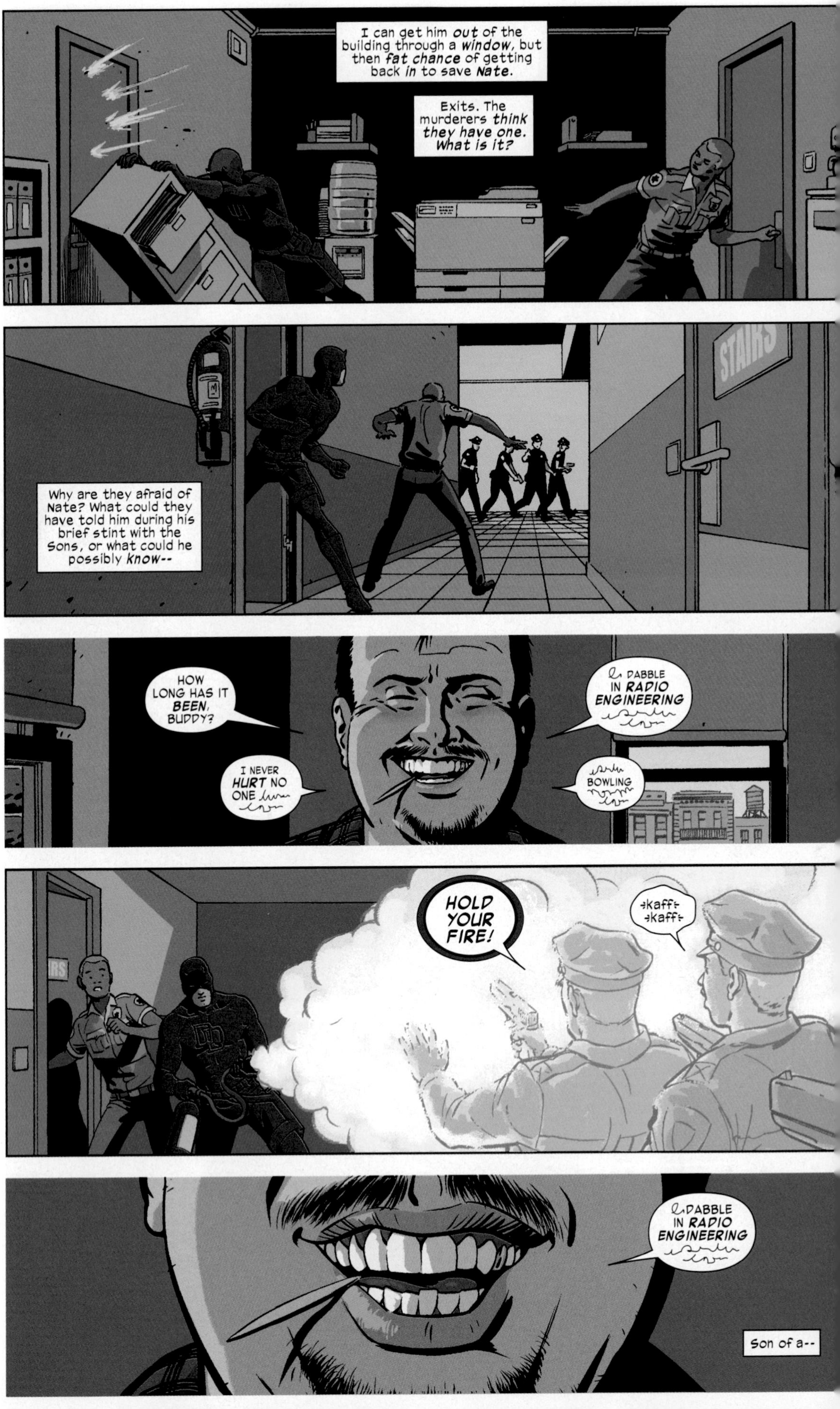

I can get him out of the building through a window, but then fat chance of getting back in to save Nate.
Exits. The murderers think they have one. What is it?
STAIRS
Why are they afraid of Nate? What could they have told him during his brief stint with the Sons, or what could he possibly know--
HOW LONG HAS IT BEEN, BUDDY?
DABBLE IN RADIO ENGINEERING
I NEVER HURT NO ONE
BOWLING
HOLD YOUR FIRE!
kaff kaff
DABBLE IN RADIO ENGINEERING
Son of a--

The whine of the radio jammer. It's coming from down *low*.

YOU EVER *BUNGEE JUMP?*

NO!

DOES IT SOUND MORE *INVITING* THAN GETTING *SHOT?*

WHAT'S *HAPPENING?*

I'LL TAKE THAT AS A *"YES."*

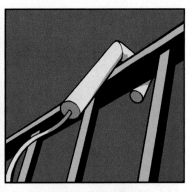

BLAM BLAM BLAM BLAM BLAM BLAM BLAM

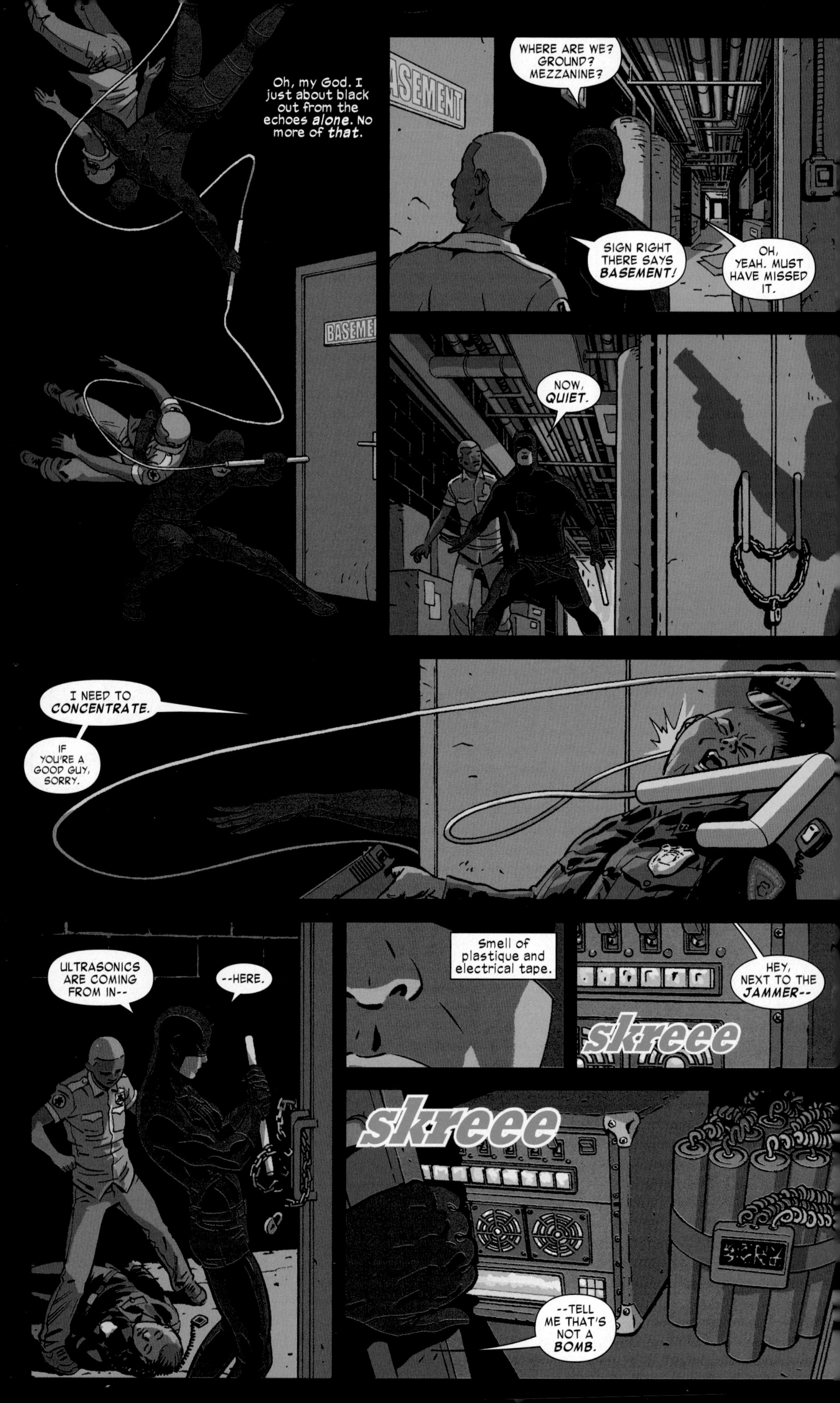
Oh, my God. I just about black out from the echoes *alone*. No more of *that*.
BASEMENT
WHERE ARE WE? GROUND? MEZZANINE?
SIGN RIGHT THERE SAYS *BASEMENT!*
OH, YEAH. MUST HAVE MISSED IT.
NOW, *QUIET*.
I NEED TO *CONCENTRATE*.
IF YOU'RE A GOOD GUY, SORRY.
ULTRASONICS ARE COMING FROM IN--
--HERE.
Smell of plastique and electrical tape.
HEY, NEXT TO THE *JAMMER*--
skreee
skreee
--TELL ME THAT'S NOT A *BOMB*.

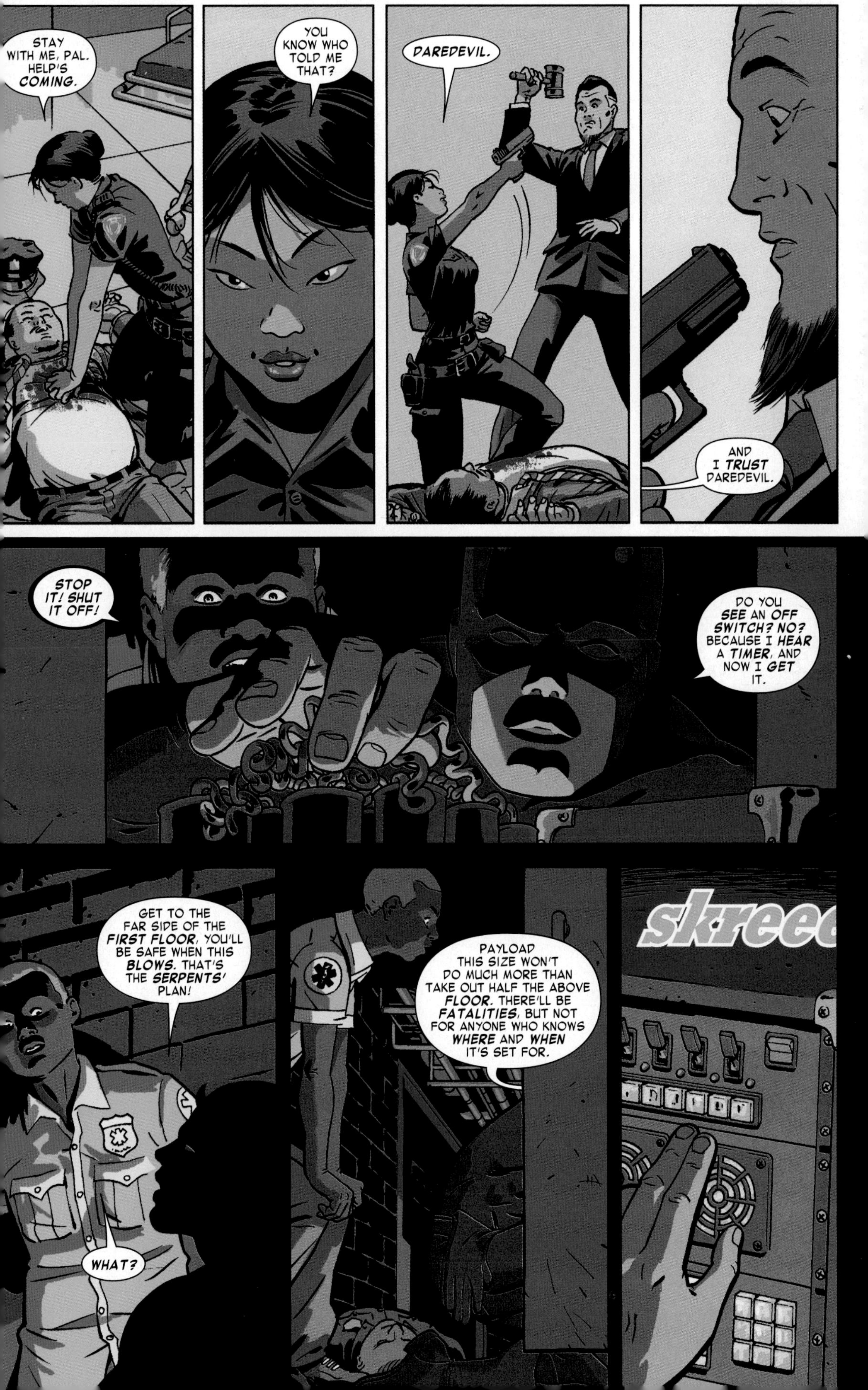
STAY WITH ME, PAL. HELP'S COMING.
YOU KNOW WHO TOLD ME THAT?
DAREDEVIL.
AND I TRUST DAREDEVIL.
STOP IT! SHUT IT OFF!
DO YOU SEE AN OFF SWITCH? NO? BECAUSE I HEAR A TIMER, AND NOW I GET IT.
GET TO THE FAR SIDE OF THE FIRST FLOOR, YOU'LL BE SAFE WHEN THIS BLOWS. THAT'S THE SERPENTS' PLAN!
WHAT?
PAYLOAD THIS SIZE WON'T DO MUCH MORE THAN TAKE OUT HALF THE ABOVE FLOOR. THERE'LL BE FATALITIES, BUT NOT FOR ANYONE WHO KNOWS WHERE AND WHEN IT'S SET FOR.
skreee

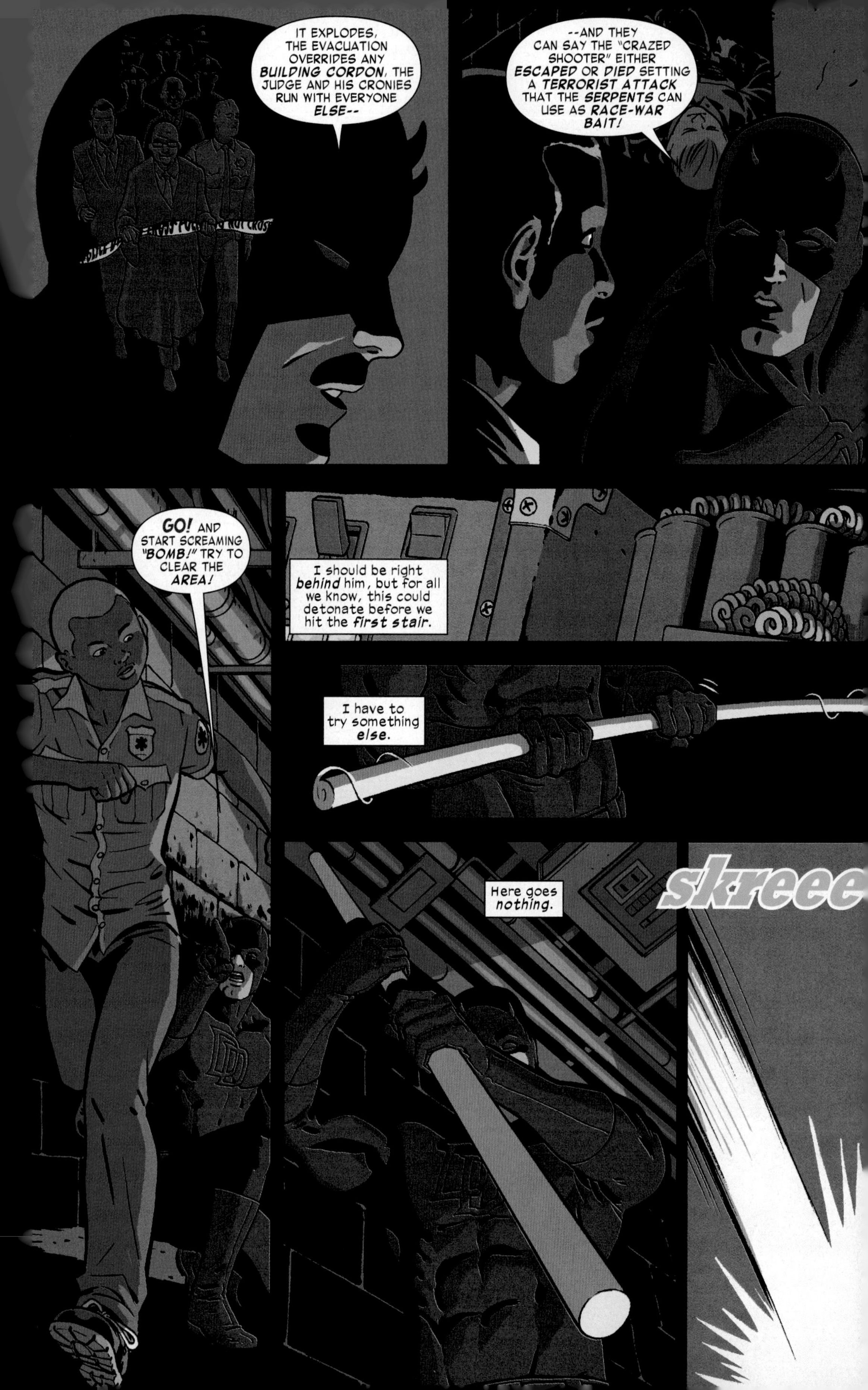
IT EXPLODES, THE EVACUATION OVERRIDES ANY BUILDING CORDON, THE JUDGE AND HIS CRONIES RUN WITH EVERYONE ELSE--
--AND THEY CAN SAY THE "CRAZED SHOOTER" EITHER ESCAPED OR DIED SETTING A TERRORIST ATTACK THAT THE SERPENTS CAN USE AS RACE-WAR BAIT!
GO! AND START SCREAMING "BOMB!" TRY TO CLEAR THE AREA!
I should be right behind him, but for all we know, this could detonate before we hit the first stair.
I have to try something else.
Here goes nothing.
skreee

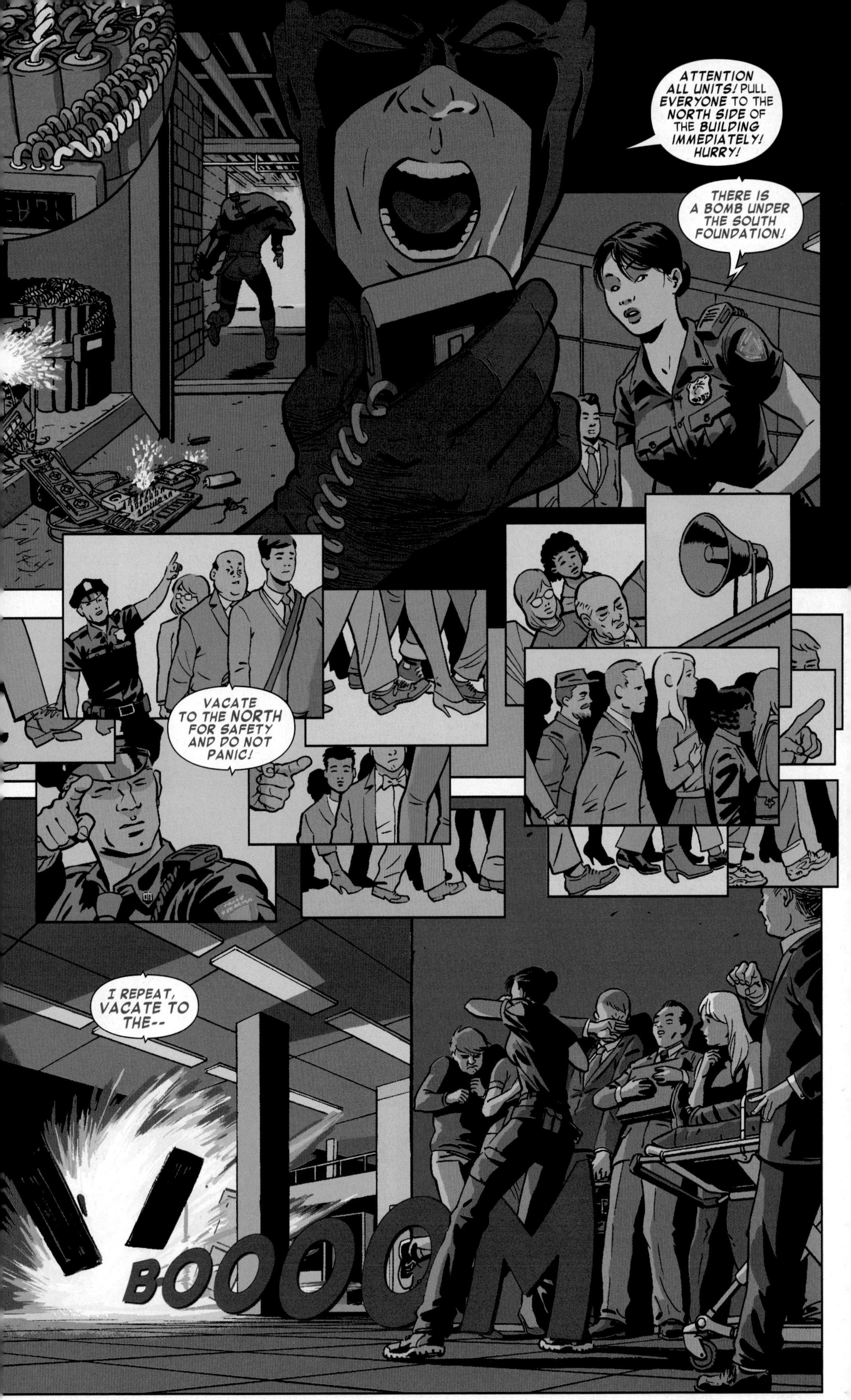
ATTENTION ALL UNITS! PULL EVERYONE TO THE NORTH SIDE OF THE BUILDING IMMEDIATELY! HURRY!
THERE IS A BOMB UNDER THE SOUTH FOUNDATION!
VACATE TO THE NORTH FOR SAFETY AND DO NOT PANIC!
I REPEAT, VACATE TO THE--
BOOOOOM

24 HOURS LATER.

...nnnhhh...

SAY, LOOK WHO'S AWAKE.

THE RADIO ENGINEER WHO MIGHT HAVE REMEMBERED HAVING A DETAILED CONVERSATION ABOUT FREQUENCY JAMMERS WITH A SERPENT BROTHER.

HERE'S THE BAD NEWS: I WON'T HELP YOU SUE THE CITY NOW THAT WE KNOW IT WASN'T THE NYPD BEHIND THE FALSE ARREST, BUT RATHER THE SERPENTS.

THEY SUMMONED YOU NOT TO COURT SO MUCH AS TO AN INQUISITION THAT BECAME A NEAR-EXECUTION WHEN THE JUDGE GOT COCKY.

YOU'LL BE HAPPY TO KNOW H WAS JAILED ONC DAREDEVIL BACKE THE CLAIMS OF T MAN HE TRIED TO FRAME.

...YOU'RE... KIDDING...

I'M SORRY, NATE. YOU WANTED A FRESH START, AND THIS ISN'T IT. BUT LET'S CONCENTRATE ON GETTING YOU WELL FIRST.

I KNOW YOU'RE BROKE. DON'T SWEAT THAT.

I HAVE THE BEST DOCTORS WORKING WITH YOU, AND THEY SAY YOU'LL PULL THROUGH.

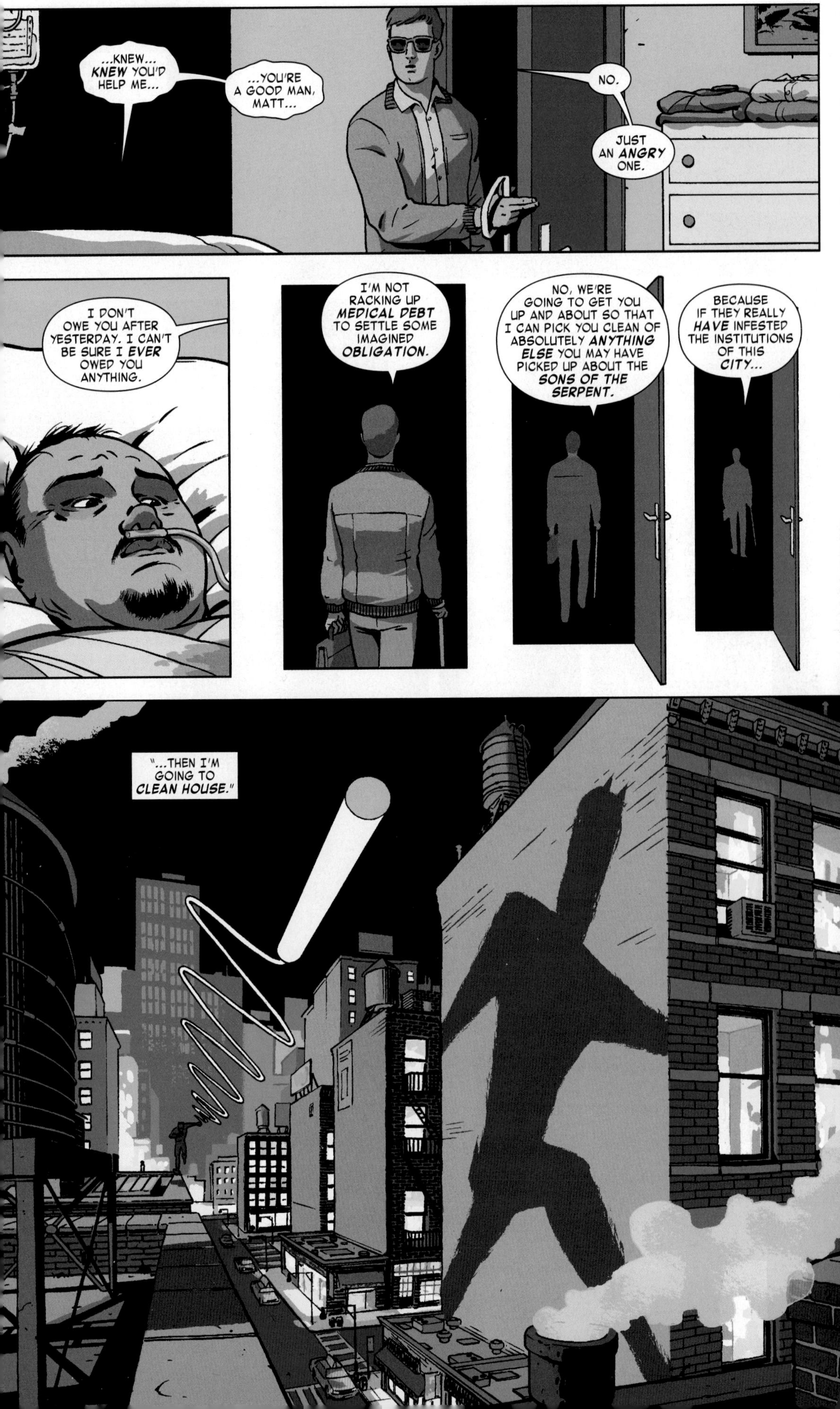
...KNEW... KNEW YOU'D HELP ME...
...YOU'RE A GOOD MAN, MATT...
NO.
JUST AN ANGRY ONE.
I DON'T OWE YOU AFTER YESTERDAY. I CAN'T BE SURE I EVER OWED YOU ANYTHING.
I'M NOT RACKING UP MEDICAL DEBT TO SETTLE SOME IMAGINED OBLIGATION.
NO, WE'RE GOING TO GET YOU UP AND ABOUT SO THAT I CAN PICK YOU CLEAN OF ABSOLUTELY ANYTHING ELSE YOU MAY HAVE PICKED UP ABOUT THE SONS OF THE SERPENT.
BECAUSE IF THEY REALLY HAVE INFESTED THE INSTITUTIONS OF THIS CITY...
"...THEN I'M GOING TO CLEAN HOUSE."

Terrific. Just what I need on my shoulders right now.

More crippling *expenses*.

With Foggy out of the office, I'm stretched to my *limit* with our mutual *caseload*—

—and that would be true even if being a *lawyer* were my *only* responsibility.

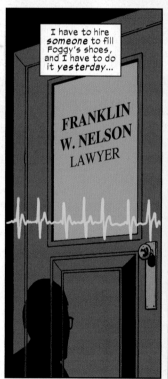

I have to hire *someone* to fill Foggy's shoes, and I have to do it *yesterday*...

FRANKLIN W. NELSON
LAWYER

...

...unless the *last person I'd ever expect* had already *taken* the job while I wasn't *looking!*

FRANKLIN
W. NELSON
LAWYER

HELLO?

MAY I *HELP* YOU?

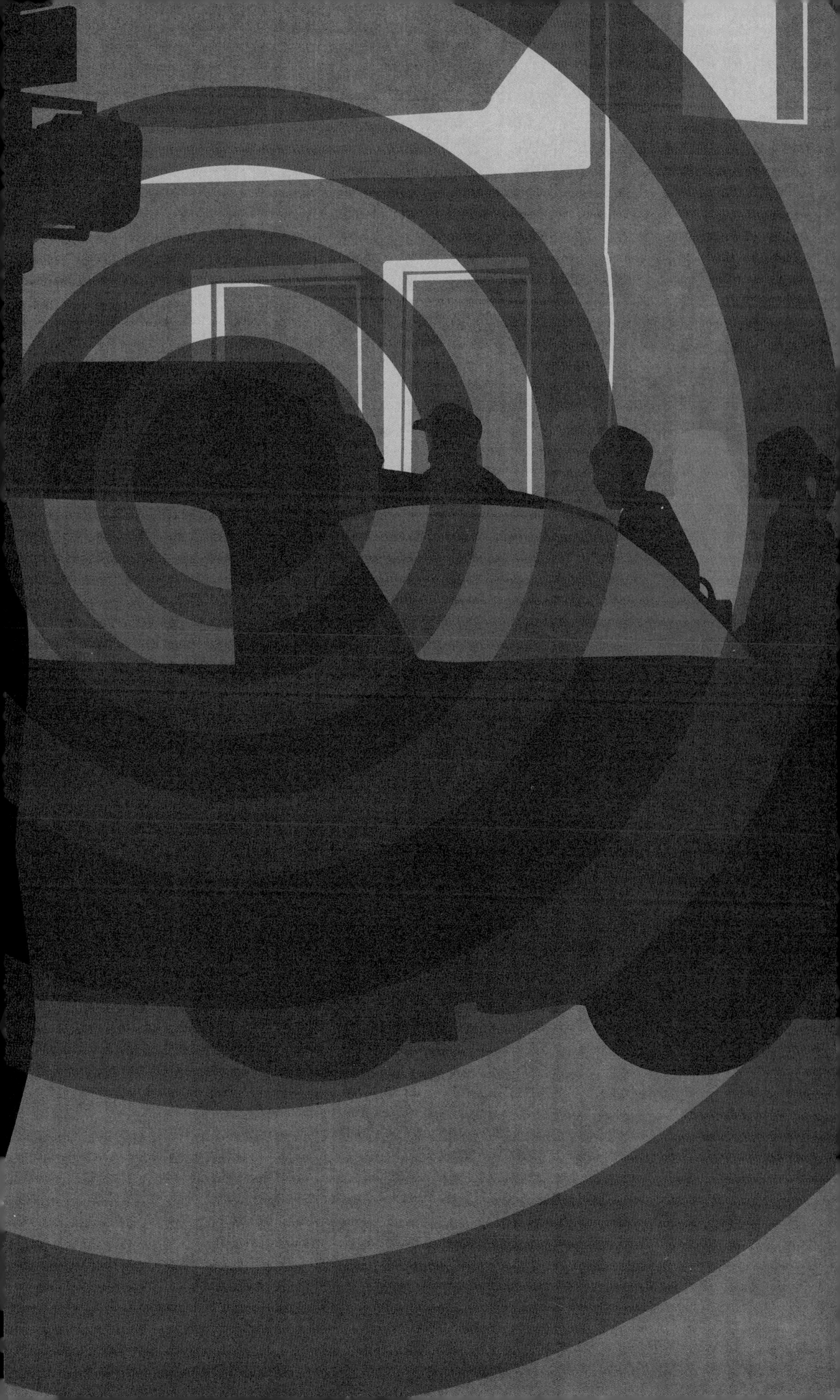

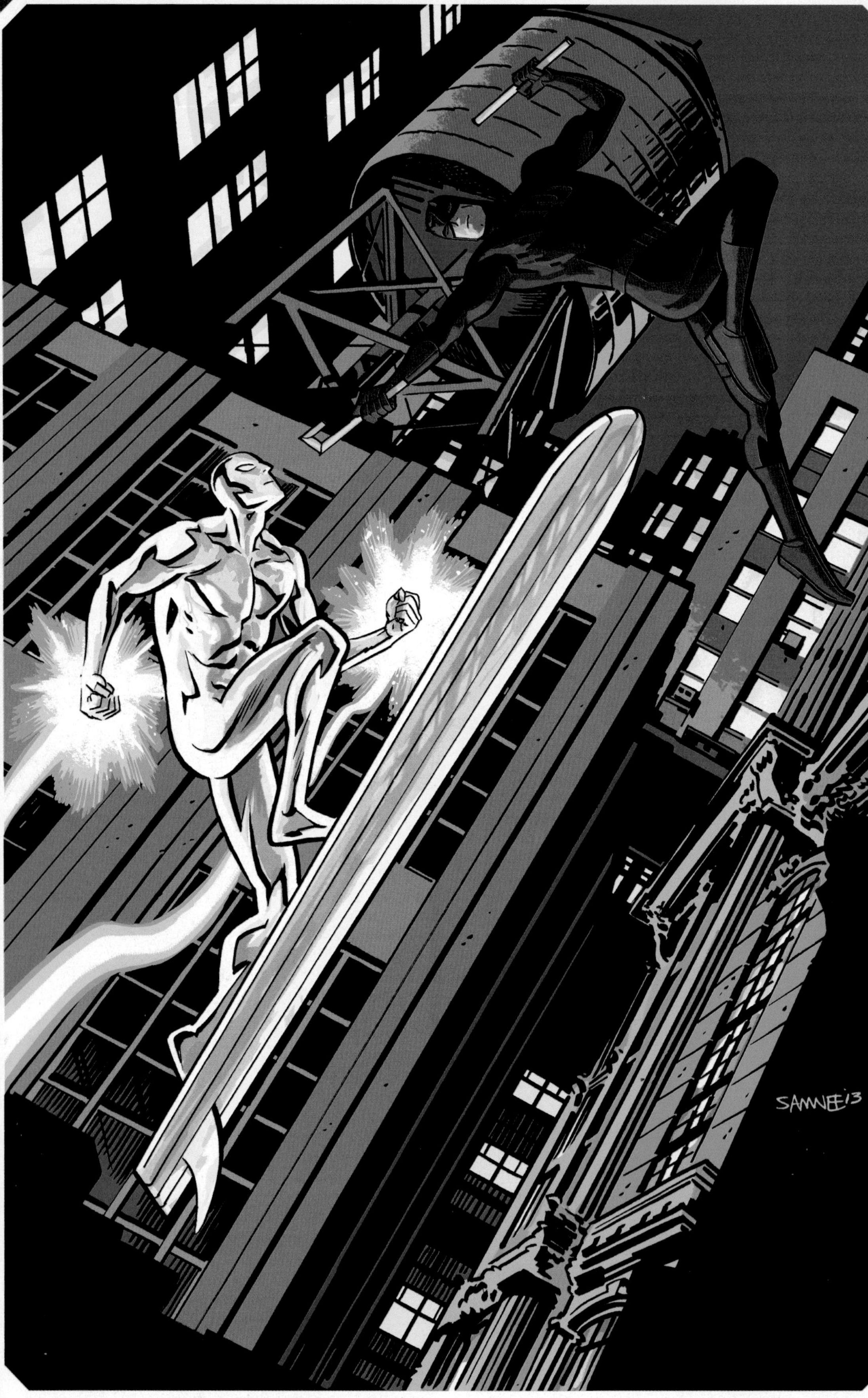
SAMNEE '13

DAREDEVIL #30

Since the start, our law firm has opened its doors to many notable women.

Karen Page was Nelson & Murdock's first office manager and the love of my life.

Karen smelled of milk and lavender.

Heather Glenn convinced us to work as storefront lawyers for a while.

Heather's laugh was a symphony orchestra of joy.

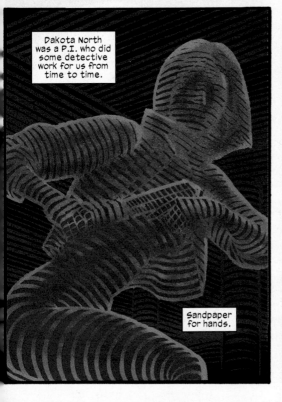

Dakota North was a P.I. who did some detective work for us from time to time.

Sandpaper for hands.

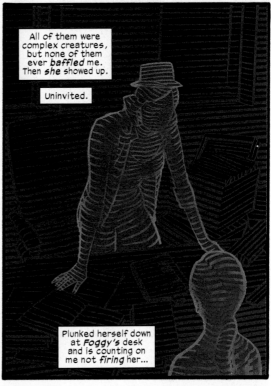

All of them were complex creatures, but none of them ever *baffled* me. Then *she* showed up.

Uninvited.

Plunked herself down at *Foggy's* desk and is counting on me not *firing* her...

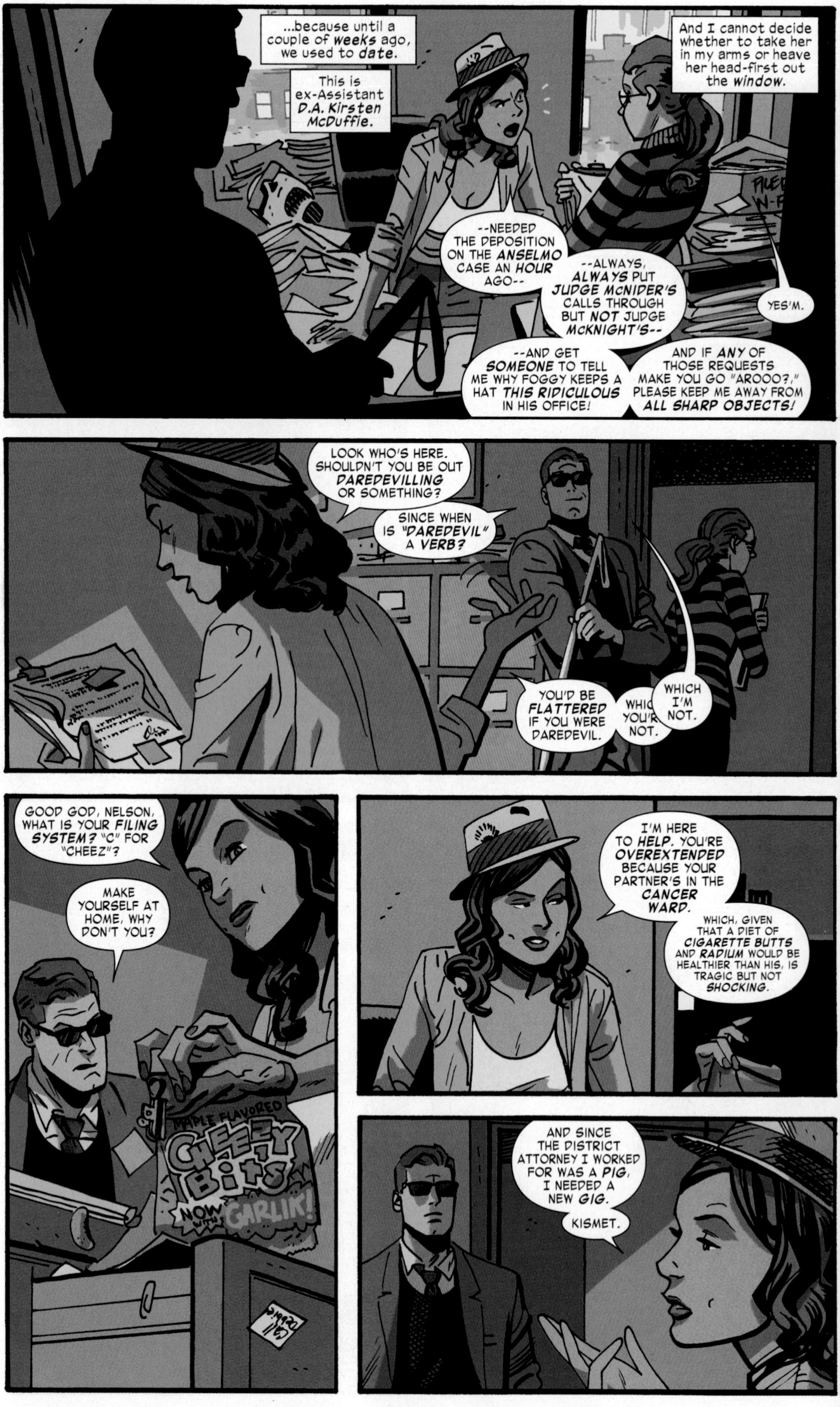
...because until a couple of *weeks* ago, we used to *date*.
This is ex-Assistant *D.A. Kirsten McDuffie*.
And I cannot decide whether to take her in my arms or heave her head-first out the *window*.
--NEEDED THE DEPOSITION ON THE **ANSELMO** CASE AN **HOUR** AGO--
--ALWAYS, **ALWAYS** PUT **JUDGE McNIDER'S** CALLS THROUGH BUT **NOT** JUDGE **McKNIGHT'S**--
YES'M.
--AND GET **SOMEONE** TO TELL ME WHY FOGGY KEEPS A HAT **THIS RIDICULOUS** IN HIS OFFICE!
AND IF **ANY** OF THOSE REQUESTS MAKE YOU GO "AROOO?," PLEASE KEEP ME AWAY FROM **ALL SHARP OBJECTS!**
LOOK WHO'S HERE. SHOULDN'T YOU BE OUT **DAREDEVILLING** OR SOMETHING?
SINCE WHEN IS **"DAREDEVIL"** A **VERB?**
YOU'D BE **FLATTERED** IF YOU WERE DAREDEVIL.
WHIC YOU'R NOT.
WHICH I'M NOT.
GOOD GOD, NELSON, WHAT IS YOUR **FILING SYSTEM?** "C" FOR "CHEEZ"?
MAKE YOURSELF AT HOME, WHY DON'T YOU?
MAPLE FLAVORED CHEEZY BITS NOW WITH GARLIK!
I'M HERE TO **HELP.** YOU'RE **OVEREXTENDED** BECAUSE YOUR PARTNER'S IN THE **CANCER WARD.**
WHICH, GIVEN THAT A DIET OF **CIGARETTE BUTTS** AND **RADIUM** WOULD BE HEALTHIER THAN HIS, IS TRAGIC BUT NOT **SHOCKING.**
AND SINCE THE DISTRICT ATTORNEY I WORKED FOR WAS A **PIG,** I NEEDED A NEW **GIG.**
KISMET.

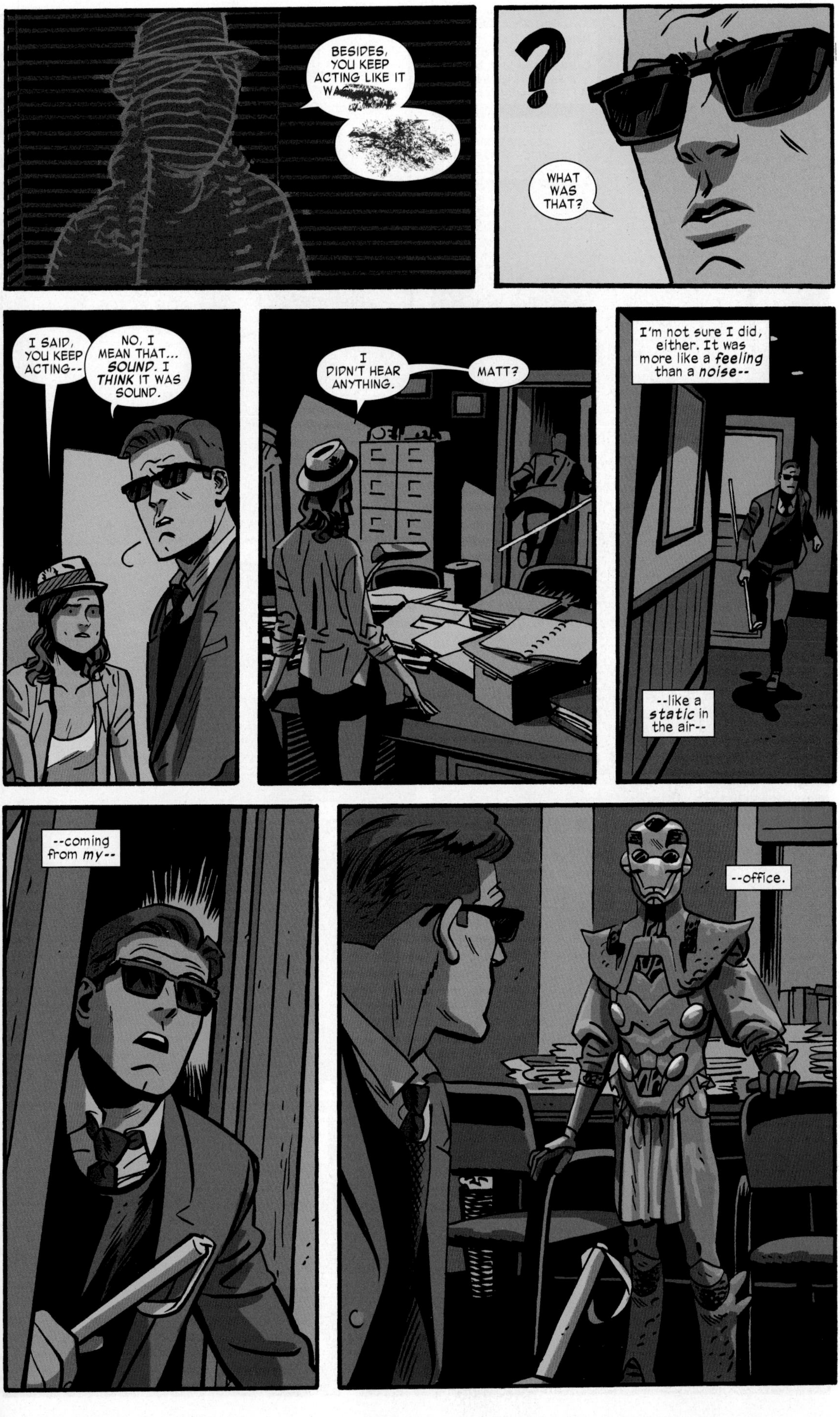

BESIDES, YOU KEEP ACTING LIKE IT WA
?
WHAT WAS THAT?
I SAID, YOU KEEP ACTING--
NO, I MEAN THAT... SOUND. I THINK IT WAS SOUND.
I DIDN'T HEAR ANYTHING.
MATT?
I'm not sure I did, either. It was more like a feeling than a noise--
--like a static in the air--
--coming from my--
--office.

Whatever it is, it has a voice like *ground glass*, and just being *close* to it gives me an instant *migraine.*

Naturally--an occupational *hazard*--I assume I'm under *attack.*

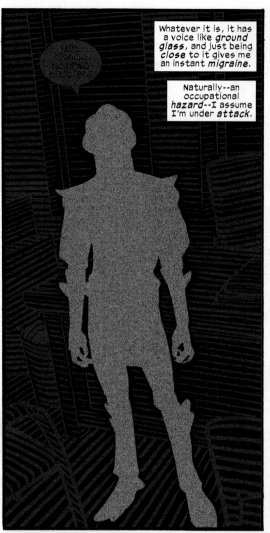

Then it *adjusts.*

ᔓᏨᏔᑫ ᗯ8Ꮸ᙭ᏋᏫ 8CTIVATE *VOICEWASH TRANSLATOR.*

ARE YOU NOW *COMPREHENDING* ME, MATTMURDOCK?

YOUR... YOUR *WORDS,* ANYWAY. WHAT... *ARE* YOU?

WAIT. *FIRST* QUESTION. I HAVE *EMPLOYEES* OUT THERE. ARE THEY *SAFE?*

I AM THE ONE IN *DANGER,* MATTMURDOCK.

MY...MY *SELF*...SELF- *DESIGNATION*--?

NAME?

THAT! MY NAME IS *RU'ACH.* I AM FROM MANY *PARSECS ON,* AND I REQUIRE YOUR *AID*...

...FOR I SEEK *ASYLUM* ON YOUR WORLD. YOU ARE *DAREDEVIL,* YES?

I cannot *wait* to hear what *that* has to do with anything.

HOW DO *YOU KNOW ME?*

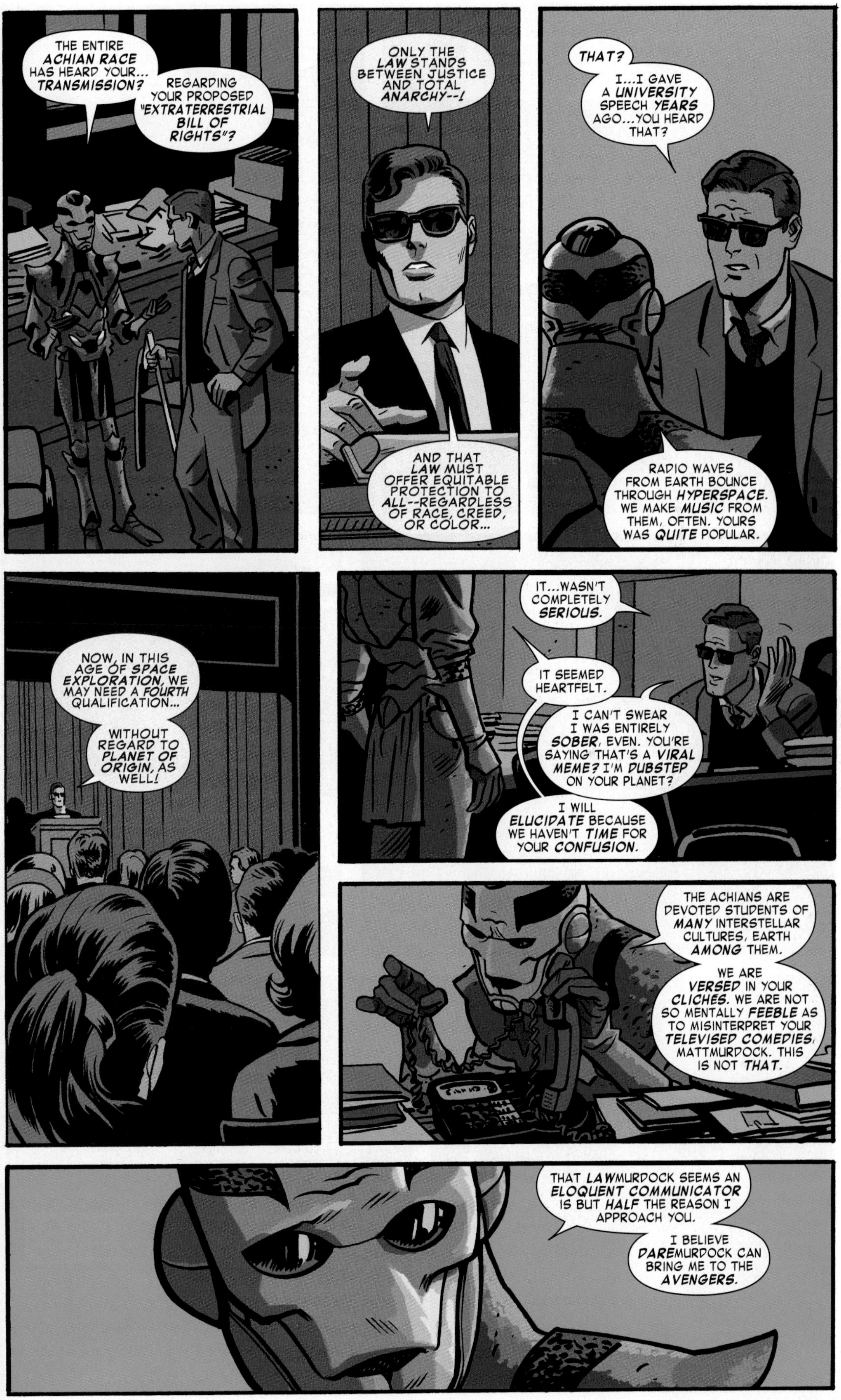
THE ENTIRE ACHIAN RACE HAS HEARD YOUR... TRANSMISSION?
REGARDING YOUR PROPOSED "EXTRATERRESTRIAL BILL OF RIGHTS"?
ONLY THE LAW STANDS BETWEEN JUSTICE AND TOTAL ANARCHY--!
AND THAT LAW MUST OFFER EQUITABLE PROTECTION TO ALL--REGARDLESS OF RACE, CREED, OR COLOR...
THAT?
I...I GAVE A UNIVERSITY SPEECH YEARS AGO...YOU HEARD THAT?
RADIO WAVES FROM EARTH BOUNCE THROUGH HYPERSPACE. WE MAKE MUSIC FROM THEM, OFTEN. YOURS WAS QUITE POPULAR.
NOW, IN THIS AGE OF SPACE EXPLORATION, WE MAY NEED A FOURTH QUALIFICATION...
WITHOUT REGARD TO PLANET OF ORIGIN, AS WELL!
IT...WASN'T COMPLETELY SERIOUS.
IT SEEMED HEARTFELT.
I CAN'T SWEAR I WAS ENTIRELY SOBER, EVEN. YOU'RE SAYING THAT'S A VIRAL MEME? I'M DUBSTEP ON YOUR PLANET?
I WILL ELUCIDATE BECAUSE WE HAVEN'T TIME FOR YOUR CONFUSION.
THE ACHIANS ARE DEVOTED STUDENTS OF MANY INTERSTELLAR CULTURES, EARTH AMONG THEM.
WE ARE VERSED IN YOUR CLICHES. WE ARE NOT SO MENTALLY FEEBLE AS TO MISINTERPRET YOUR TELEVISED COMEDIES, MATTMURDOCK. THIS IS NOT THAT.
THAT LAWMURDOCK SEEMS AN ELOQUENT COMMUNICATOR IS BUT HALF THE REASON I APPROACH YOU.
I BELIEVE DAREMURDOCK CAN BRING ME TO THE AVENGERS.

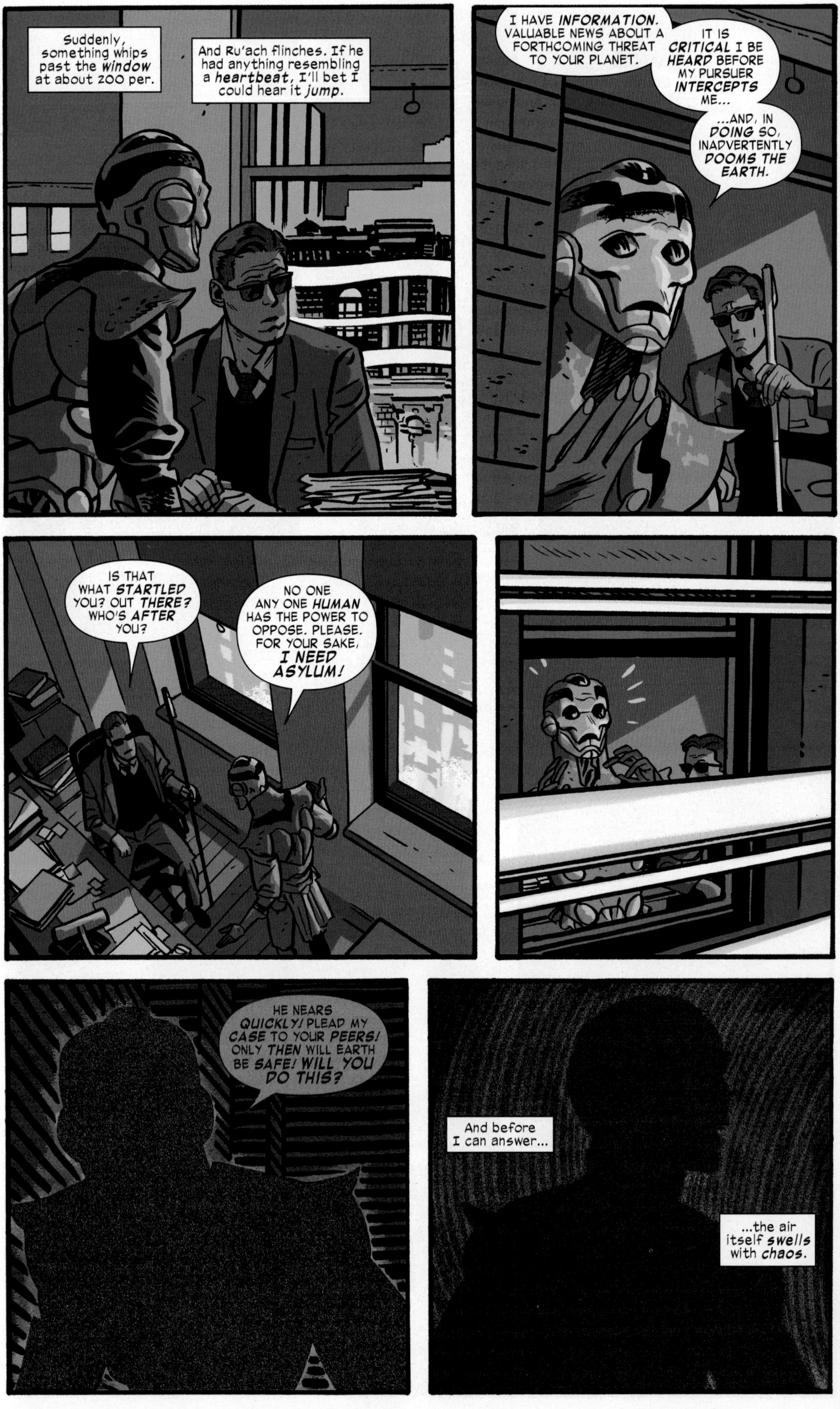
Suddenly, something whips past the window at about 200 per.
And Ru'ach flinches. If he had anything resembling a heartbeat, I'll bet I could hear it jump.
I HAVE INFORMATION. VALUABLE NEWS ABOUT A FORTHCOMING THREAT TO YOUR PLANET.
IT IS CRITICAL I BE HEARD BEFORE MY PURSUER INTERCEPTS ME...
...AND, IN DOING SO, INADVERTENTLY DOOMS THE EARTH.
IS THAT WHAT STARTLED YOU? OUT THERE? WHO'S AFTER YOU?
NO ONE ANY ONE HUMAN HAS THE POWER TO OPPOSE. PLEASE. FOR YOUR SAKE, I NEED ASYLUM!
HE NEARS QUICKLY! PLEAD MY CASE TO YOUR PEERS! ONLY THEN WILL EARTH BE SAFE! WILL YOU DO THIS?
And before I can answer...
...the air itself swells with chaos.

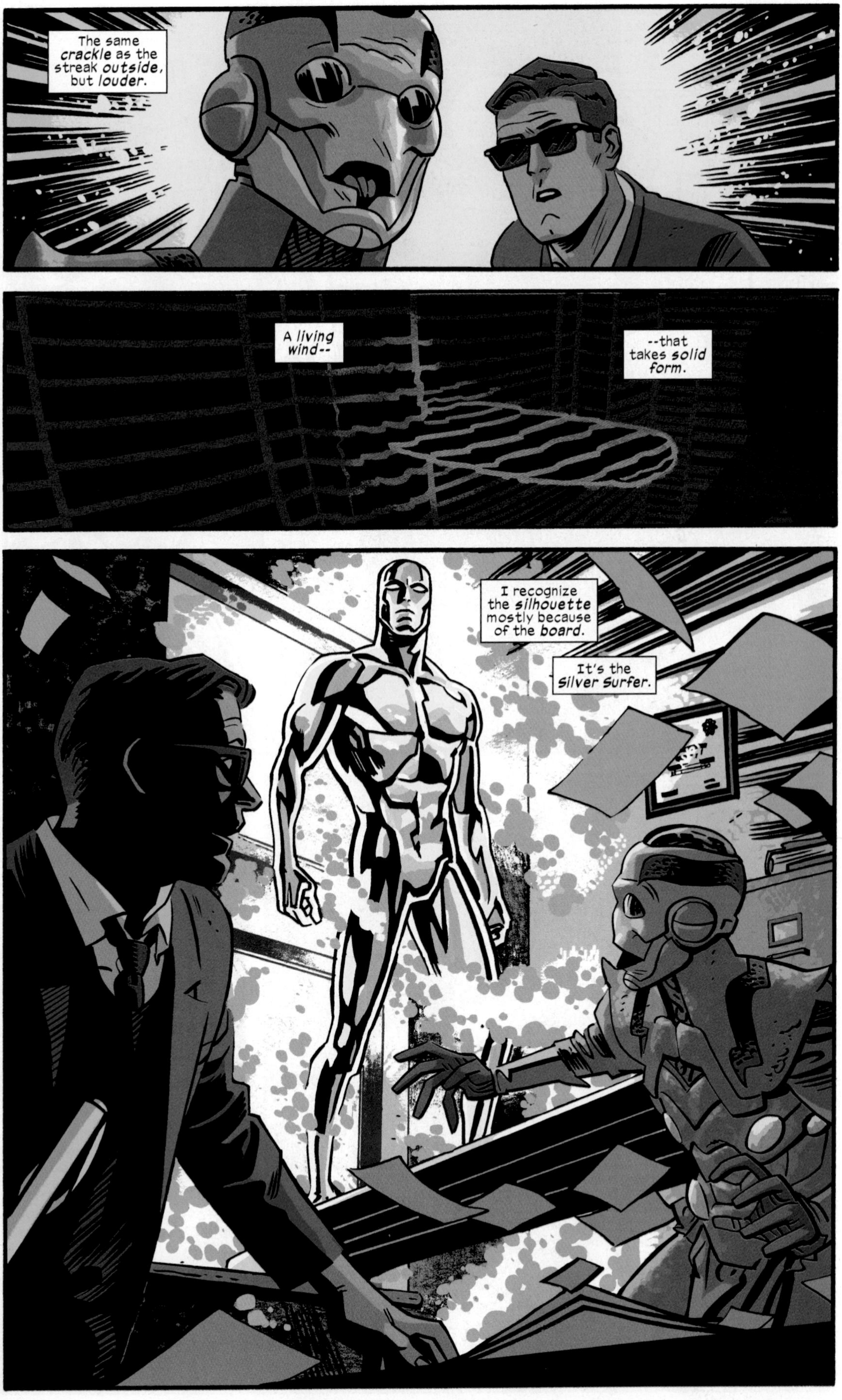
The same crackle as the streak outside, but louder.
A living wind--
--that takes solid form.
I recognize the silhouette mostly because of the board.
It's the Silver Surfer.

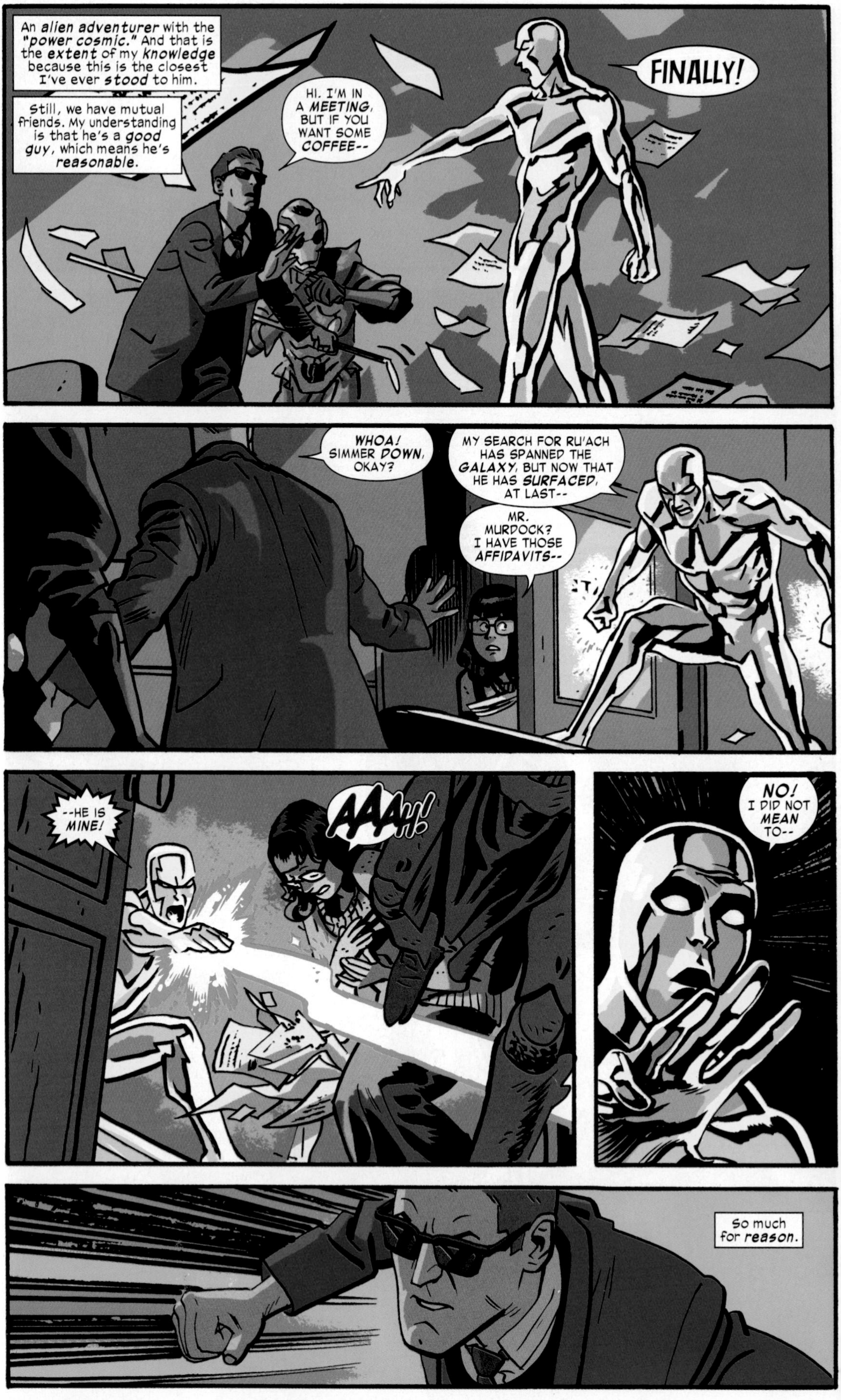

An alien adventurer with the "power cosmic." And that is the extent of my knowledge because this is the closest I've ever stood to him.
Still, we have mutual friends. My understanding is that he's a good guy, which means he's reasonable.
HI. I'M IN A MEETING, BUT IF YOU WANT SOME COFFEE--
FINALLY!
WHOA! SIMMER DOWN, OKAY?
MY SEARCH FOR RU'ACH HAS SPANNED THE GALAXY, BUT NOW THAT HE HAS SURFACED, AT LAST--
MR. MURDOCK? I HAVE THOSE AFFIDAVITS--
--HE IS MINE!
AAAH!
NO! I DID NOT MEAN TO--
So much for reason.

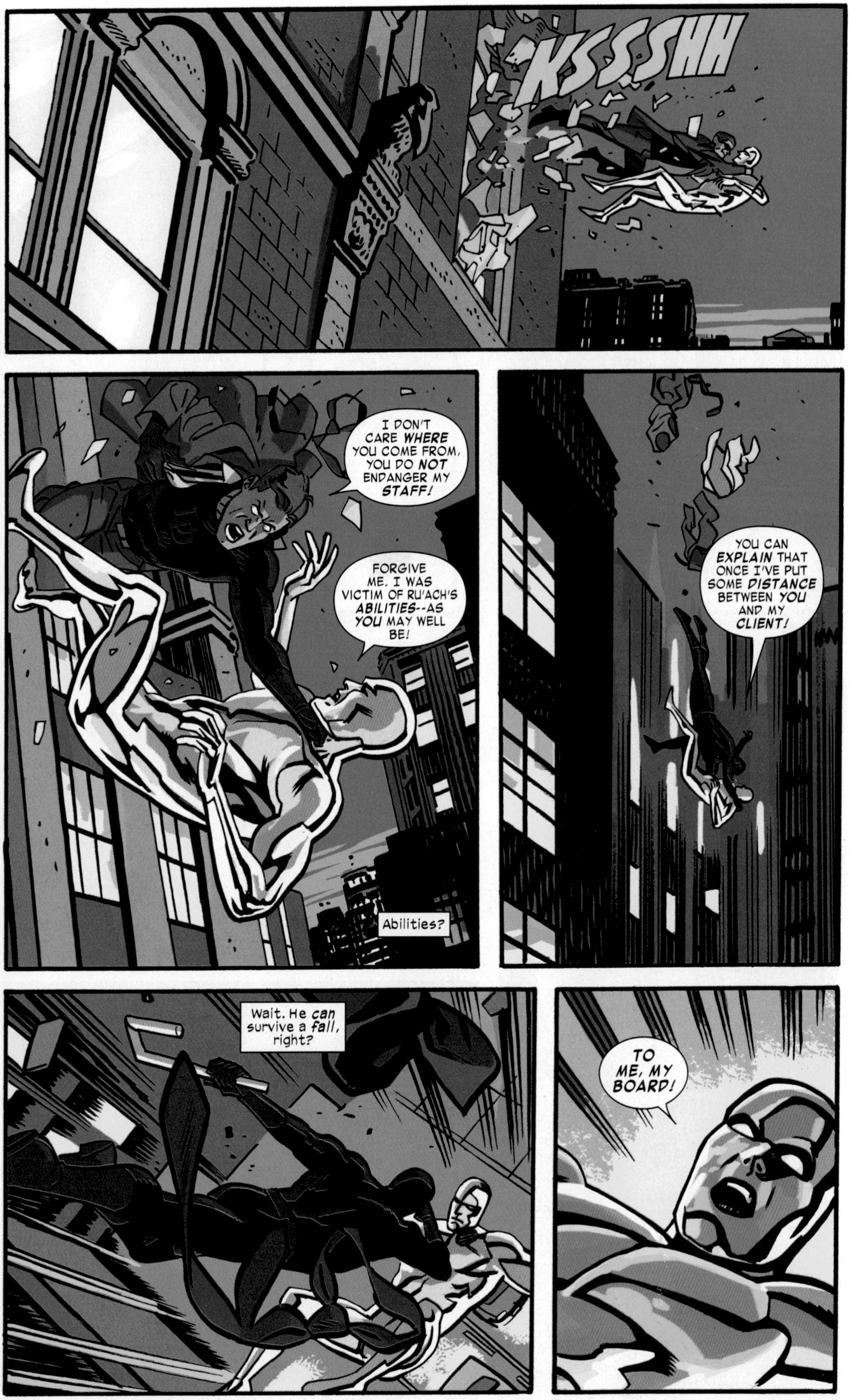
KSSSHH
I DON'T CARE WHERE YOU COME FROM, YOU DO NOT ENDANGER MY STAFF!
FORGIVE ME. I WAS VICTIM OF RU'ACH'S ABILITIES--AS YOU MAY WELL BE!
Abilities?
YOU CAN EXPLAIN THAT ONCE I'VE PUT SOME DISTANCE BETWEEN YOU AND MY CLIENT!
Wait. He can survive a fall, right?
TO ME, MY BOARD!

KSSSH

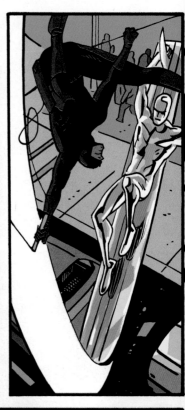

YOU KNOW *NOT* WHAT YOU *DO* OR WHO YOU *SHIELD!*

RU'ACH IS A *DECEIVER* OF THE *HIGHEST ORDER!*

TNG

YOU KNOW, YOU COULD HAVE *STARTED* WITH *THAT!* TELL ME *YOUR* SIDE OF THE STORY!

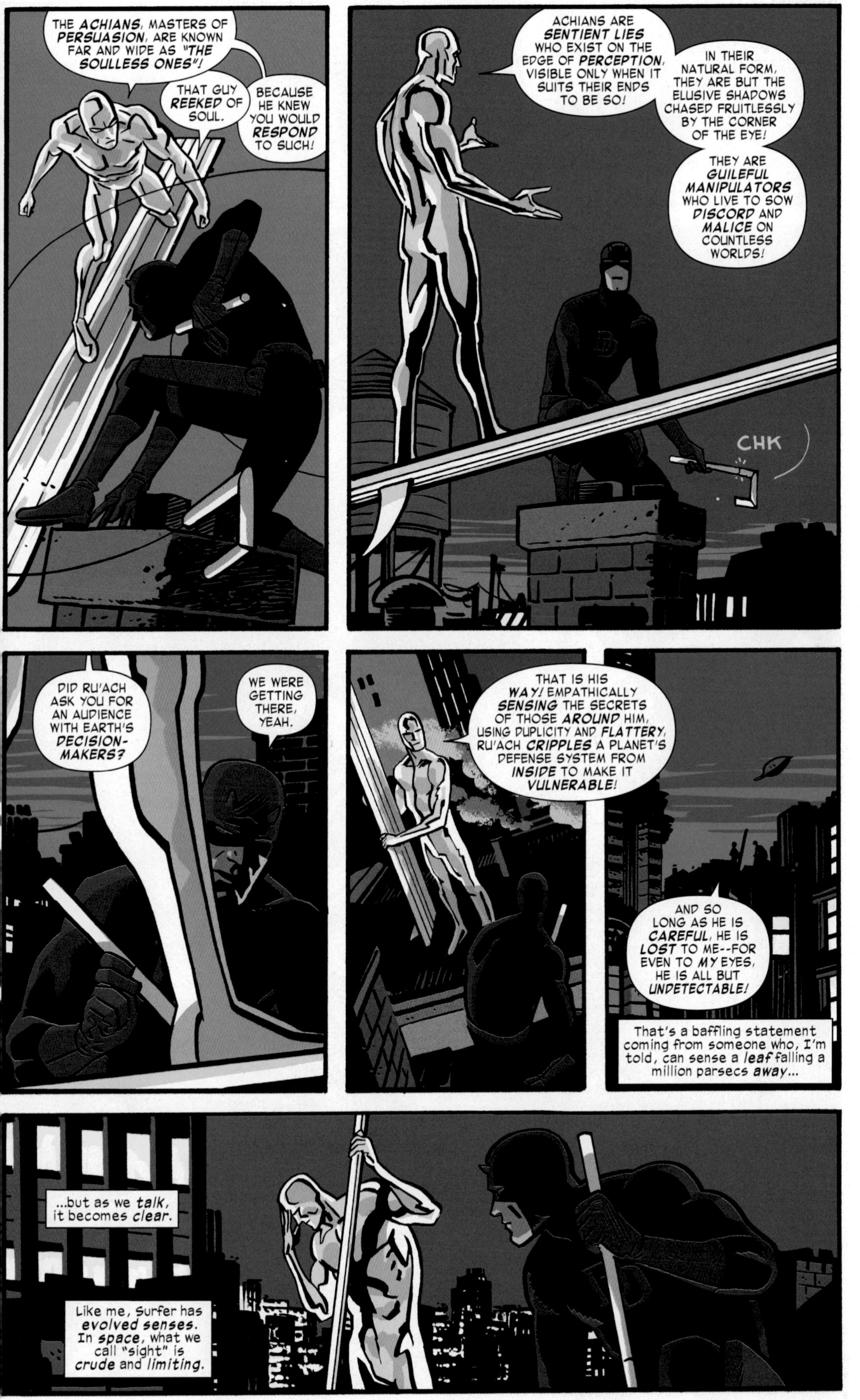
THE ACHIANS, MASTERS OF PERSUASION, ARE KNOWN FAR AND WIDE AS "THE SOULLESS ONES"!
THAT GUY REEKED OF SOUL.
BECAUSE HE KNEW YOU WOULD RESPOND TO SUCH!
ACHIANS ARE SENTIENT LIES WHO EXIST ON THE EDGE OF PERCEPTION, VISIBLE ONLY WHEN IT SUITS THEIR ENDS TO BE SO!
IN THEIR NATURAL FORM, THEY ARE BUT THE ELUSIVE SHADOWS CHASED FRUITLESSLY BY THE CORNER OF THE EYE!
THEY ARE GUILEFUL MANIPULATORS WHO LIVE TO SOW DISCORD AND MALICE ON COUNTLESS WORLDS!
CHK
DID RU'ACH ASK YOU FOR AN AUDIENCE WITH EARTH'S DECISION-MAKERS?
WE WERE GETTING THERE, YEAH.
THAT IS HIS WAY! EMPATHICALLY SENSING THE SECRETS OF THOSE AROUND HIM, USING DUPLICITY AND FLATTERY, RU'ACH CRIPPLES A PLANET'S DEFENSE SYSTEM FROM INSIDE TO MAKE IT VULNERABLE!
AND SO LONG AS HE IS CAREFUL, HE IS LOST TO ME--FOR EVEN TO MY EYES, HE IS ALL BUT UNDETECTABLE!
That's a baffling statement coming from someone who, I'm told, can sense a leaf falling a million parsecs away...
...but as we talk, it becomes clear.
Like me, Surfer has evolved senses. In space, what we call "sight" is crude and limiting.

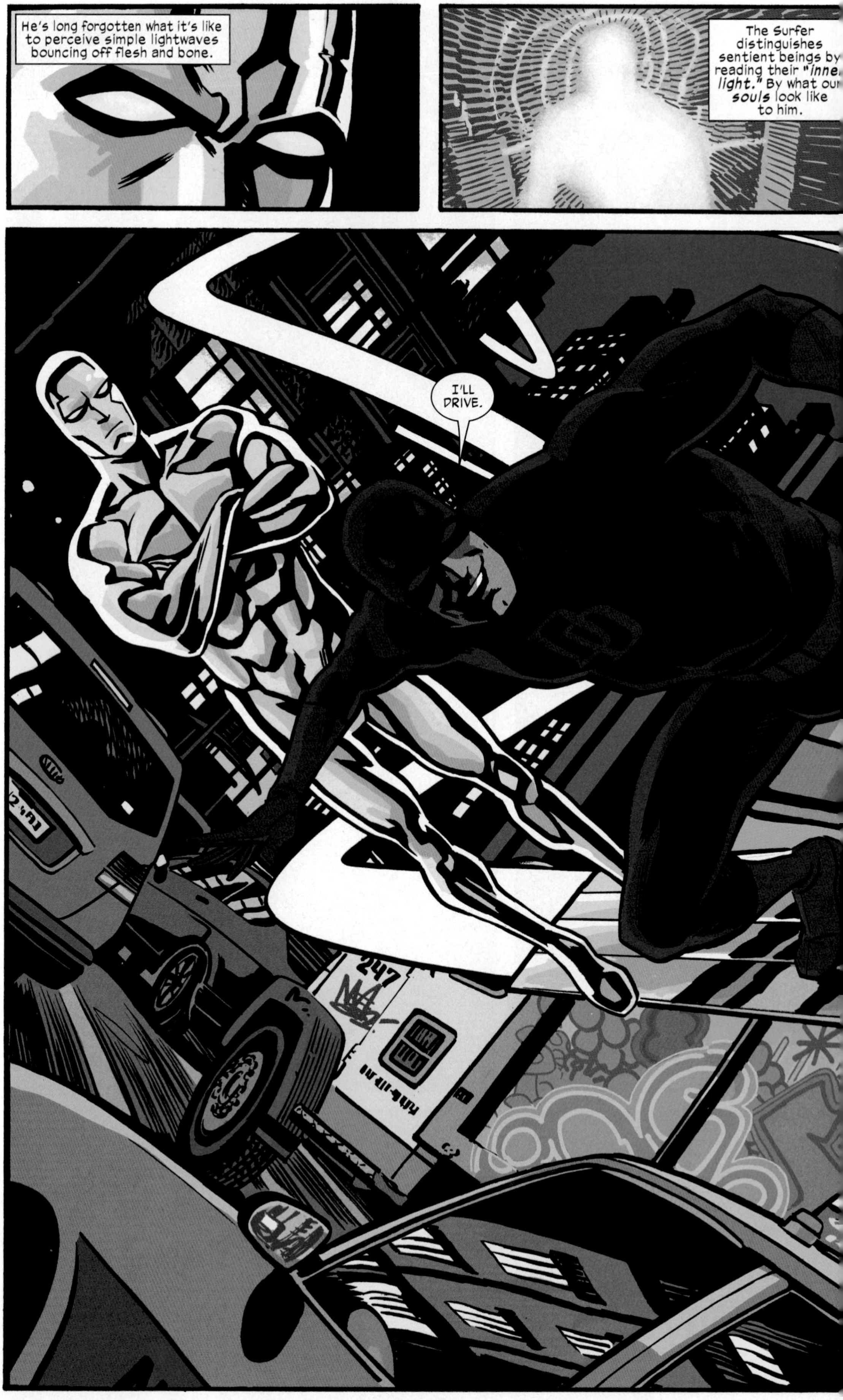

He's long forgotten what it's like to perceive simple lightwaves bouncing off flesh and bone.
The Surfer distinguishes sentient beings by reading their "inne light." By what our souls look like to him.
I'LL DRIVE.

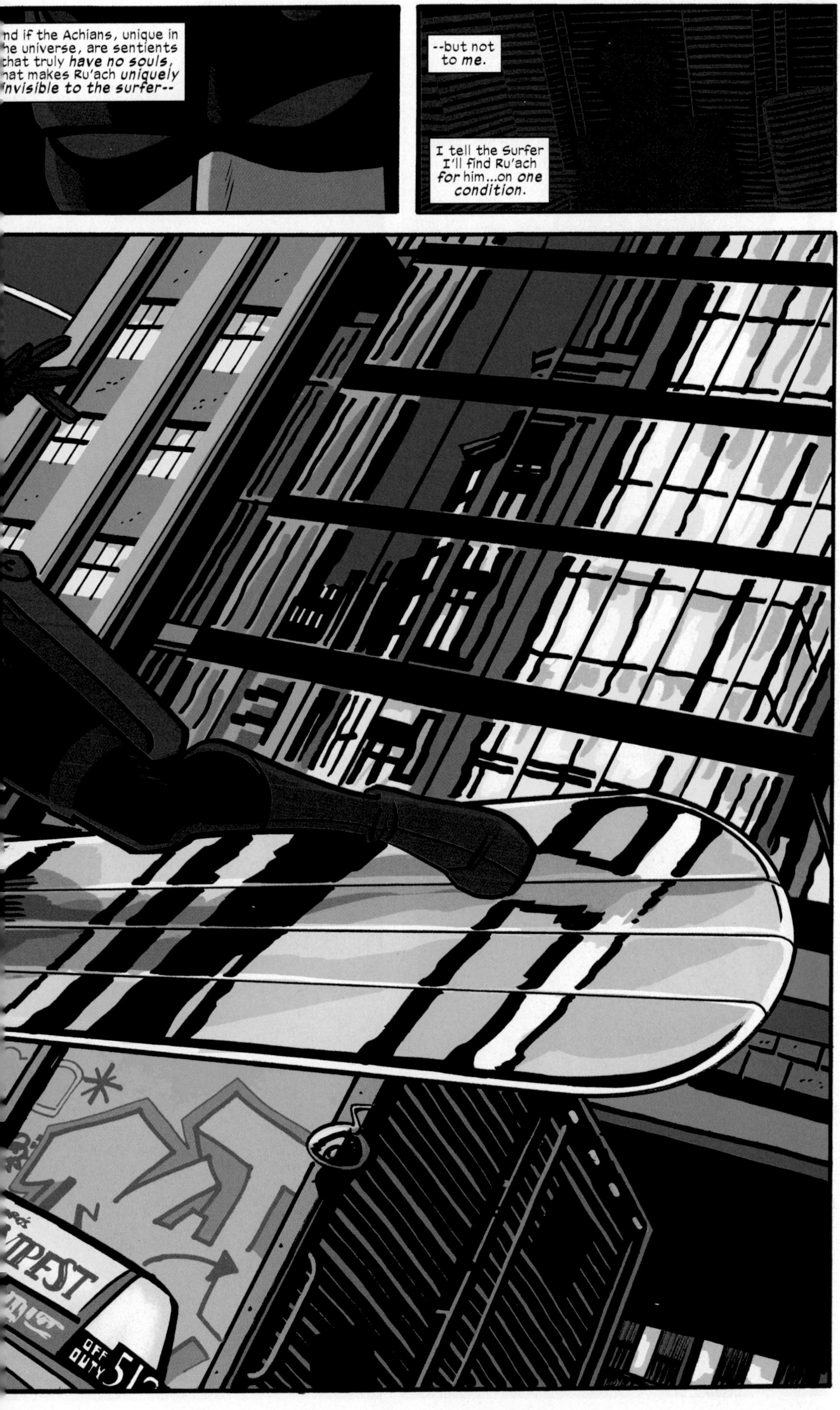

nd if the Achians, unique in he universe, are sentients that truly *have no souls*, hat makes Ru'ach *uniquely invisible to the surfer*--
--but not to *me*.
I tell the Surfer I'll find Ru'ach *for* him...on *one* condition.
OFF DUTY

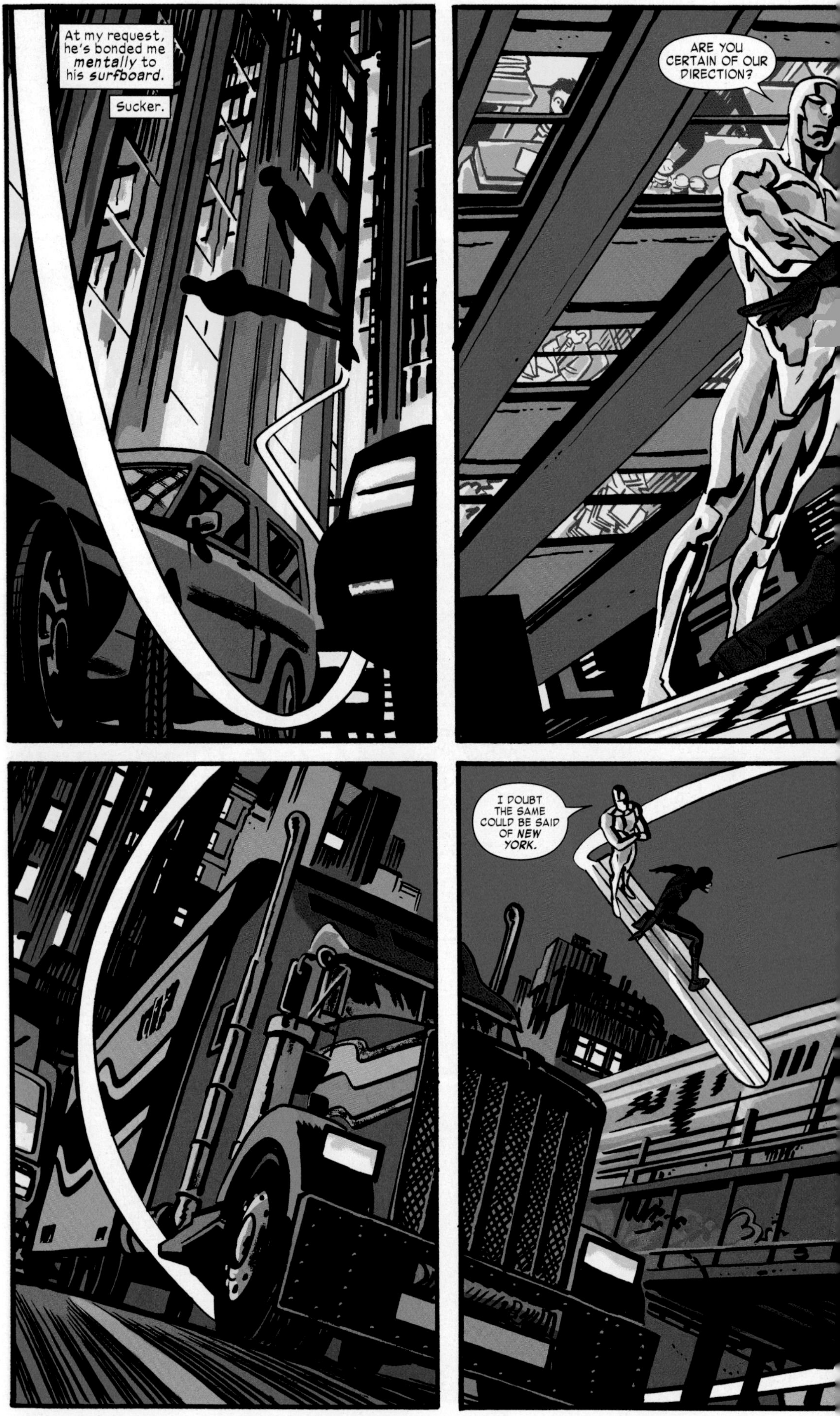
At my request, he's bonded me *mentally* to his *surfboard*.
Sucker.
ARE YOU CERTAIN OF OUR DIRECTION?
I DOUBT THE SAME COULD BE SAID OF *NEW YORK*.

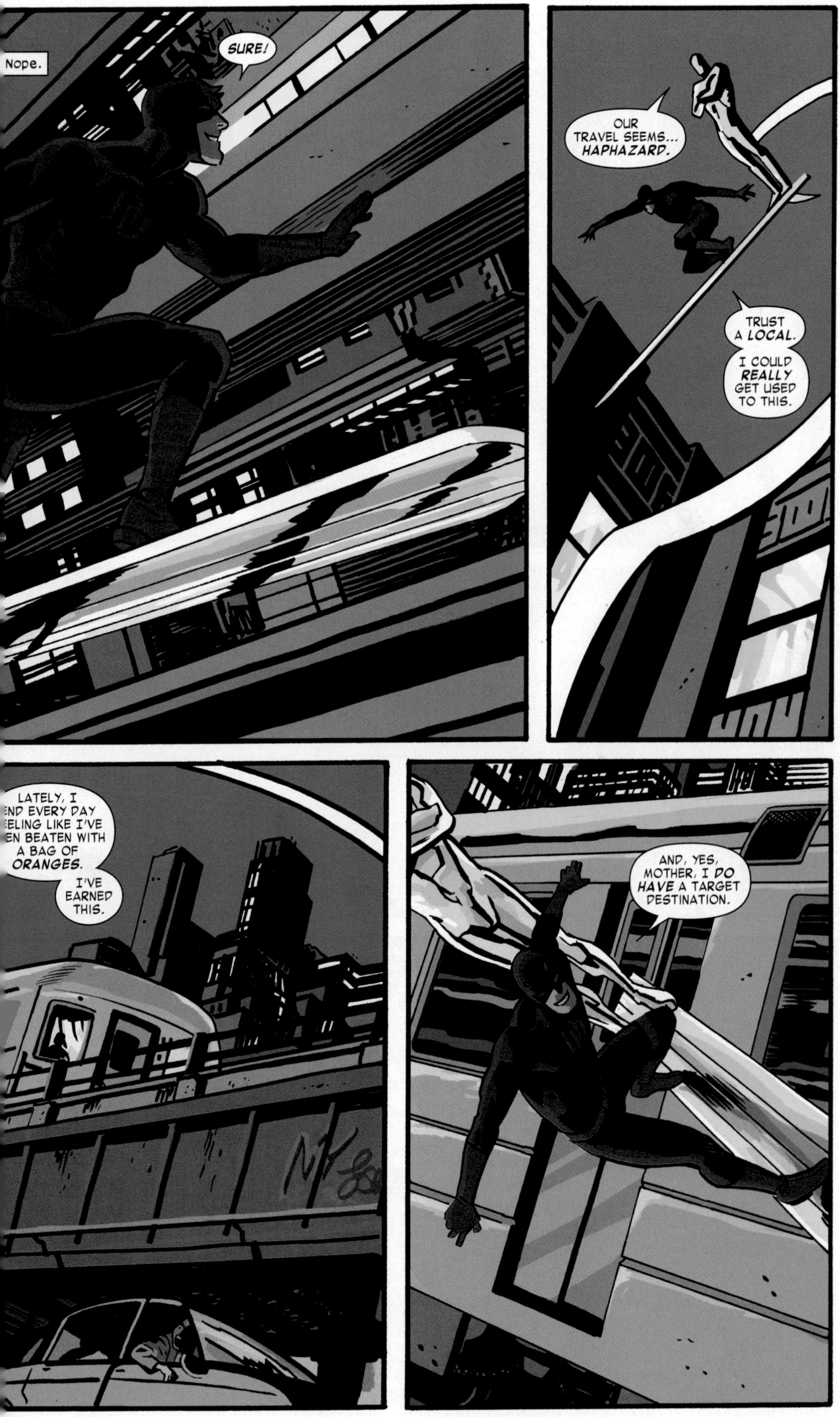
Nope.
SURE!
OUR TRAVEL SEEMS... HAPHAZARD.
TRUST A LOCAL.
I COULD REALLY GET USED TO THIS.
LATELY, I END EVERY DAY FEELING LIKE I'VE BEEN BEATEN WITH A BAG OF ORANGES.
I'VE EARNED THIS.
AND, YES, MOTHER, I DO HAVE A TARGET DESTINATION.

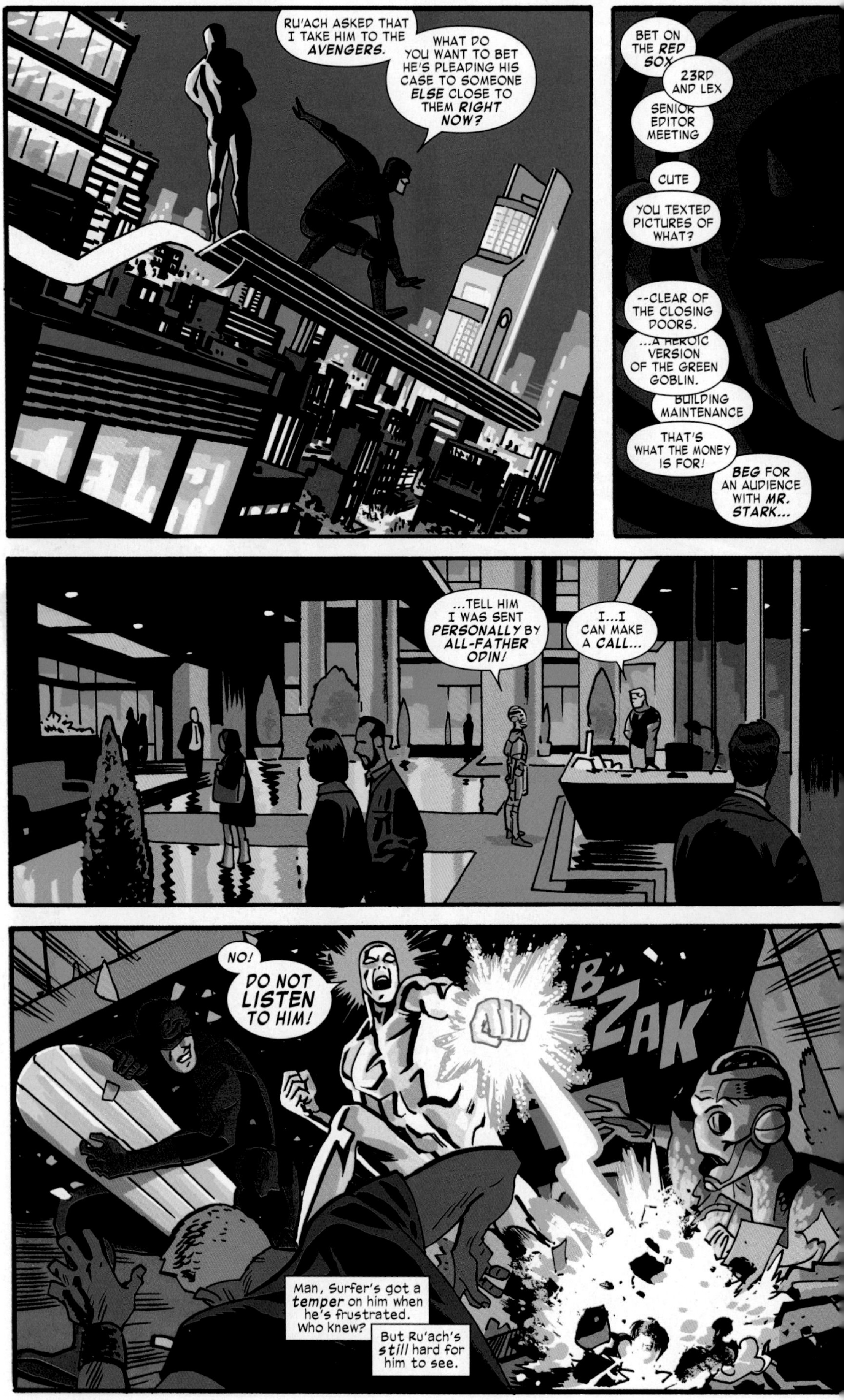

RU'ACH ASKED THAT I TAKE HIM TO THE AVENGERS.
WHAT DO YOU WANT TO BET HE'S PLEADING HIS CASE TO SOMEONE ELSE CLOSE TO THEM RIGHT NOW?
BET ON THE RED SOX
23RD AND LEX
SENIOR EDITOR MEETING
CUTE
YOU TEXTED PICTURES OF WHAT?
--CLEAR OF THE CLOSING DOORS.
...A HEROIC VERSION OF THE GREEN GOBLIN.
BUILDING MAINTENANCE
THAT'S WHAT THE MONEY IS FOR!
BEG FOR AN AUDIENCE WITH MR. STARK...
...TELL HIM I WAS SENT PERSONALLY BY ALL-FATHER ODIN!
I...I CAN MAKE A CALL...
NO!
DO NOT LISTEN TO HIM!
BZAK
Man, Surfer's got a temper on him when he's frustrated. Who knew?
But Ru'ach's still hard for him to see.

No wonder his aim *sucks.*

STOP FIRING *BLIND!* I'LL HANDLE *THIS!*

Easier *said.*

Even this close, it's like trying to grab *smoke.*

Ru'ach has a way of staying on the periphery of vision...

...even though my radar-sense *range* is *360* degrees.

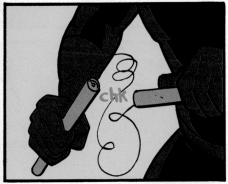

chk

zzzz zzzz zzzzzzz

TWANG

In desperation, he whispers something inaudible to human hearing.

ZT!

Surfer *warned* me that Ru'ach senses the secrets of those he *nears.*

But I refuse to be distracted.

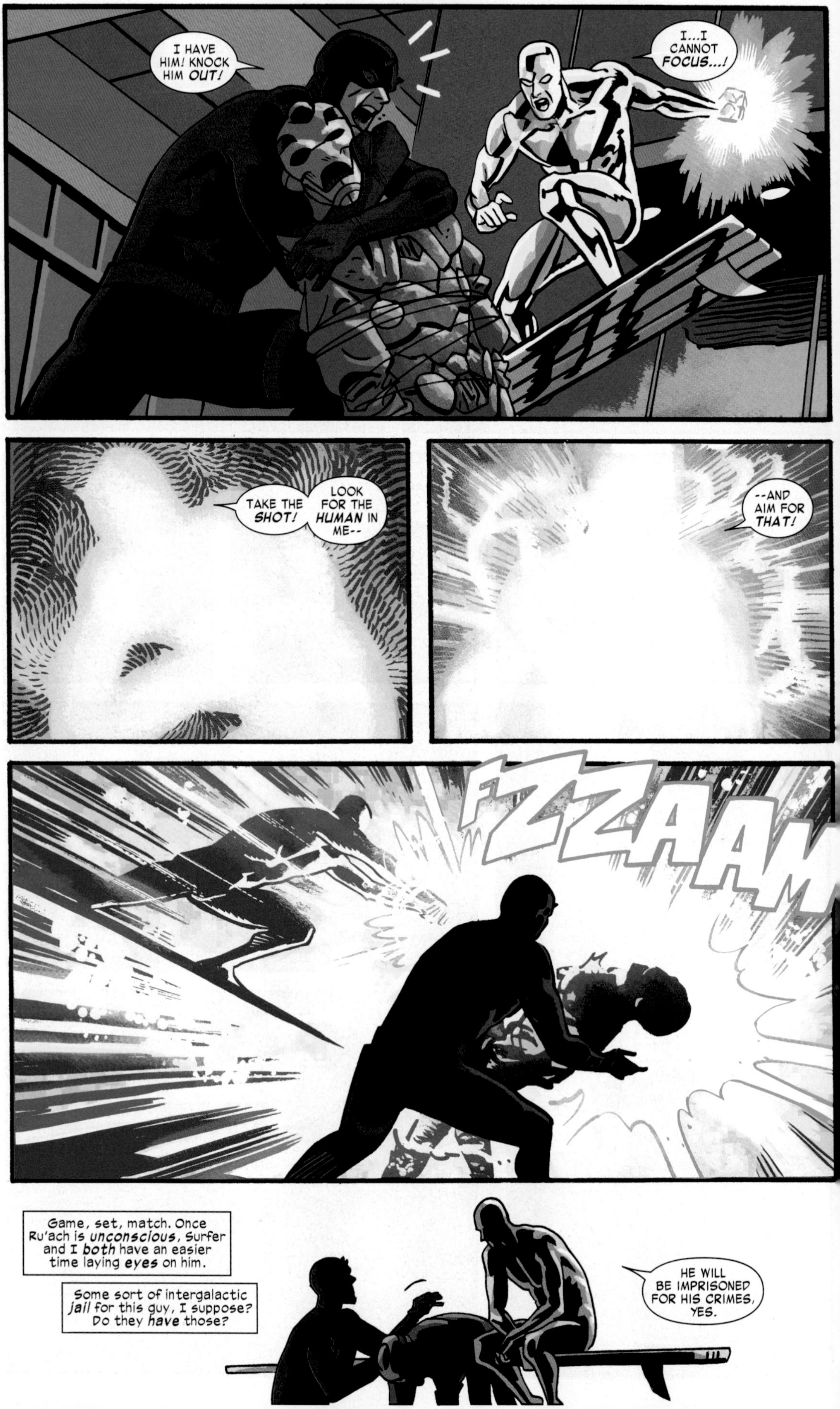
I HAVE HIM! KNOCK HIM OUT!
I...I CANNOT FOCUS...!
TAKE THE SHOT!
LOOK FOR THE HUMAN IN ME--
--AND AIM FOR THAT!
FZZAAM
Game, set, match. Once Ru'ach is unconscious, Surfer and I both have an easier time laying eyes on him.
Some sort of intergalactic jail for this guy, I suppose? Do they have those?
HE WILL BE IMPRISONED FOR HIS CRIMES, YES.

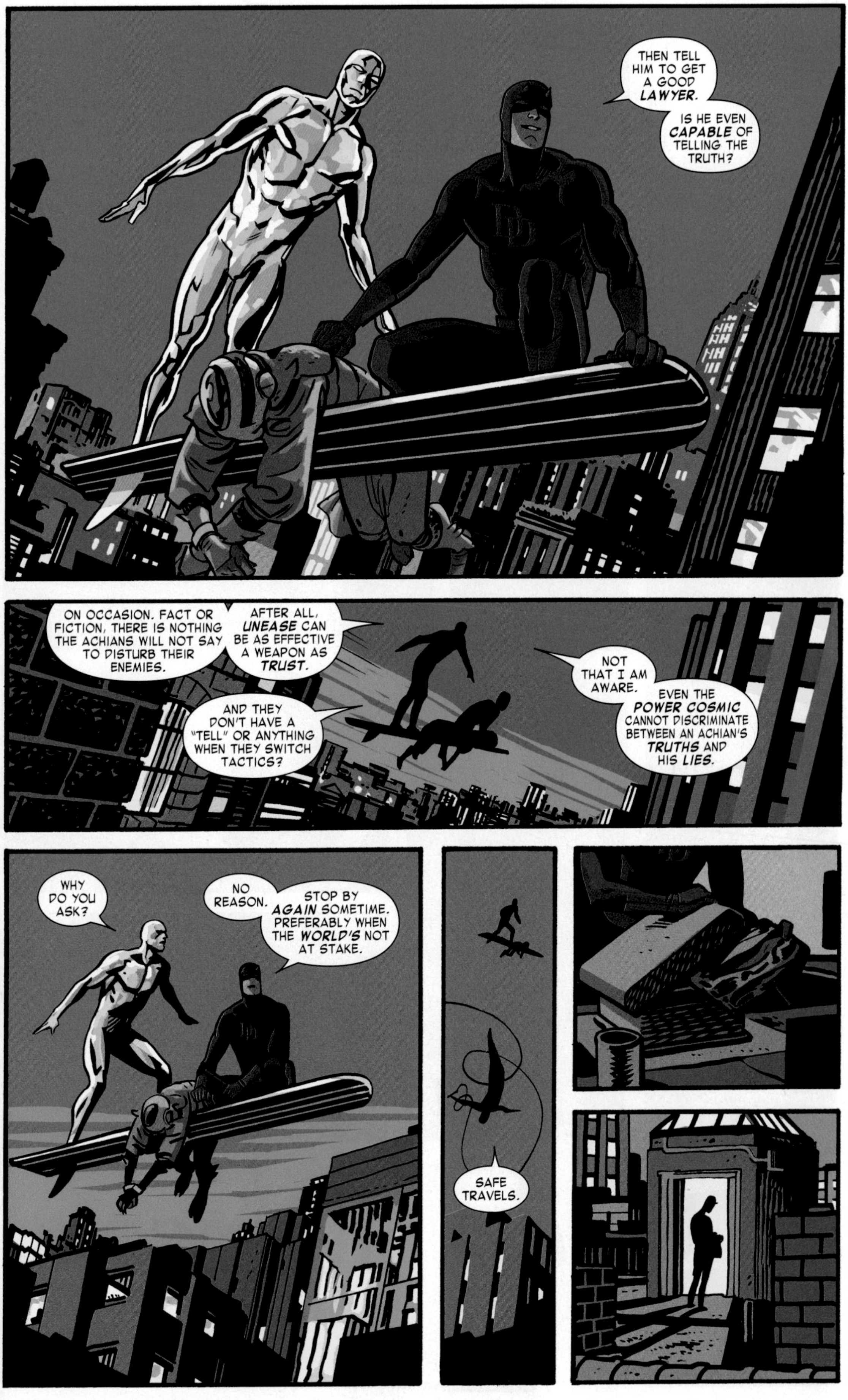
THEN TELL HIM TO GET A GOOD LAWYER.
IS HE EVEN CAPABLE OF TELLING THE TRUTH?
ON OCCASION. FACT OR FICTION, THERE IS NOTHING THE ACHIANS WILL NOT SAY TO DISTURB THEIR ENEMIES.
AFTER ALL, UNEASE CAN BE AS EFFECTIVE A WEAPON AS TRUST.
AND THEY DON'T HAVE A "TELL" OR ANYTHING WHEN THEY SWITCH TACTICS?
NOT THAT I AM AWARE.
EVEN THE POWER COSMIC CANNOT DISCRIMINATE BETWEEN AN ACHIAN'S TRUTHS AND HIS LIES.
WHY DO YOU ASK?
NO REASON.
STOP BY AGAIN SOMETIME. PREFERABLY WHEN THE WORLD'S NOT AT STAKE.
SAFE TRAVELS.

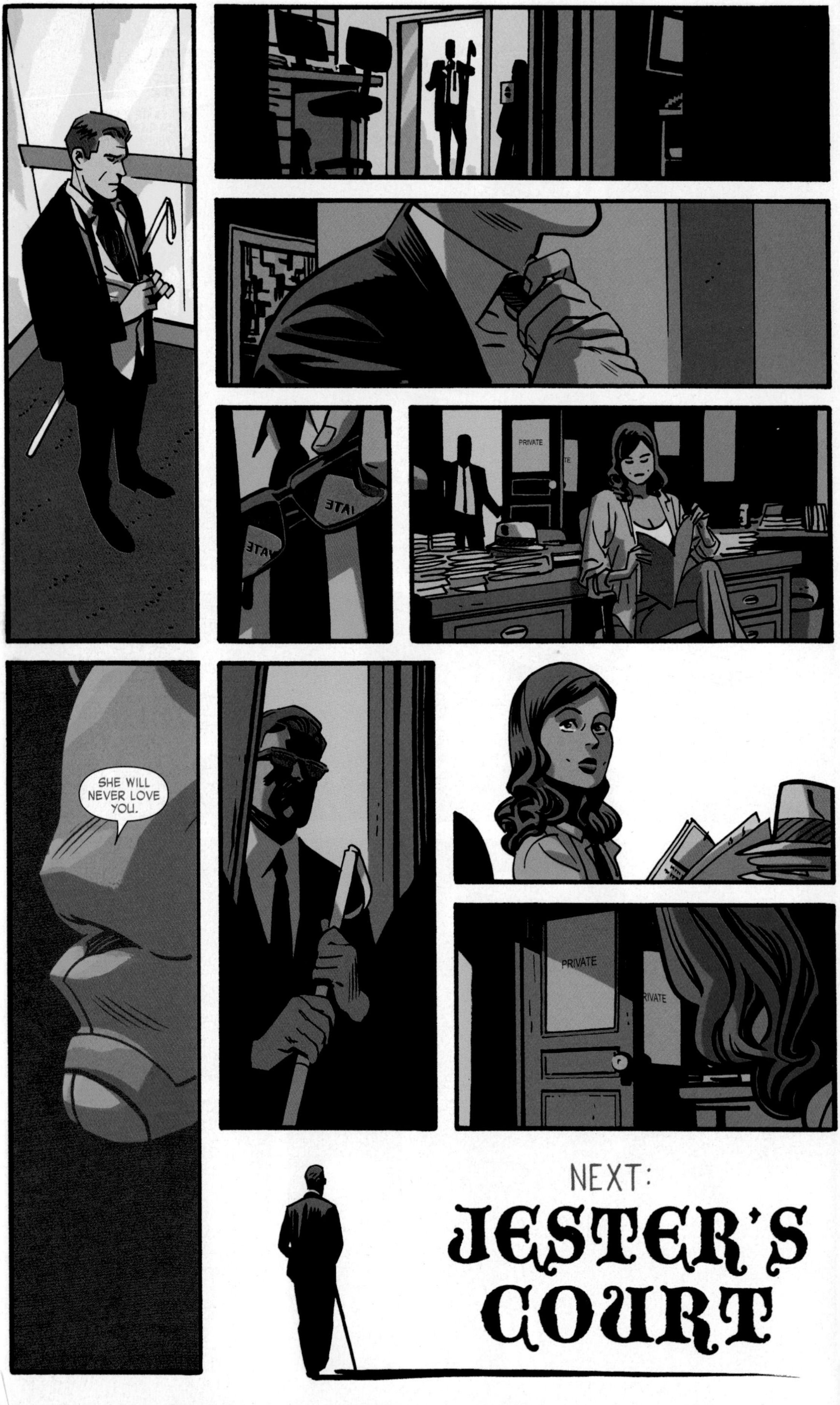
PRIVATE
SHE WILL NEVER LOVE YOU.
PRIVATE
NEXT:
JESTER'S COURT

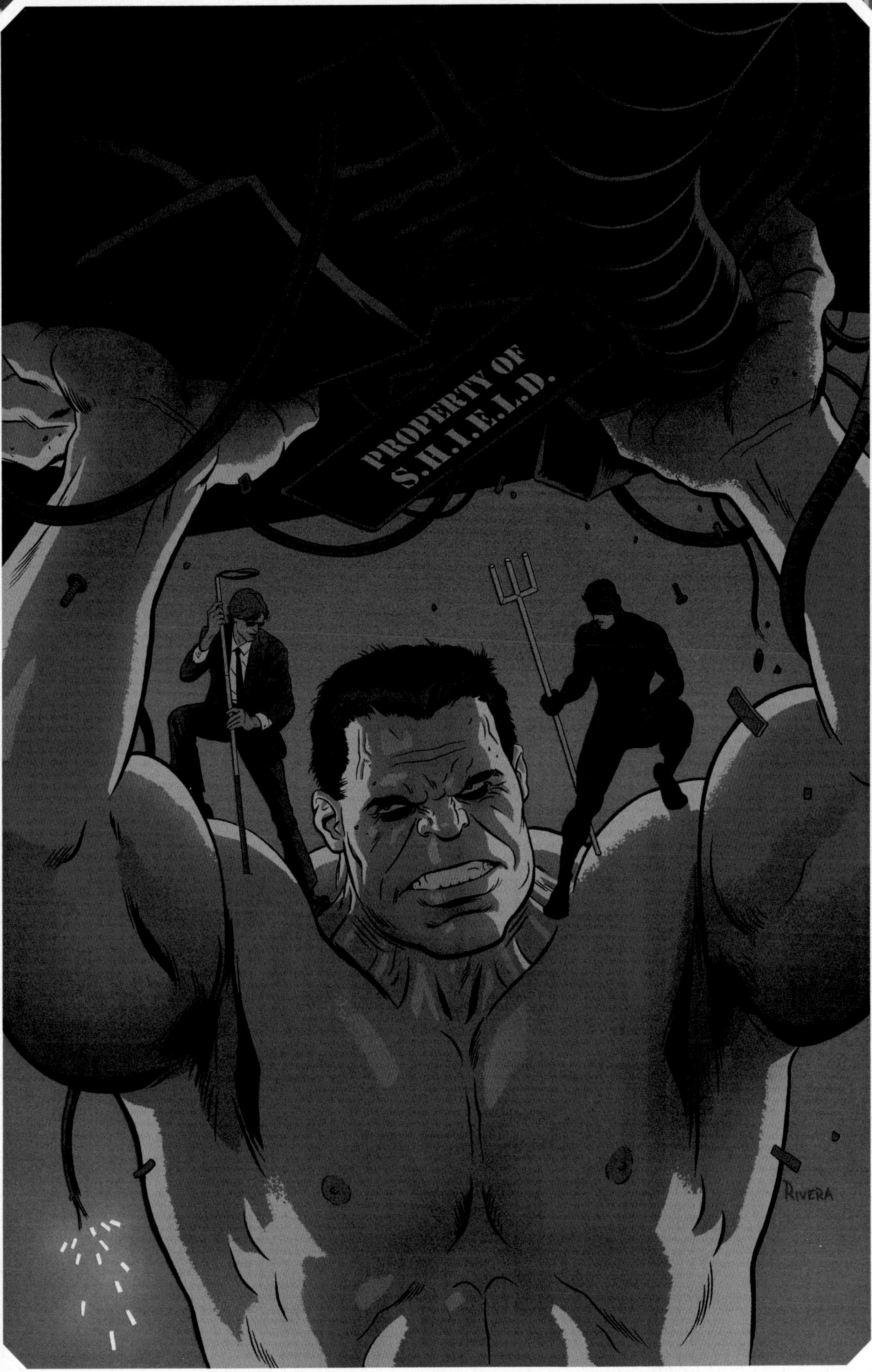
PROPERTY OF
S.H.I.E.L.D.
RIVERA

INDESTRUCTIBLE HULK #9

THE HULK WILL ALWAYS BE A PART OF DR. BRUCE BANNER, BUT BANNER WANTS TO BE REMEMBERED FOR HIS CONTRIBUTIONS TO SCIENCE AND NOT FOR TURNING INTO A BIG, GREEN FORCE OF RAGE AND DESTRUCTION. TO ACHIEVE THAT GOAL, BANNER HAS STRUCK A MUTUALLY BENEFICIAL DEAL WITH MARIA HILL, THE DIRECTOR OF S.H.I.E.L.D. SHE PROVIDES BANNER WITH A LAB, STAFF, EQUIPMENT AND ALL OF THE RESOURCES HE NEEDS TO BETTER MANKIND, AND BANNER PROVIDES S.H.I.E.L.D. WITH THE HULK FOR ANY MISSIONS THAT MIGHT NEED THAT EXTRA MUSCLE.

INDESTRUCTIBLE HULK

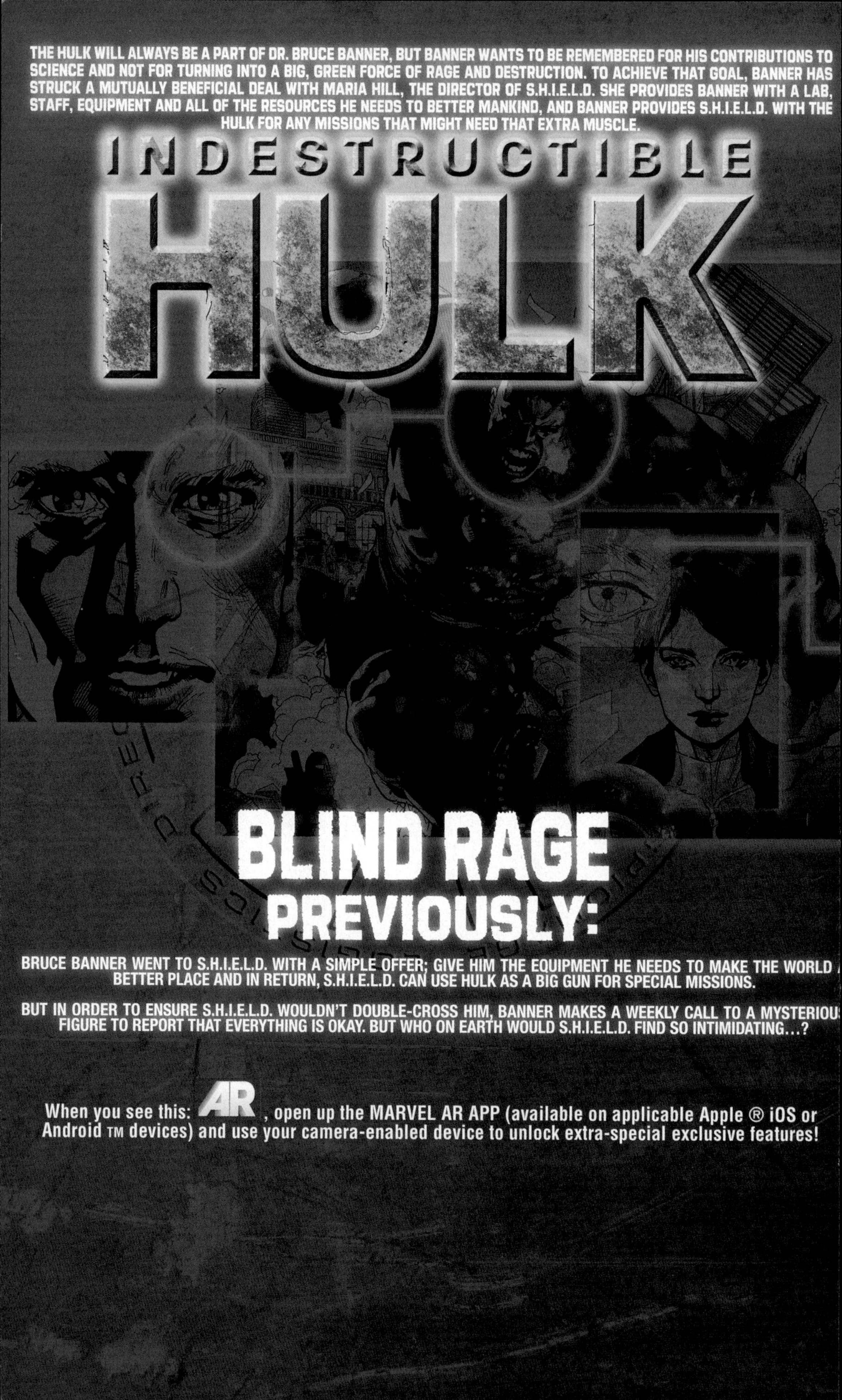

BLIND RAGE

PREVIOUSLY:

BRUCE BANNER WENT TO S.H.I.E.L.D. WITH A SIMPLE OFFER; GIVE HIM THE EQUIPMENT HE NEEDS TO MAKE THE WORLD A BETTER PLACE AND IN RETURN, S.H.I.E.L.D. CAN USE HULK AS A BIG GUN FOR SPECIAL MISSIONS.

BUT IN ORDER TO ENSURE S.H.I.E.L.D. WOULDN'T DOUBLE-CROSS HIM, BANNER MAKES A WEEKLY CALL TO A MYSTERIOU FIGURE TO REPORT THAT EVERYTHING IS OKAY. BUT WHO ON EARTH WOULD S.H.I.E.L.D. FIND SO INTIMIDATING...?

When you see this: AR, open up the MARVEL AR APP (available on applicable Apple ® iOS or Android TM devices) and use your camera-enabled device to unlock extra-special exclusive features!

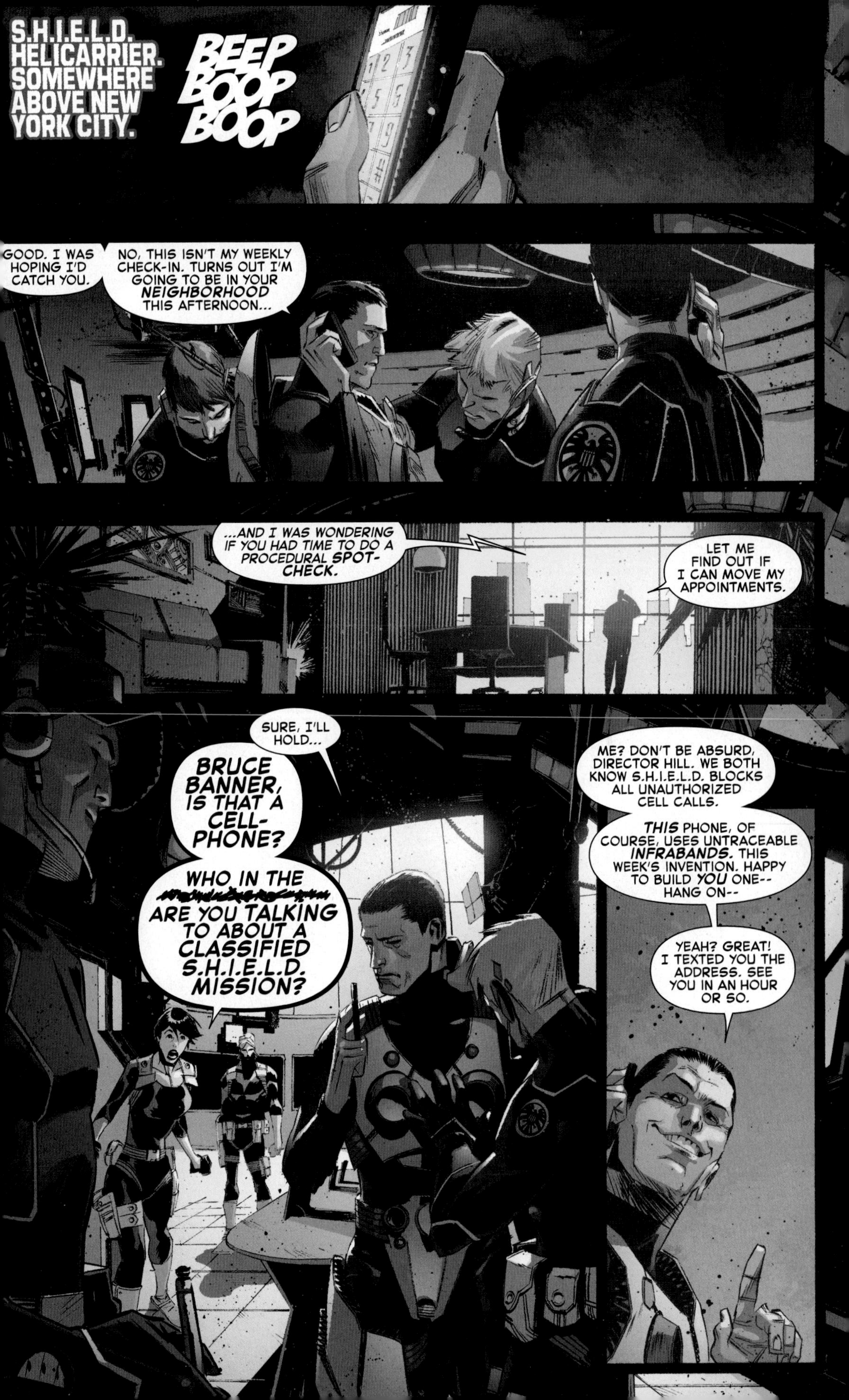
S.H.I.E.L.D. HELICARRIER. SOMEWHERE ABOVE NEW YORK CITY.
BEEP BOOP BOOP
GOOD. I WAS HOPING I'D CATCH YOU.
NO, THIS ISN'T MY WEEKLY CHECK-IN. TURNS OUT I'M GOING TO BE IN YOUR NEIGHBORHOOD THIS AFTERNOON...
...AND I WAS WONDERING IF YOU HAD TIME TO DO A PROCEDURAL SPOT-CHECK.
LET ME FIND OUT IF I CAN MOVE MY APPOINTMENTS.
SURE, I'LL HOLD...
BRUCE BANNER, IS THAT A CELL-PHONE?
WHO IN THE ARE YOU TALKING TO ABOUT A CLASSIFIED S.H.I.E.L.D. MISSION?
ME? DON'T BE ABSURD, DIRECTOR HILL. WE BOTH KNOW S.H.I.E.L.D. BLOCKS ALL UNAUTHORIZED CELL CALLS.
THIS PHONE, OF COURSE, USES UNTRACEABLE INFRABANDS. THIS WEEK'S INVENTION. HAPPY TO BUILD YOU ONE-- HANG ON--
YEAH? GREAT! I TEXTED YOU THE ADDRESS. SEE YOU IN AN HOUR OR SO.

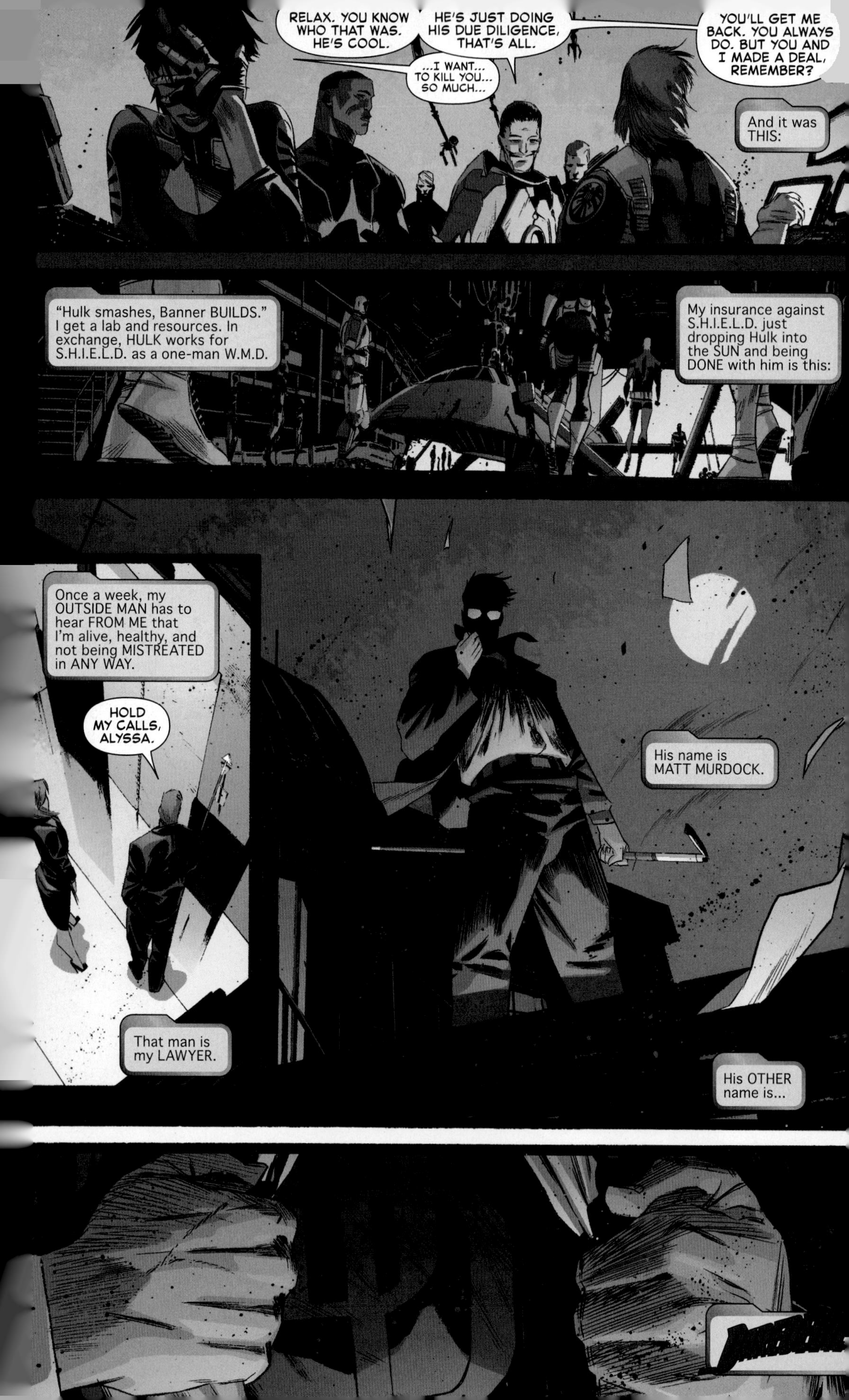
RELAX. YOU KNOW WHO THAT WAS. HE'S COOL.
HE'S JUST DOING HIS DUE DILIGENCE, THAT'S ALL.
...I WANT... TO KILL YOU... SO MUCH...
YOU'LL GET ME BACK. YOU ALWAYS DO. BUT YOU AND I MADE A DEAL, REMEMBER?
And it was THIS:
"Hulk smashes, Banner BUILDS." I get a lab and resources. In exchange, HULK works for S.H.I.E.L.D. as a one-man W.M.D.
My insurance against S.H.I.E.L.D. just dropping Hulk into the SUN and being DONE with him is this:
Once a week, my OUTSIDE MAN has to hear FROM ME that I'm alive, healthy, and not being MISTREATED in ANY WAY.
HOLD MY CALLS, ALYSSA.
That man is my LAWYER.
His name is MATT MURDOCK.
His OTHER name is...

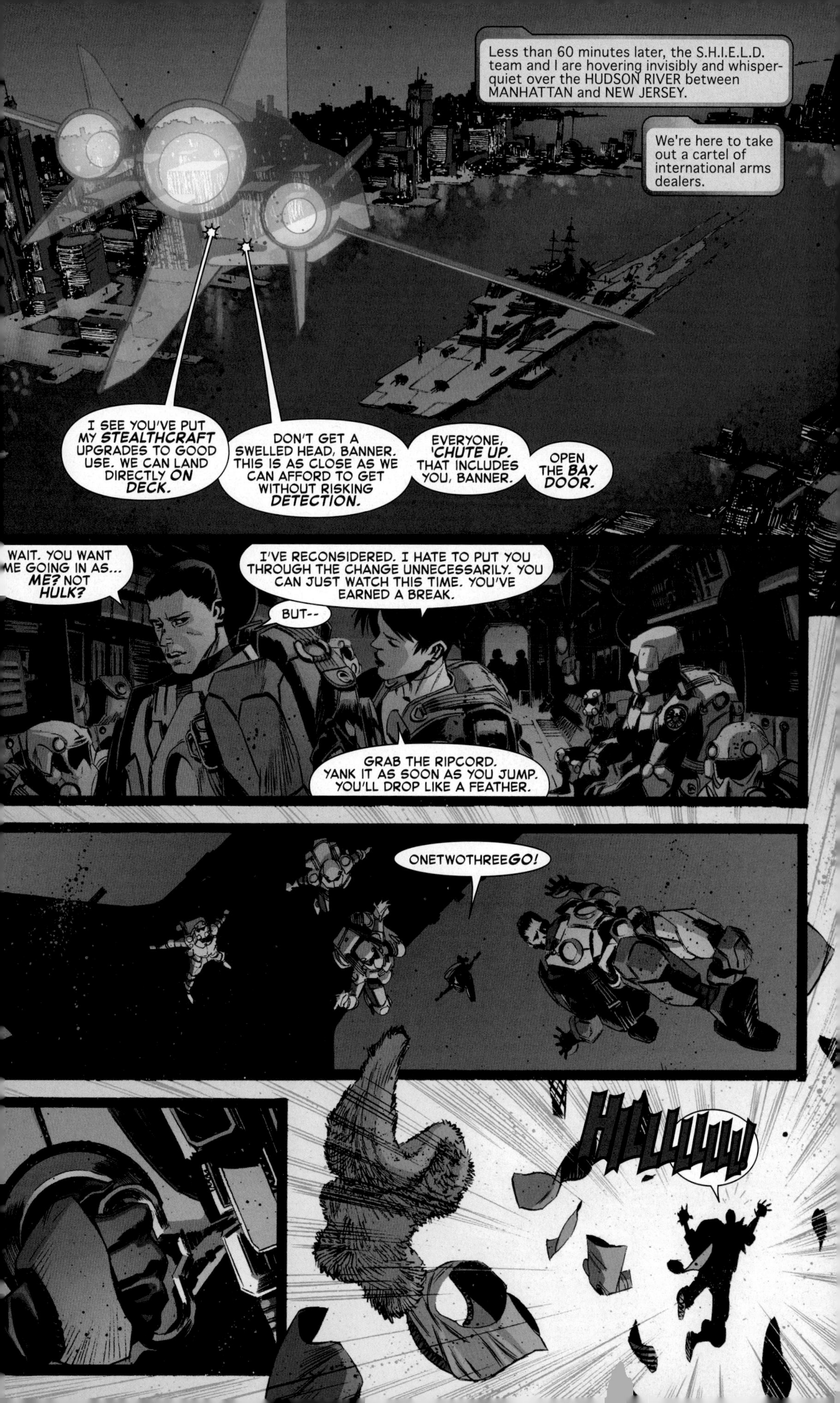

Less than 60 minutes later, the S.H.I.E.L.D. team and I are hovering invisibly and whisper-quiet over the HUDSON RIVER between MANHATTAN and NEW JERSEY.
We're here to take out a cartel of international arms dealers.
I SEE YOU'VE PUT MY STEALTHCRAFT UPGRADES TO GOOD USE. WE CAN LAND DIRECTLY ON DECK.
DON'T GET A SWELLED HEAD, BANNER. THIS IS AS CLOSE AS WE CAN AFFORD TO GET WITHOUT RISKING DETECTION.
EVERYONE, 'CHUTE UP. THAT INCLUDES YOU, BANNER.
OPEN THE BAY DOOR.
WAIT. YOU WANT ME GOING IN AS... ME? NOT HULK?
I'VE RECONSIDERED. I HATE TO PUT YOU THROUGH THE CHANGE UNNECESSARILY. YOU CAN JUST WATCH THIS TIME. YOU'VE EARNED A BREAK.
BUT--
GRAB THE RIPCORD. YANK IT AS SOON AS YOU JUMP. YOU'LL DROP LIKE A FEATHER.
ONETWOTHREEGO!
HIIIIIIIII!

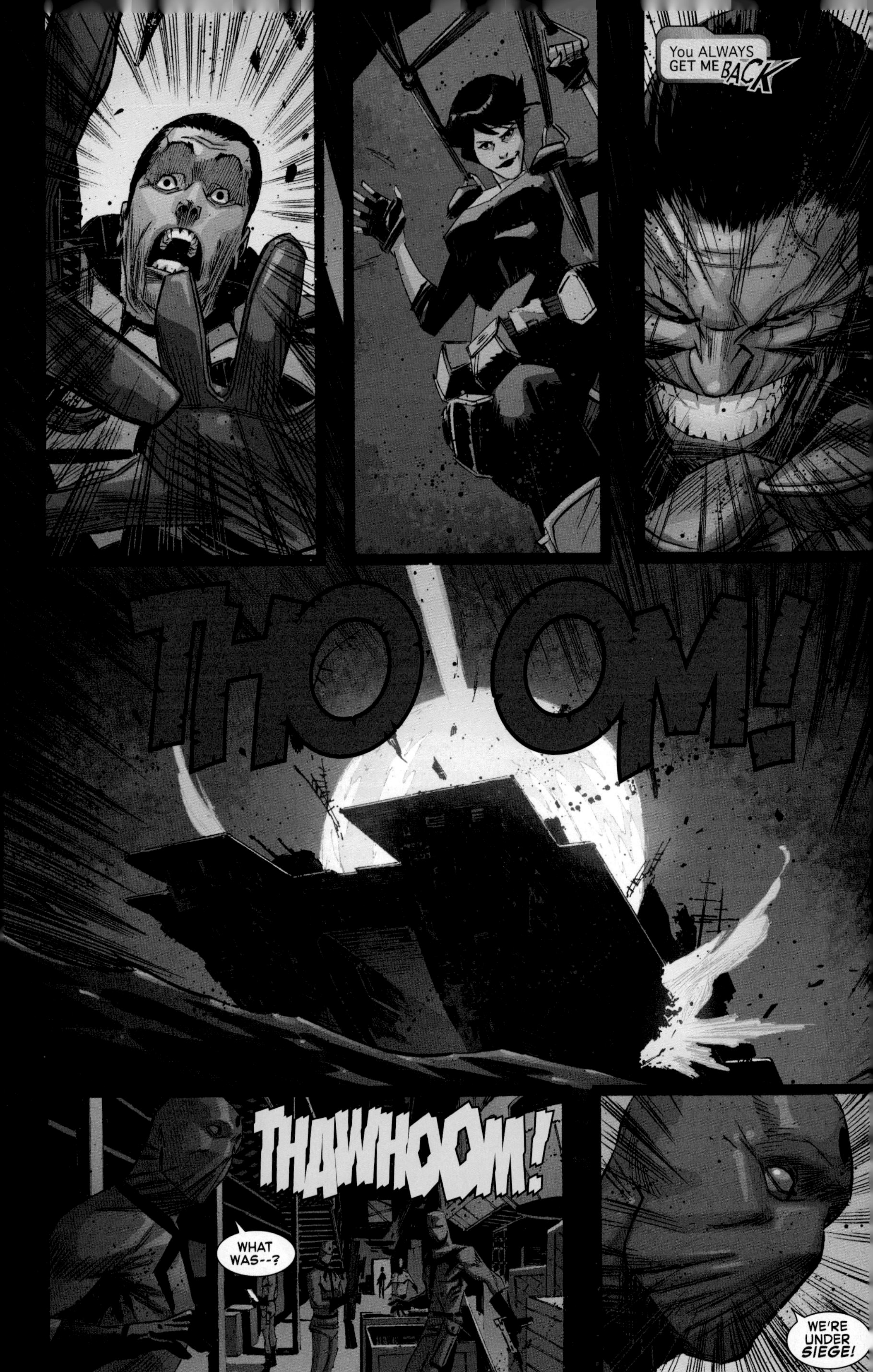
You ALWAYS GET ME BACK
THOOOM!
THAWHOOM!
WHAT WAS--?
WE'RE UNDER SIEGE!

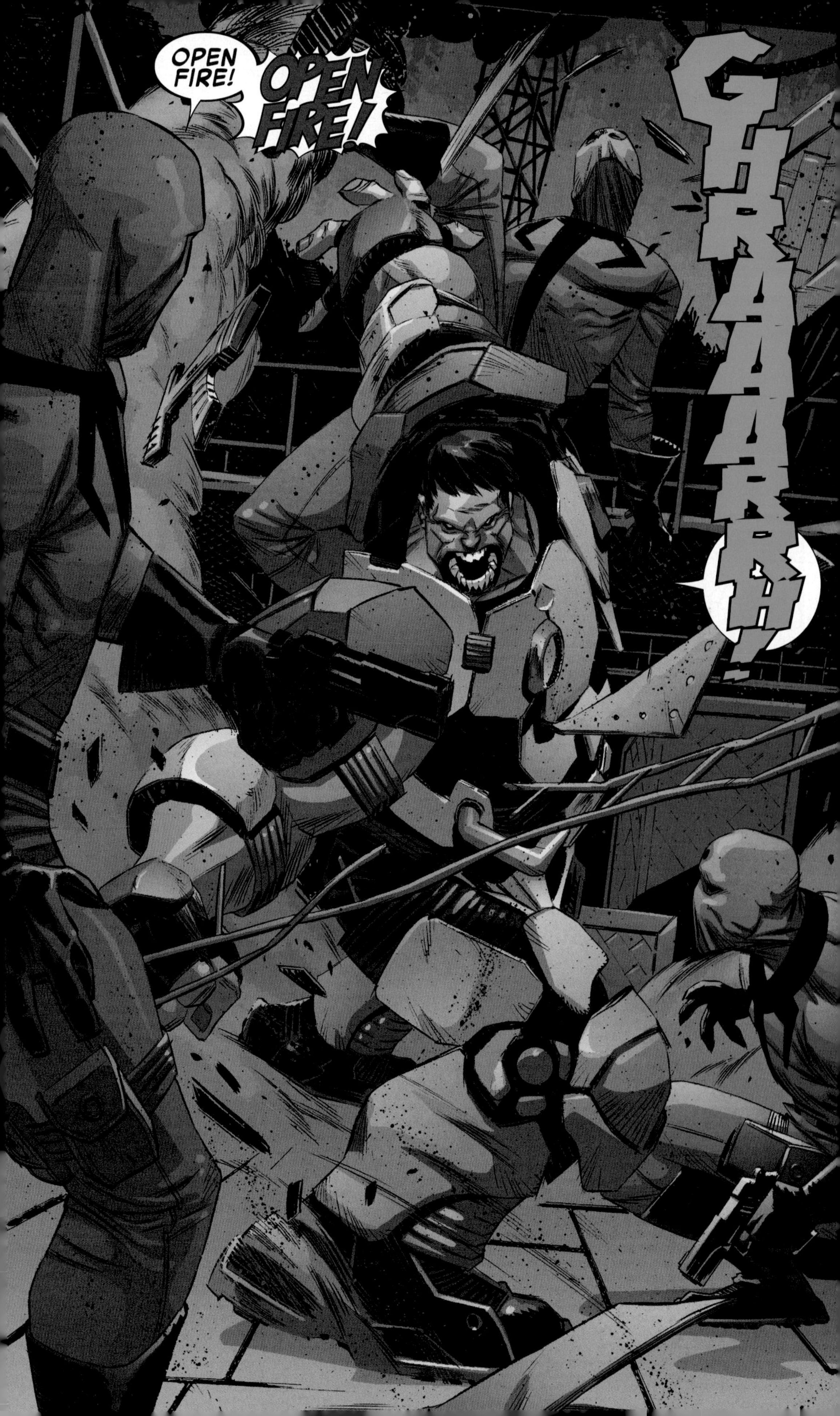
OPEN FIRE!
OPEN FIRE!
GHRAAARRH!

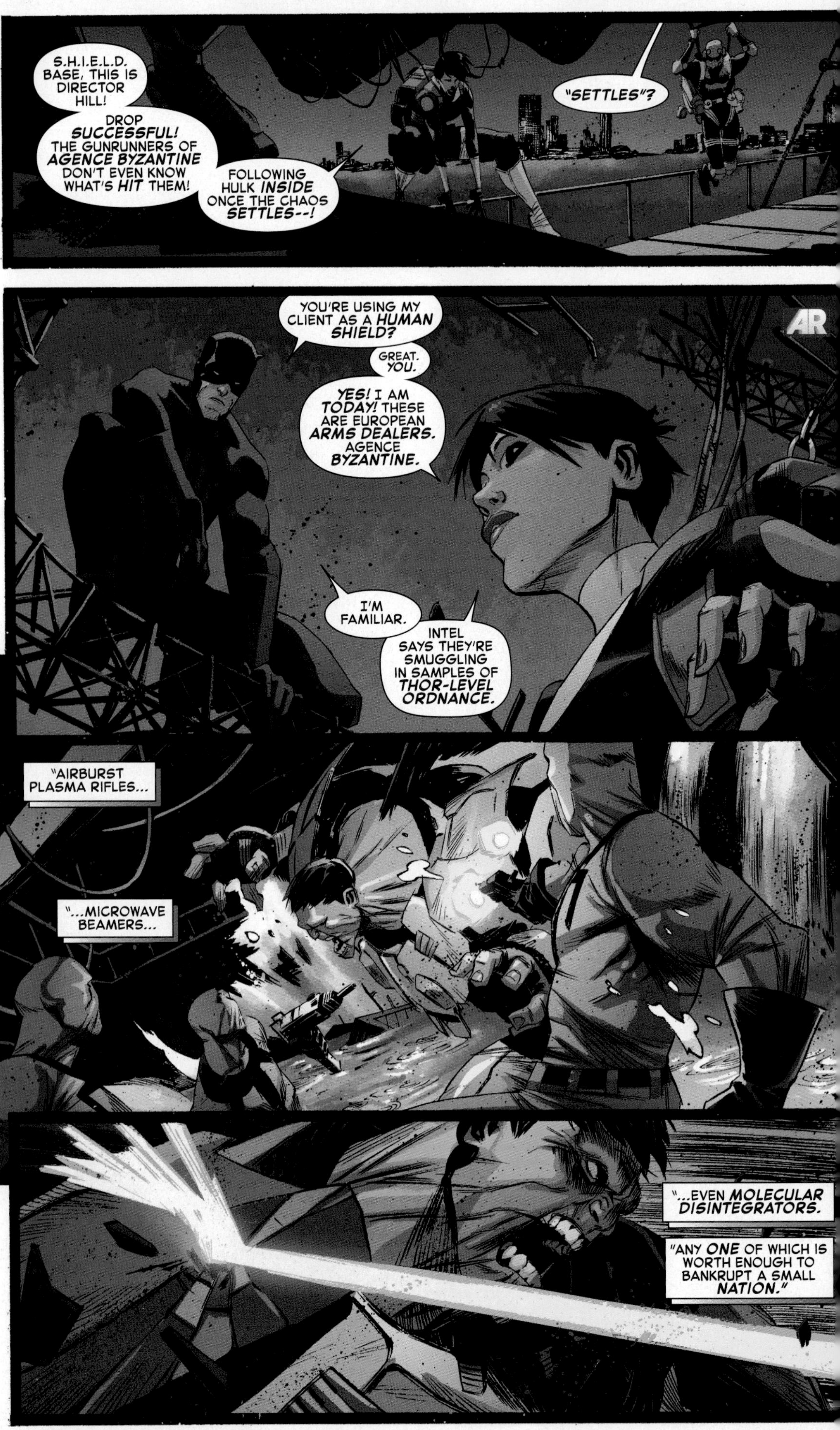
S.H.I.E.L.D. BASE, THIS IS DIRECTOR HILL!
DROP SUCCESSFUL! THE GUNRUNNERS OF AGENCE BYZANTINE DON'T EVEN KNOW WHAT'S HIT THEM!
FOLLOWING HULK INSIDE ONCE THE CHAOS SETTLES--!
"SETTLES"?
YOU'RE USING MY CLIENT AS A HUMAN SHIELD?
GREAT. YOU.
YES! I AM TODAY! THESE ARE EUROPEAN ARMS DEALERS. AGENCE BYZANTINE.
I'M FAMILIAR.
INTEL SAYS THEY'RE SMUGGLING IN SAMPLES OF THOR-LEVEL ORDNANCE.
"AIRBURST PLASMA RIFLES...
"...MICROWAVE BEAMERS...
"...EVEN MOLECULAR DISINTEGRATORS.
"ANY ONE OF WHICH IS WORTH ENOUGH TO BANKRUPT A SMALL NATION."

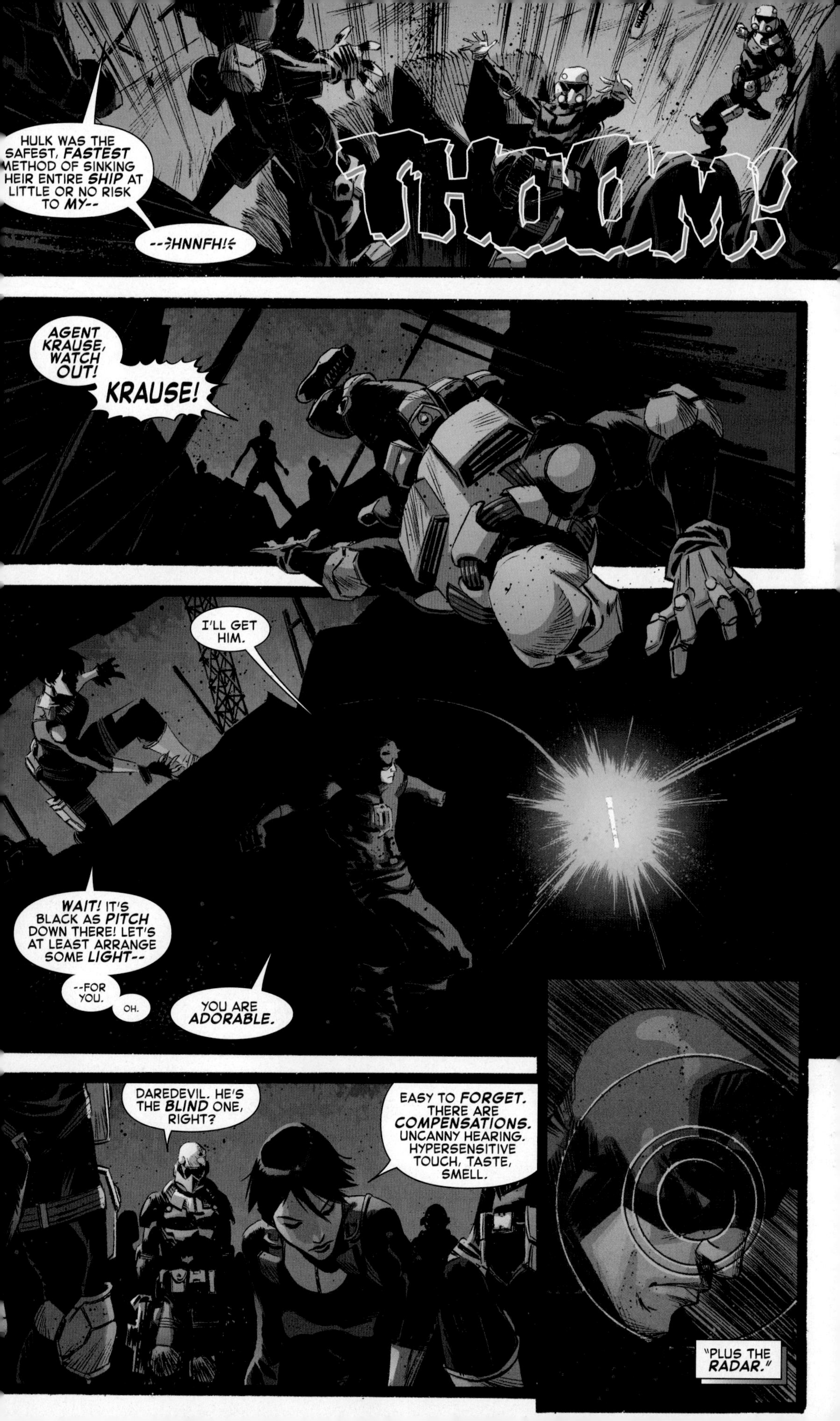

HULK WAS THE SAFEST, FASTEST METHOD OF SINKING HEIR ENTIRE SHIP AT LITTLE OR NO RISK TO MY--
--HNNFH!
THOOM!
AGENT KRAUSE, WATCH OUT!
KRAUSE!
I'LL GET HIM.
WAIT! IT'S BLACK AS PITCH DOWN THERE! LET'S AT LEAST ARRANGE SOME LIGHT--
--FOR YOU.
OH.
YOU ARE ADORABLE.
DAREDEVIL. HE'S THE BLIND ONE, RIGHT?
EASY TO FORGET. THERE ARE COMPENSATIONS. UNCANNY HEARING. HYPERSENSITIVE TOUCH, TASTE, SMELL.
"PLUS THE RADAR."

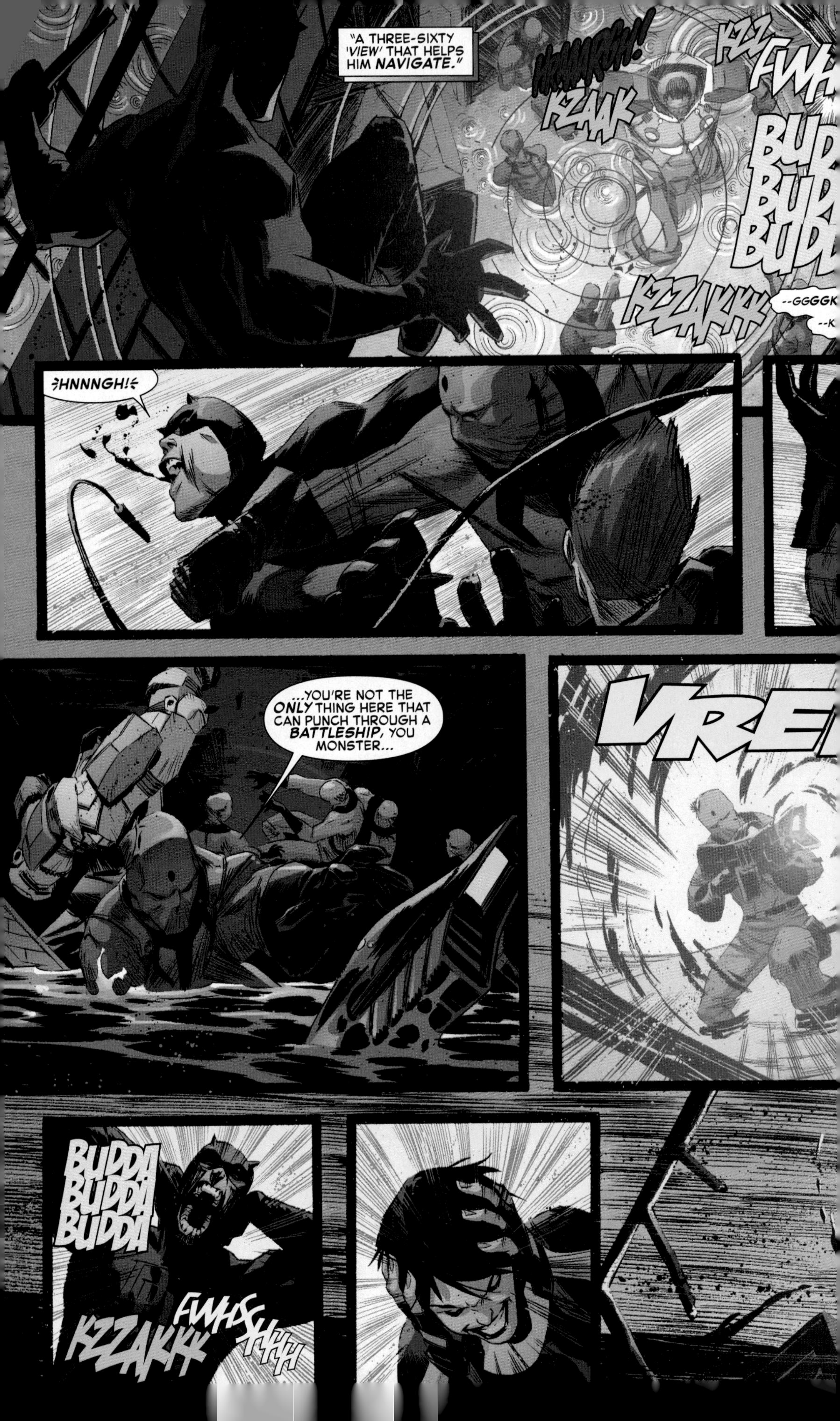
"A THREE-SIXTY 'VIEW' THAT HELPS HIM NAVIGATE."
HRAAAKROOH!!
KZZ
FWH
KZAAK
BUD
BUD
BUDD
KZZAKKK
--GGGGK
--K
HNNNGH!
...YOU'RE NOT THE ONLY THING HERE THAT CAN PUNCH THROUGH A BATTLESHIP, YOU MONSTER...
VRE
BUDDA
BUDDA
BUDDA
KZZAKKK
FWHSHHHH

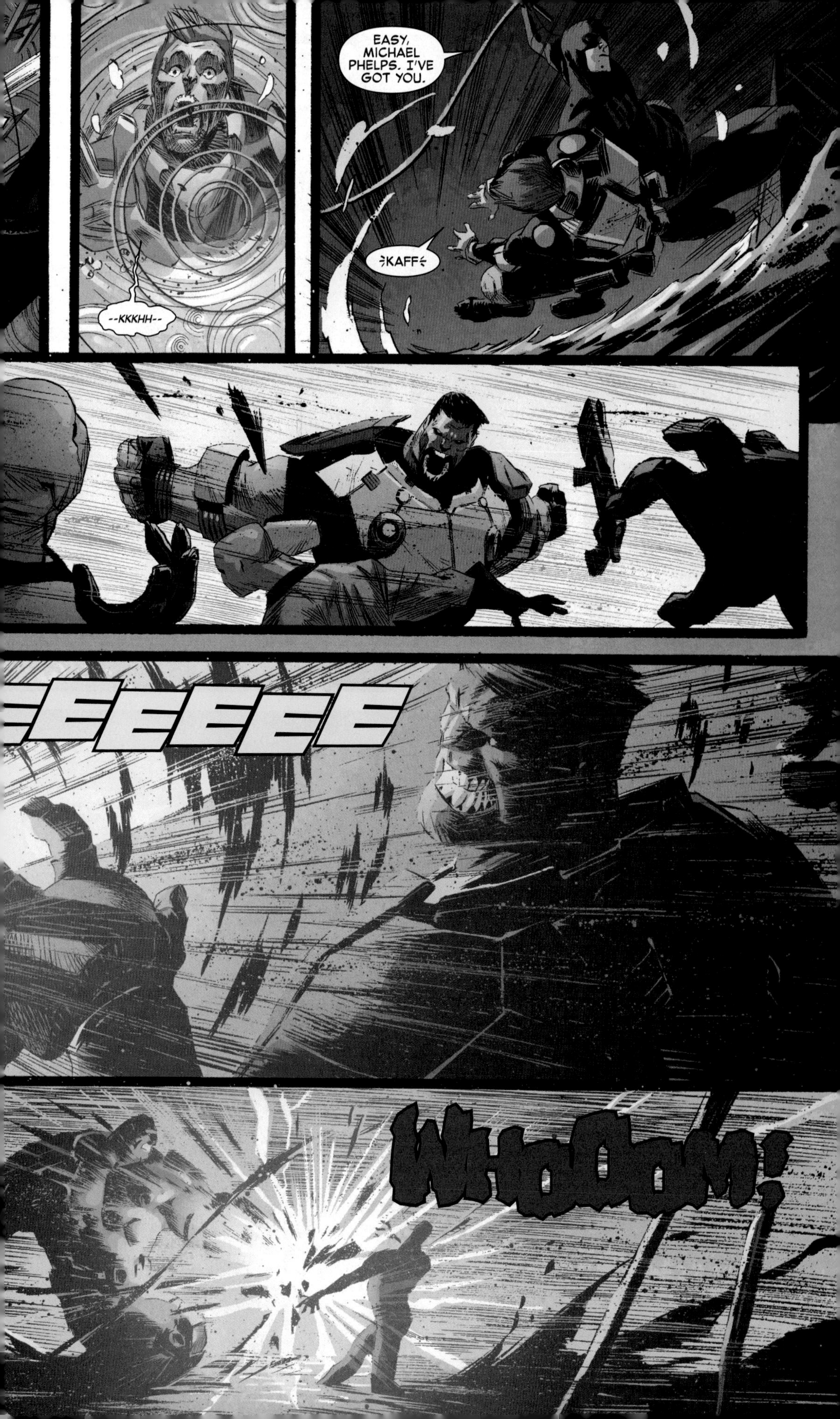
--KKKHH--
EASY, MICHAEL PHELPS. I'VE GOT YOU.
KAFF
EEEEEE
WHOOOM!

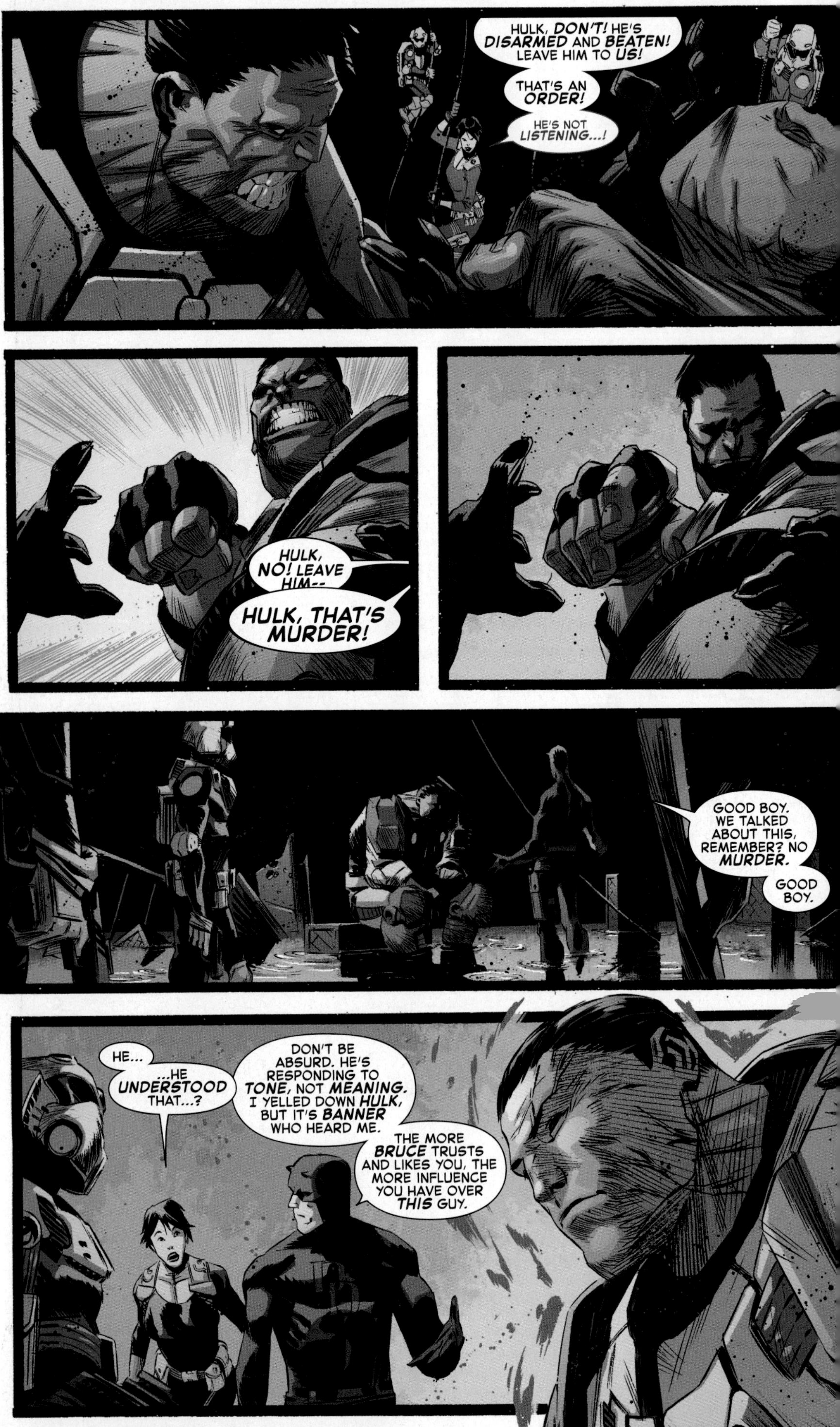
HULK, DON'T! HE'S DISARMED AND BEATEN! LEAVE HIM TO US!
THAT'S AN ORDER!
HE'S NOT LISTENING...!
HULK, NO! LEAVE HIM--
HULK, THAT'S MURDER!
GOOD BOY. WE TALKED ABOUT THIS, REMEMBER? NO MURDER.
GOOD BOY.
HE...
...HE UNDERSTOOD THAT...?
DON'T BE ABSURD. HE'S RESPONDING TO TONE, NOT MEANING. I YELLED DOWN HULK, BUT IT'S BANNER WHO HEARD ME.
THE MORE BRUCE TRUSTS AND LIKES YOU, THE MORE INFLUENCE YOU HAVE OVER THIS GUY.

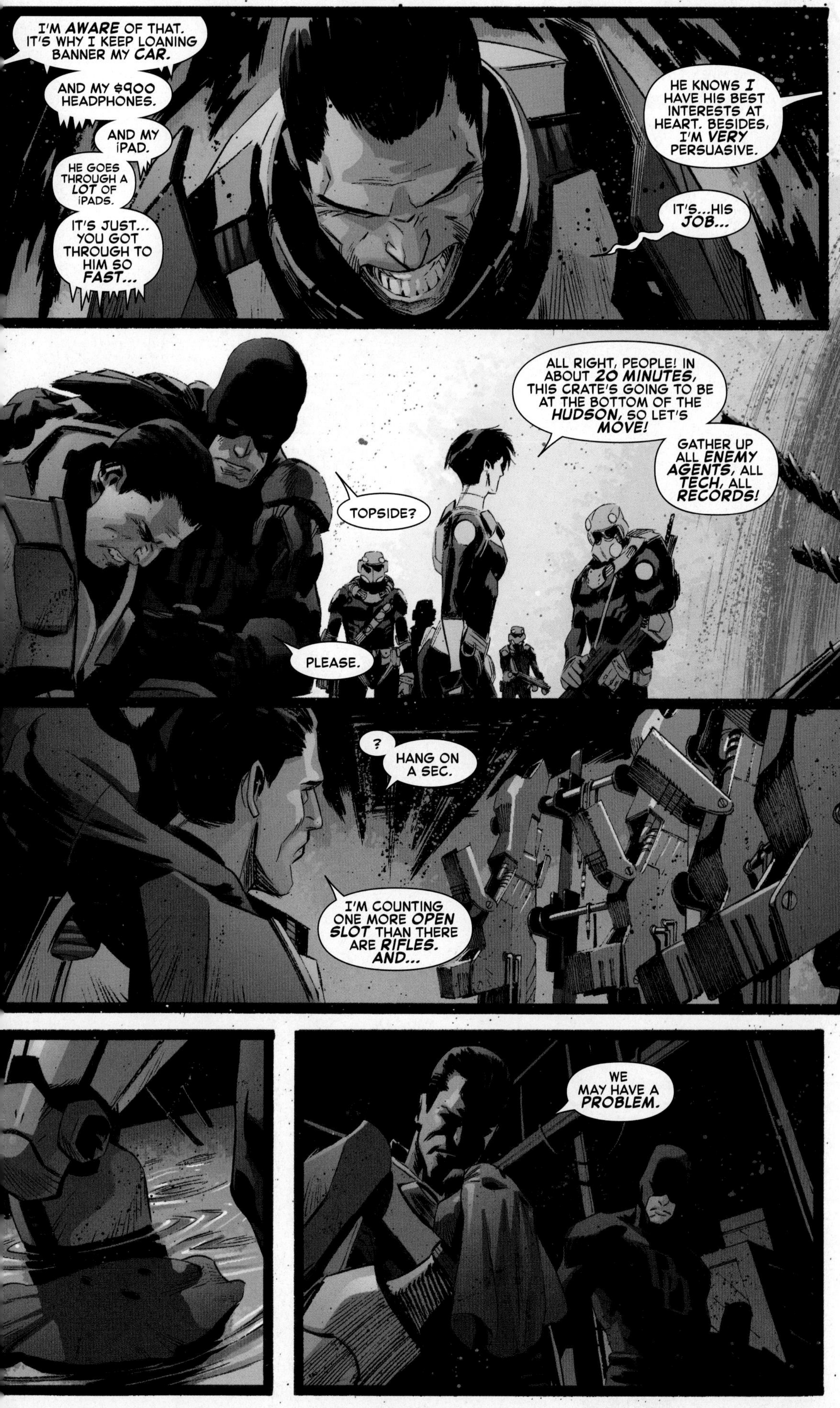
I'M AWARE OF THAT. IT'S WHY I KEEP LOANING BANNER MY CAR.
AND MY $900 HEADPHONES.
AND MY iPAD.
HE GOES THROUGH A LOT OF iPADS.
IT'S JUST... YOU GOT THROUGH TO HIM SO FAST...
HE KNOWS I HAVE HIS BEST INTERESTS AT HEART. BESIDES, I'M VERY PERSUASIVE.
IT'S...HIS JOB...
ALL RIGHT, PEOPLE! IN ABOUT 20 MINUTES, THIS CRATE'S GOING TO BE AT THE BOTTOM OF THE HUDSON, SO LET'S MOVE!
GATHER UP ALL ENEMY AGENTS, ALL TECH, ALL RECORDS!
TOPSIDE?
PLEASE.
?
HANG ON A SEC.
I'M COUNTING ONE MORE OPEN SLOT THAN THERE ARE RIFLES. AND...
WE MAY HAVE A PROBLEM.

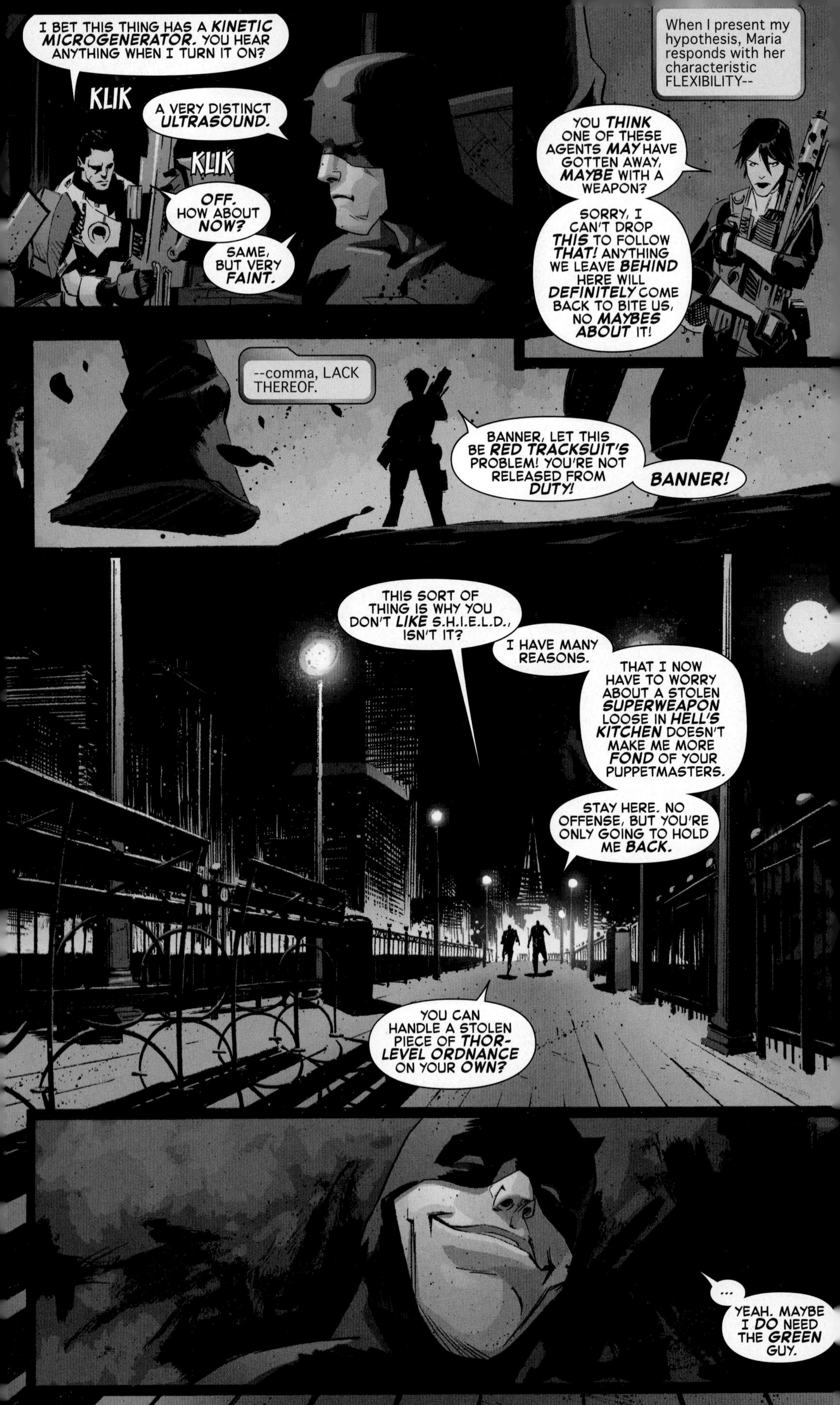
I BET THIS THING HAS A KINETIC MICROGENERATOR. YOU HEAR ANYTHING WHEN I TURN IT ON?
KLIK
A VERY DISTINCT ULTRASOUND.
KLIK
OFF. HOW ABOUT NOW?
SAME, BUT VERY FAINT.
When I present my hypothesis, Maria responds with her characteristic FLEXIBILITY--
YOU THINK ONE OF THESE AGENTS MAY HAVE GOTTEN AWAY, MAYBE WITH A WEAPON?
SORRY, I CAN'T DROP THIS TO FOLLOW THAT! ANYTHING WE LEAVE BEHIND HERE WILL DEFINITELY COME BACK TO BITE US, NO MAYBES ABOUT IT!
--comma, LACK THEREOF.
BANNER, LET THIS BE RED TRACKSUIT'S PROBLEM! YOU'RE NOT RELEASED FROM DUTY!
BANNER!
THIS SORT OF THING IS WHY YOU DON'T LIKE S.H.I.E.L.D., ISN'T IT?
I HAVE MANY REASONS.
THAT I NOW HAVE TO WORRY ABOUT A STOLEN SUPERWEAPON LOOSE IN HELL'S KITCHEN DOESN'T MAKE ME MORE FOND OF YOUR PUPPETMASTERS.
STAY HERE. NO OFFENSE, BUT YOU'RE ONLY GOING TO HOLD ME BACK.
YOU CAN HANDLE A STOLEN PIECE OF THOR-LEVEL ORDNANCE ON YOUR OWN?
...
YEAH. MAYBE I DO NEED THE GREEN GUY.

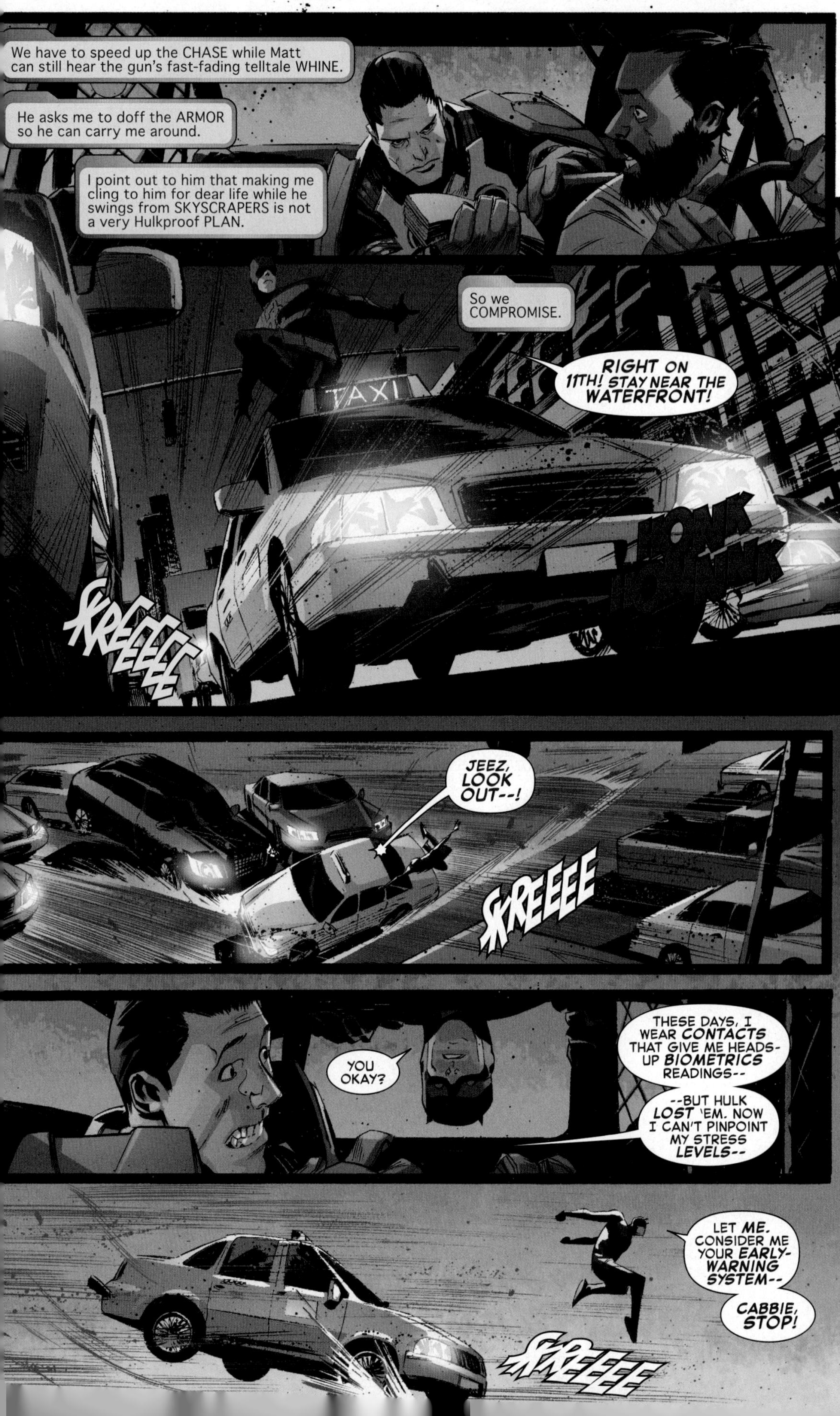

We have to speed up the CHASE while Matt can still hear the gun's fast-fading telltale WHINE.
He asks me to doff the ARMOR so he can carry me around.
I point out to him that making me cling to him for dear life while he swings from SKYSCRAPERS is not a very Hulkproof PLAN.
So we COMPROMISE.
RIGHT ON 11TH! STAY NEAR THE WATERFRONT!
TAXI
HONK HONK
SKREEEEE
JEEZ, LOOK OUT--!
SKREEEE
YOU OKAY?
THESE DAYS, I WEAR CONTACTS THAT GIVE ME HEADS-UP BIOMETRICS READINGS--
--BUT HULK LOST 'EM. NOW I CAN'T PINPOINT MY STRESS LEVELS--
LET ME. CONSIDER ME YOUR EARLY-WARNING SYSTEM--
CABBIE, STOP!
SKREEEE

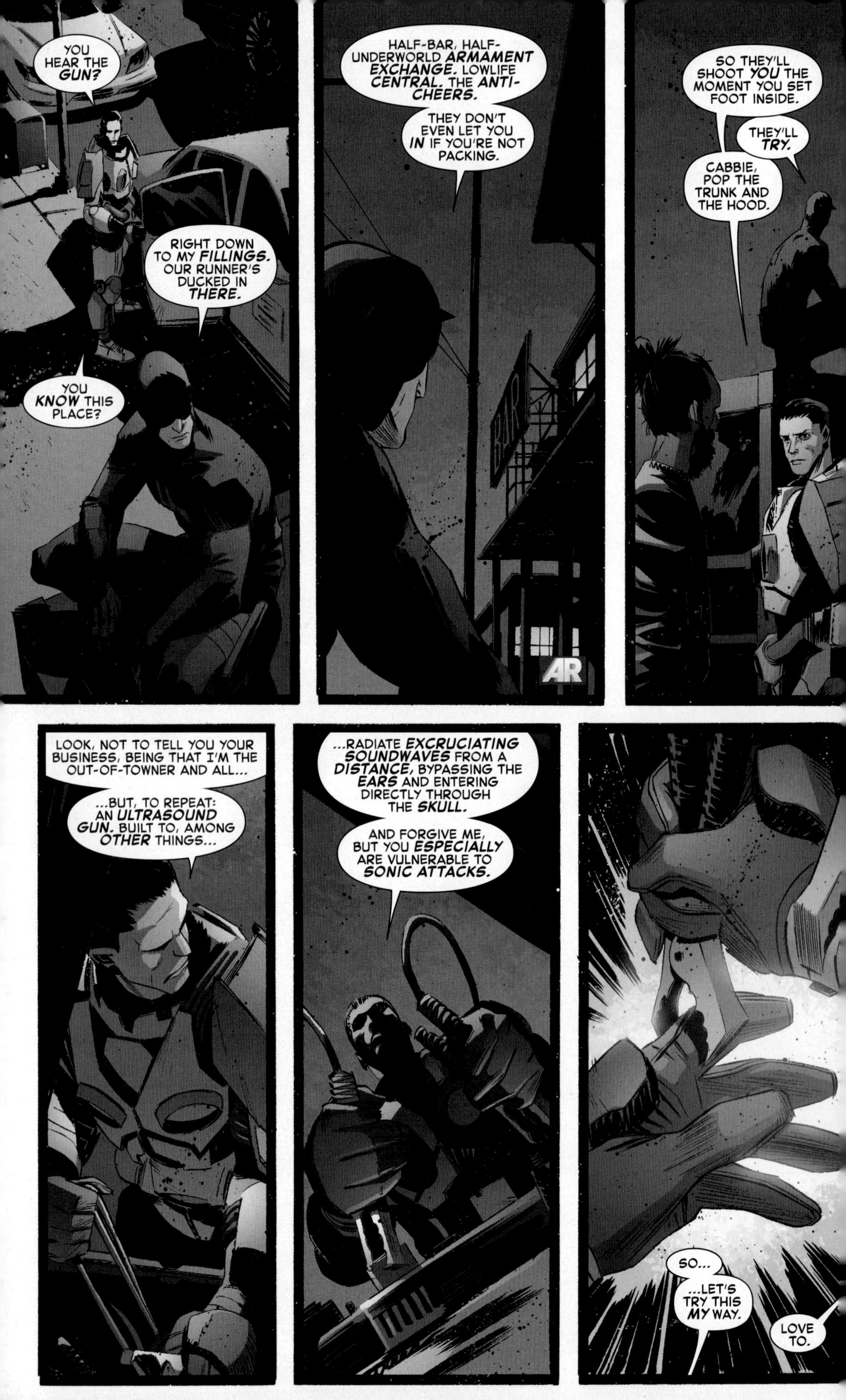
YOU HEAR THE GUN?
RIGHT DOWN TO MY FILLINGS. OUR RUNNER'S DUCKED IN THERE.
YOU KNOW THIS PLACE?
HALF-BAR, HALF-UNDERWORLD ARMAMENT EXCHANGE. LOWLIFE CENTRAL. THE ANTI-CHEERS.
THEY DON'T EVEN LET YOU IN IF YOU'RE NOT PACKING.
BAR
SO THEY'LL SHOOT YOU THE MOMENT YOU SET FOOT INSIDE.
THEY'LL TRY.
CABBIE, POP THE TRUNK AND THE HOOD.
LOOK, NOT TO TELL YOU YOUR BUSINESS, BEING THAT I'M THE OUT-OF-TOWNER AND ALL...
...BUT, TO REPEAT: AN ULTRASOUND GUN. BUILT TO, AMONG OTHER THINGS...
...RADIATE EXCRUCIATING SOUNDWAVES FROM A DISTANCE, BYPASSING THE EARS AND ENTERING DIRECTLY THROUGH THE SKULL.
AND FORGIVE ME, BUT YOU ESPECIALLY ARE VULNERABLE TO SONIC ATTACKS.
SO...
...LET'S TRY THIS MY WAY.
LOVE TO.

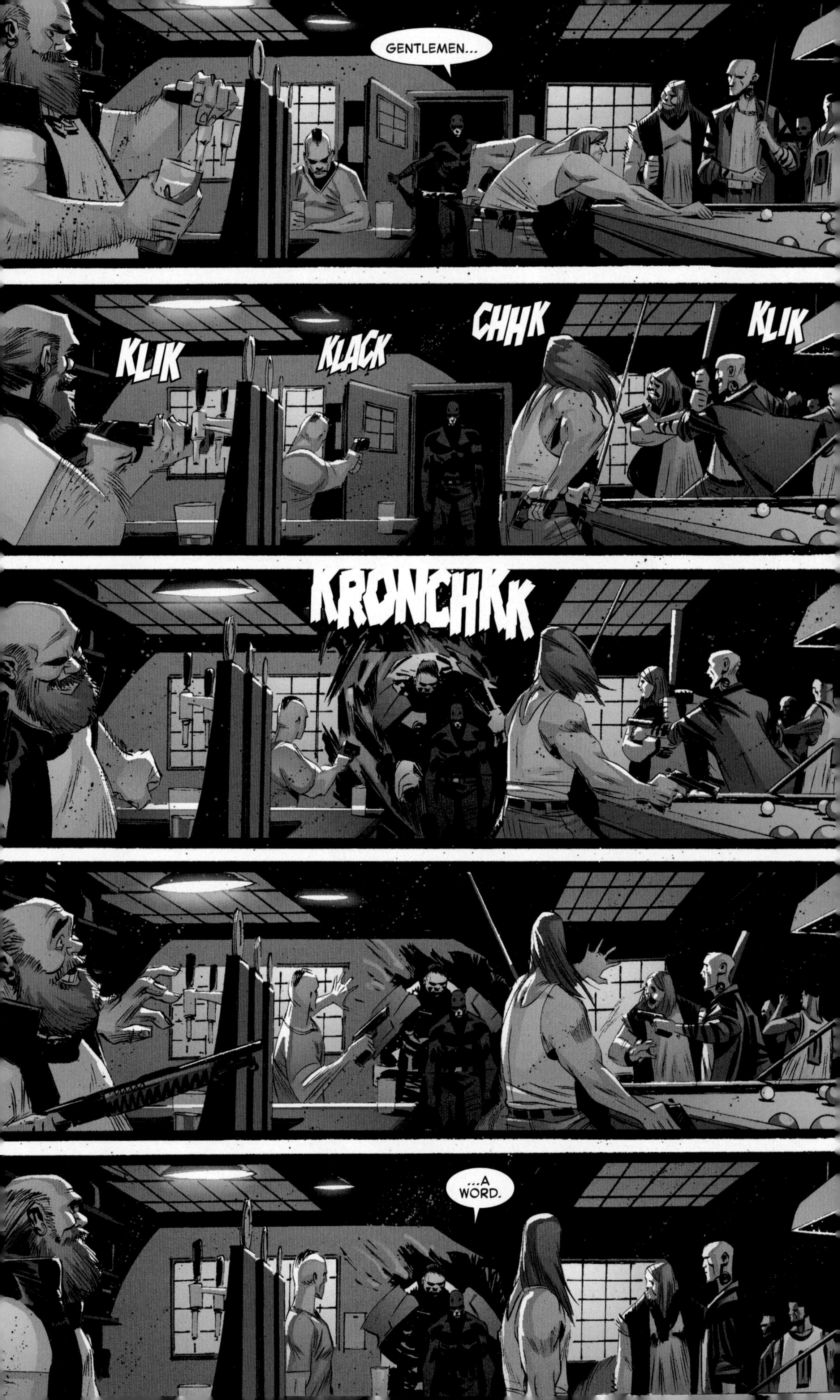
GENTLEMEN...
KLIK
KLACK
CHHK
KLIK
KRONCHKK
...A WORD.

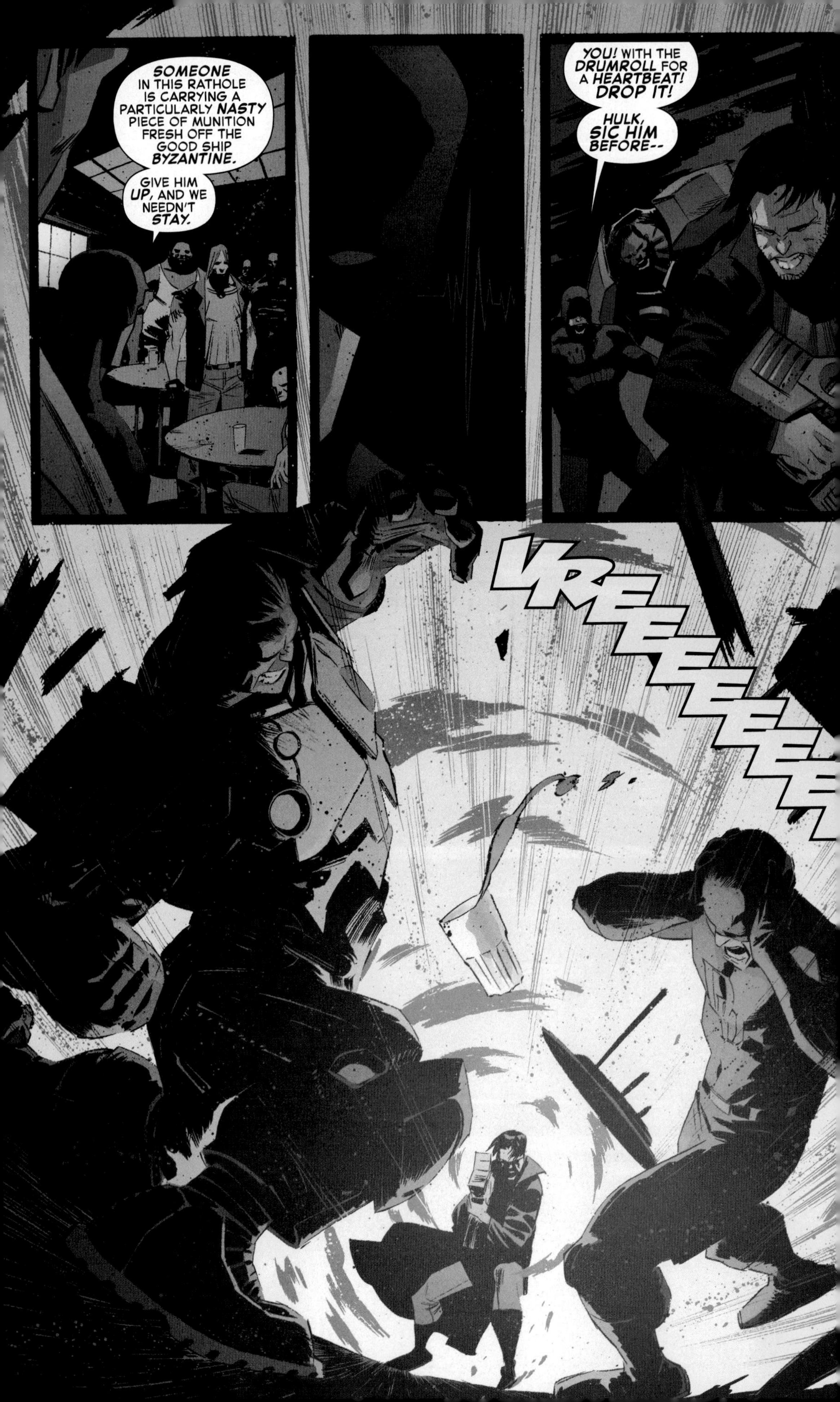

SOMEONE IN THIS RATHOLE IS CARRYING A PARTICULARLY NASTY PIECE OF MUNITION FRESH OFF THE GOOD SHIP BYZANTINE.
GIVE HIM UP, AND WE NEEDN'T STAY.
YOU! WITH THE DRUMROLL FOR A HEARTBEAT! DROP IT!
HULK, SIC HIM BEFORE--
VREEEEEEEEE

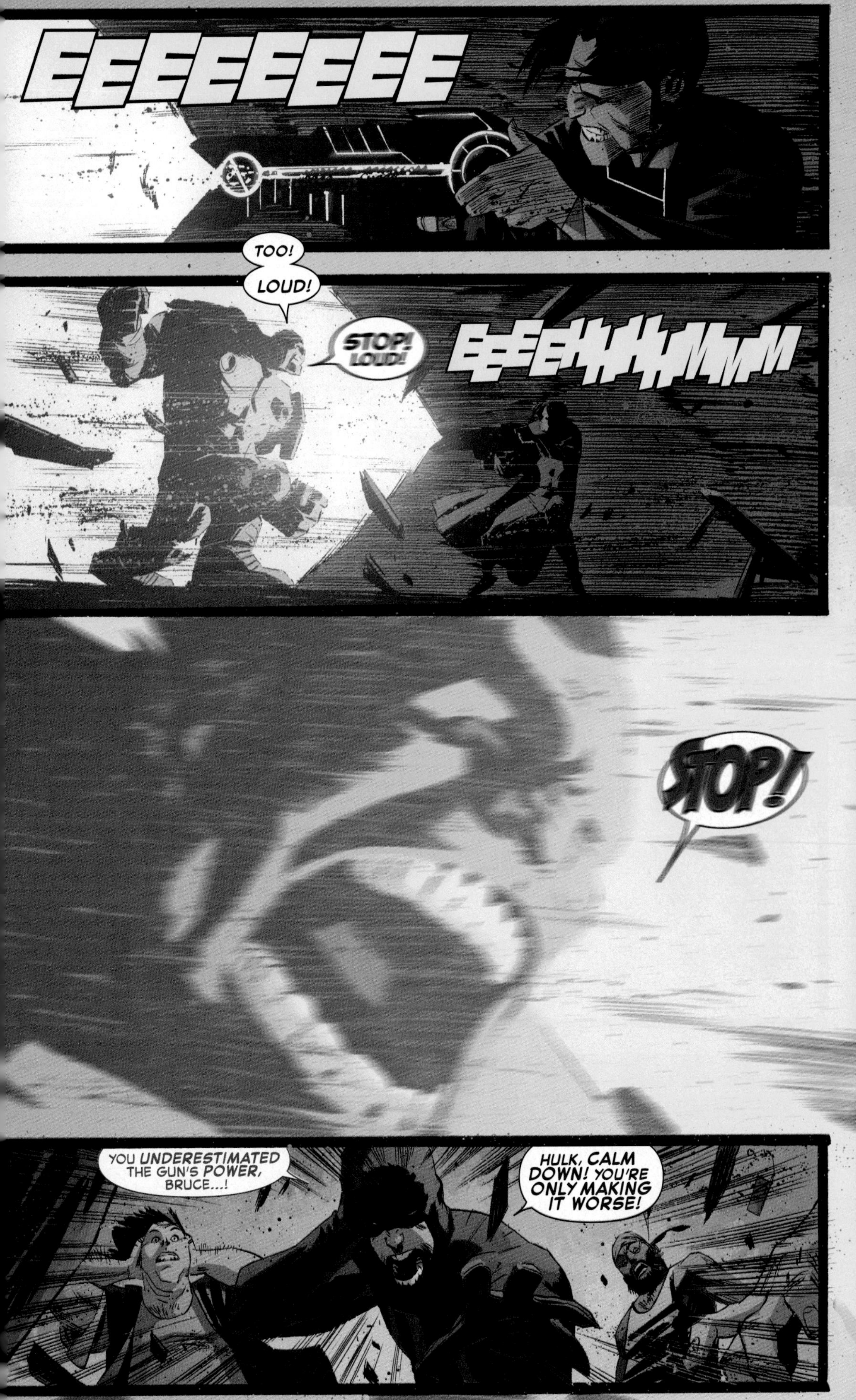
EEEEEEEEE
TOO!
LOUD!
STOP! LOUD!
EEEEHHHHMMMM
STOP!
YOU UNDERESTIMATED THE GUN'S POWER, BRUCE...!
HULK, CALM DOWN! YOU'RE ONLY MAKING IT WORSE!

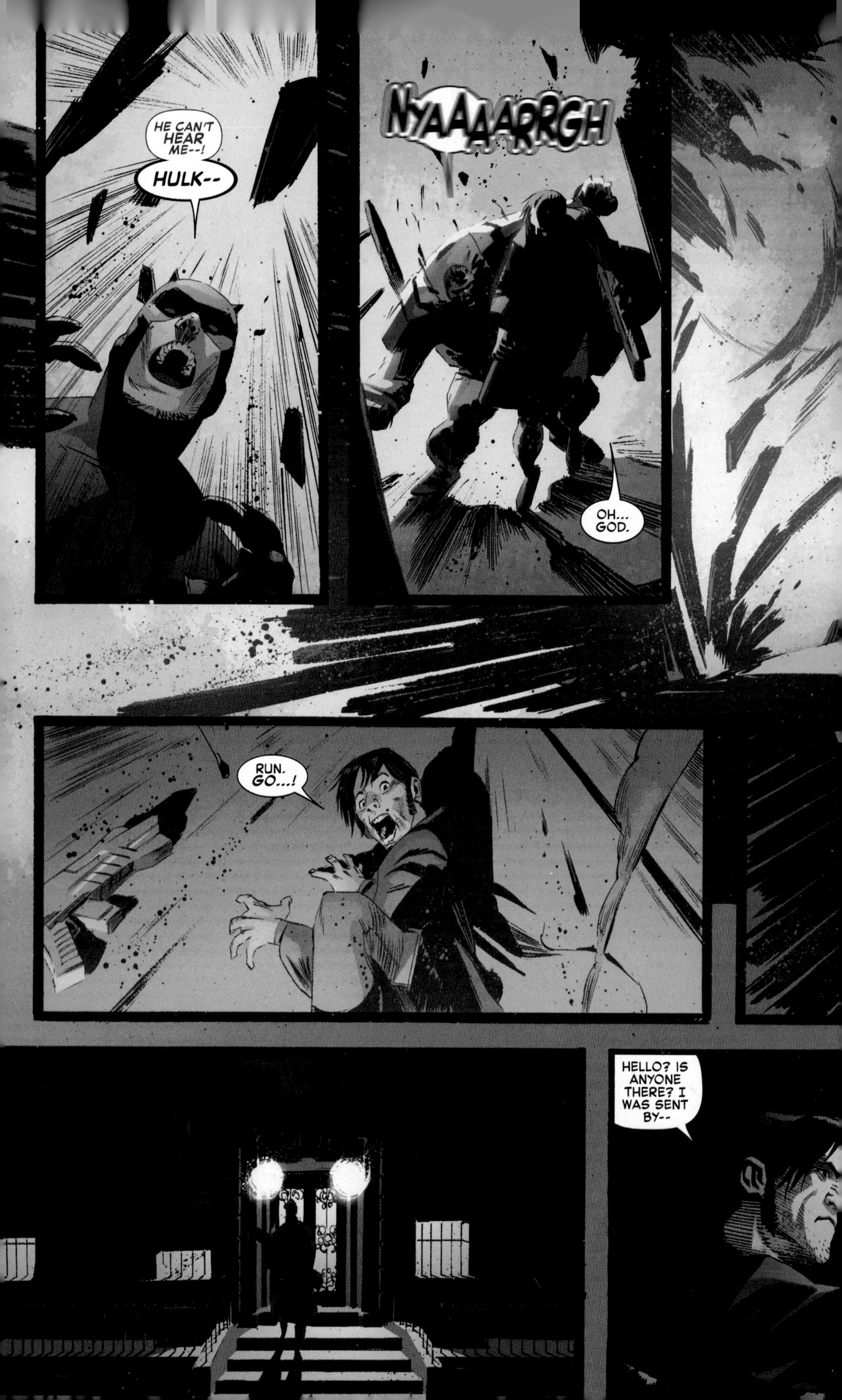
HE CAN'T HEAR ME--!
HULK--
NYAAAARRGH
OH... GOD.
RUN. GO...!
HELLO? IS ANYONE THERE? I WAS SENT BY--

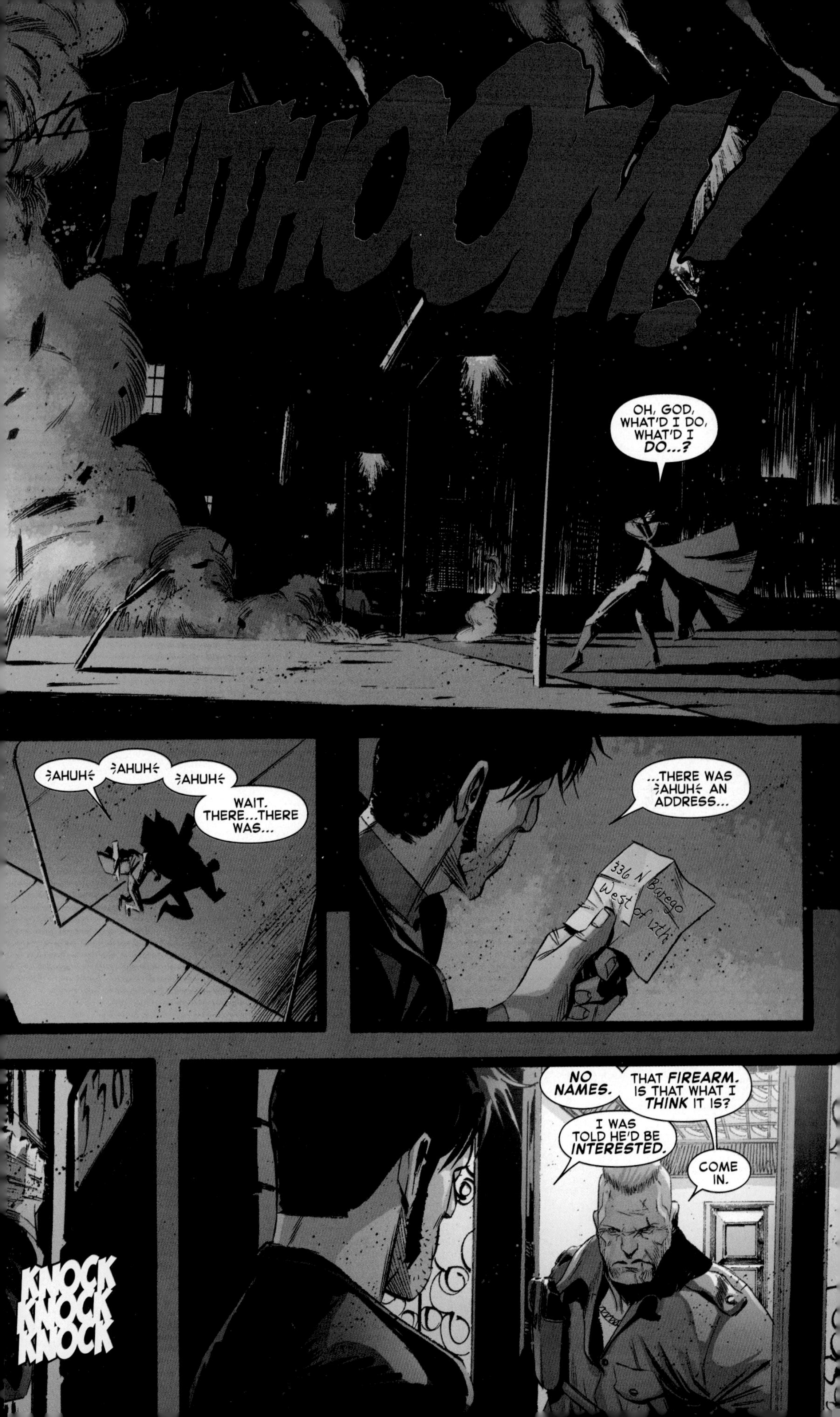
FATHOOM!
OH, GOD, WHAT'D I DO, WHAT'D I DO...?
≥AHUH≤
≥AHUH≤
≥AHUH≤
WAIT. THERE...THERE WAS...
...THERE WAS ≥AHUH≤ AN ADDRESS...
336 N Barego West of 12th
KNOCK KNOCK KNOCK
NO NAMES.
THAT FIREARM. IS THAT WHAT I THINK IT IS?
I WAS TOLD HE'D BE INTERESTED.
COME IN.

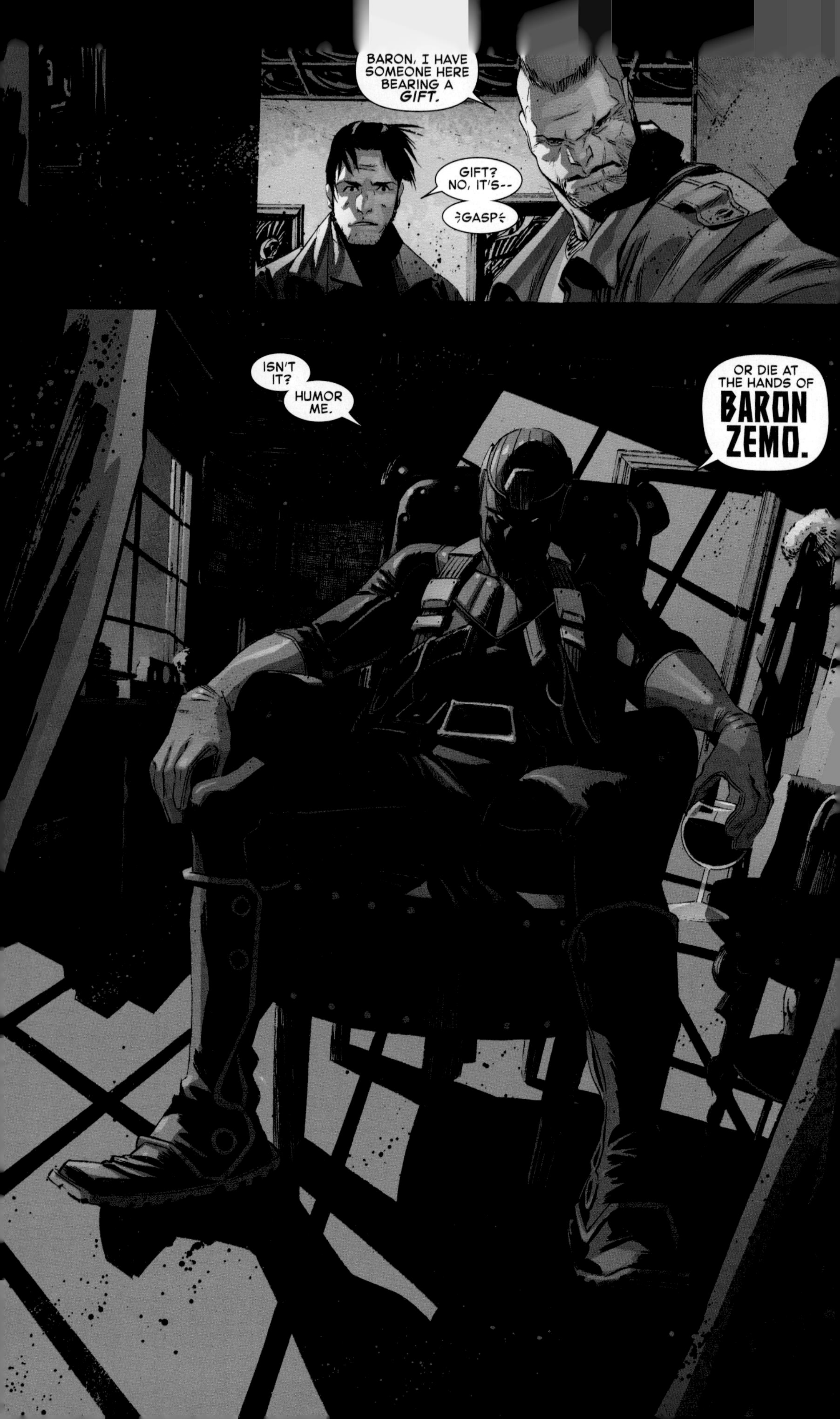
BARON, I HAVE SOMEONE HERE BEARING A GIFT.
GIFT? NO, IT'S--
GASP
ISN'T IT? HUMOR ME.
OR DIE AT THE HANDS OF BARON ZEMO.

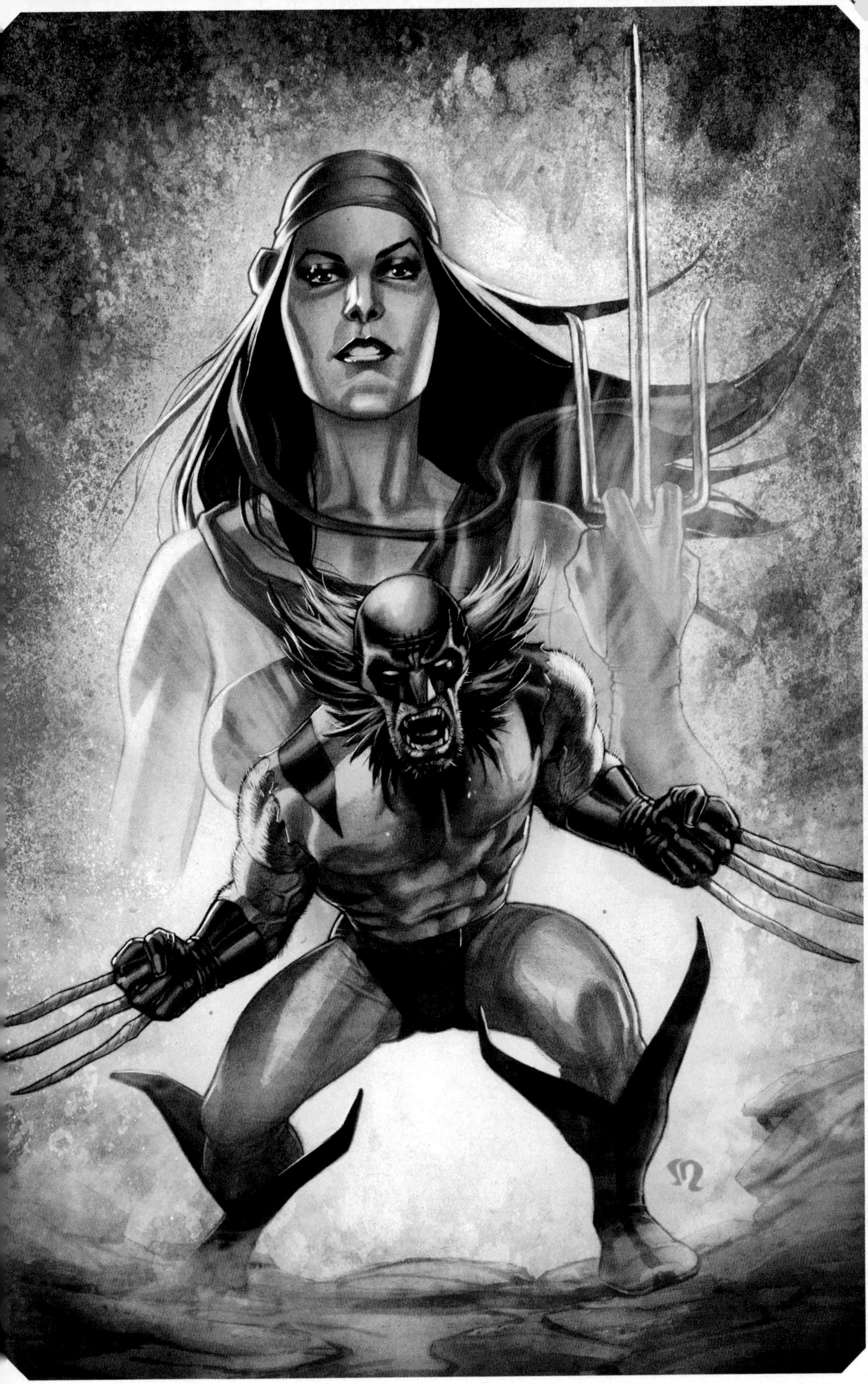

INDESTRUCTIBLE HULK #9 ***WOLVERINE THROUGH THE AGES VARIANT BY STEPHANE ROUX***

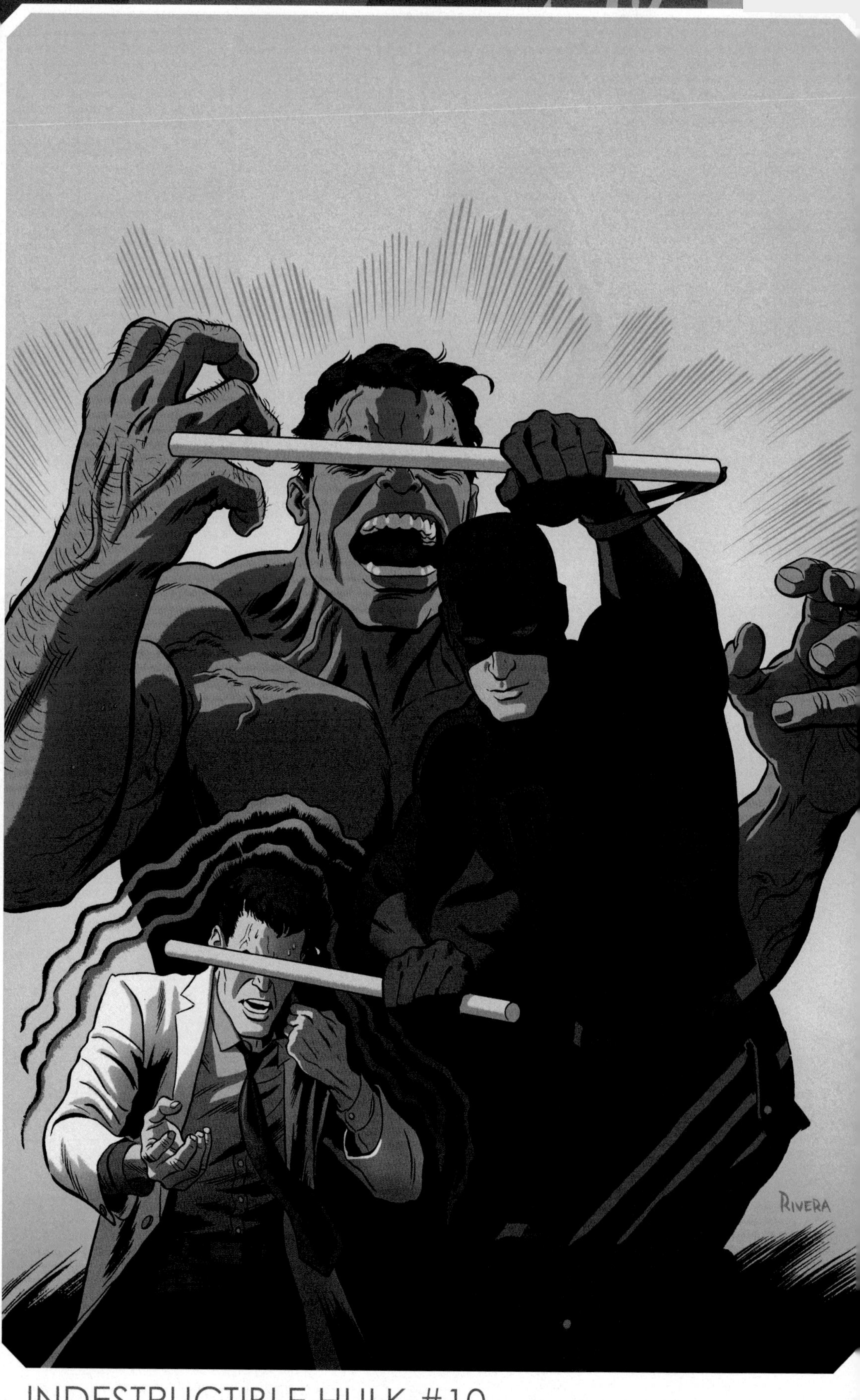
RIVERA

INDESTRUCTIBLE HULK #10

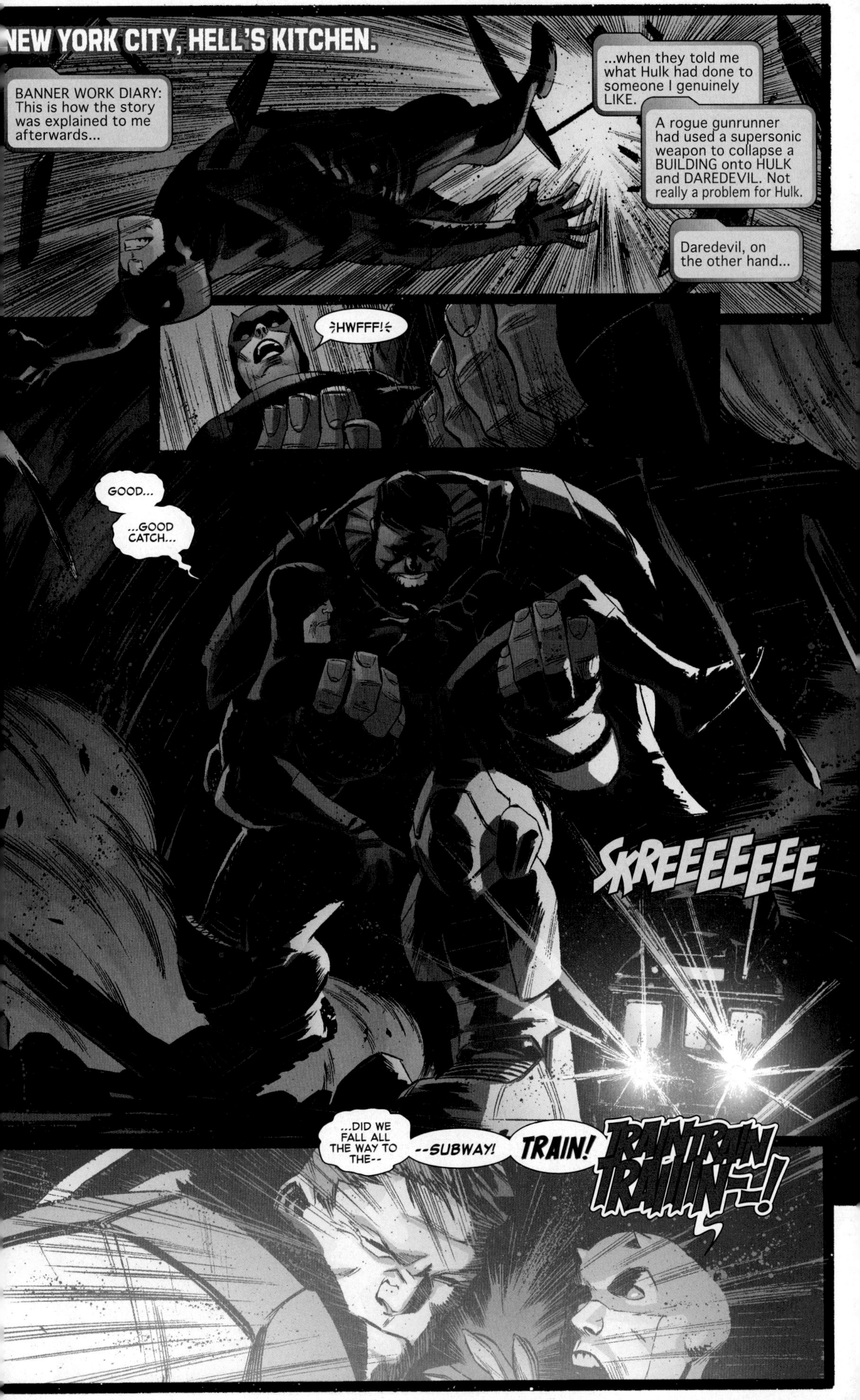

NEW YORK CITY, HELL'S KITCHEN.
BANNER WORK DIARY: This is how the story was explained to me afterwards...
...when they told me what Hulk had done to someone I genuinely LIKE.
A rogue gunrunner had used a supersonic weapon to collapse a BUILDING onto HULK and DAREDEVIL. Not really a problem for Hulk.
Daredevil, on the other hand...
HWFFF!
GOOD...
...GOOD CATCH...
SKREEEEEEEE
...DID WE FALL ALL THE WAY TO THE--
--SUBWAY!
TRAIN!
TRAINTRAIN TRAIIIN--!

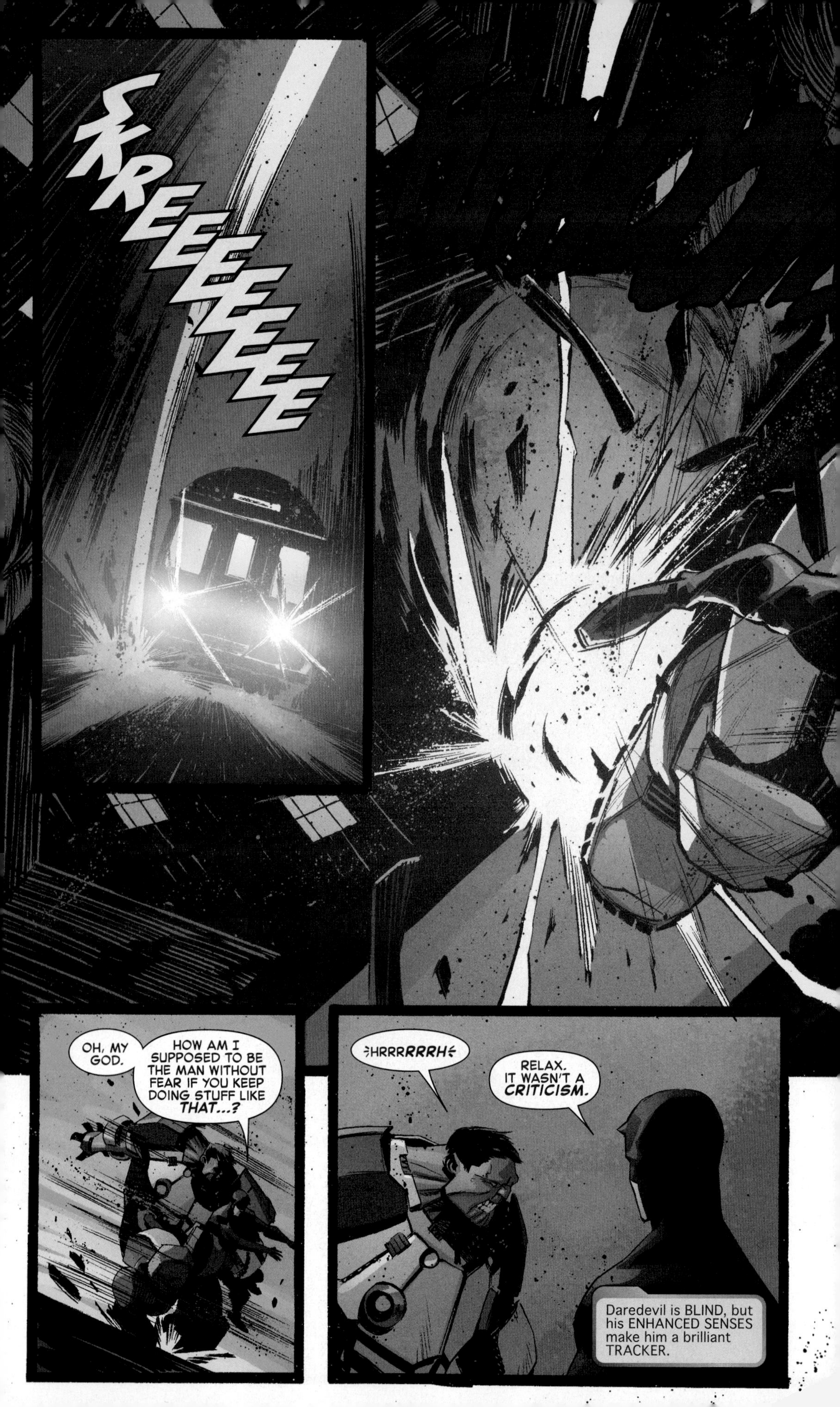
SKREEEEEEEEE
OH, MY GOD.
HOW AM I SUPPOSED TO BE THE MAN WITHOUT FEAR IF YOU KEEP DOING STUFF LIKE THAT...?
HRRRRRRH
RELAX. IT WASN'T A CRITICISM.
Daredevil is BLIND, but his ENHANCED SENSES make him a brilliant TRACKER.

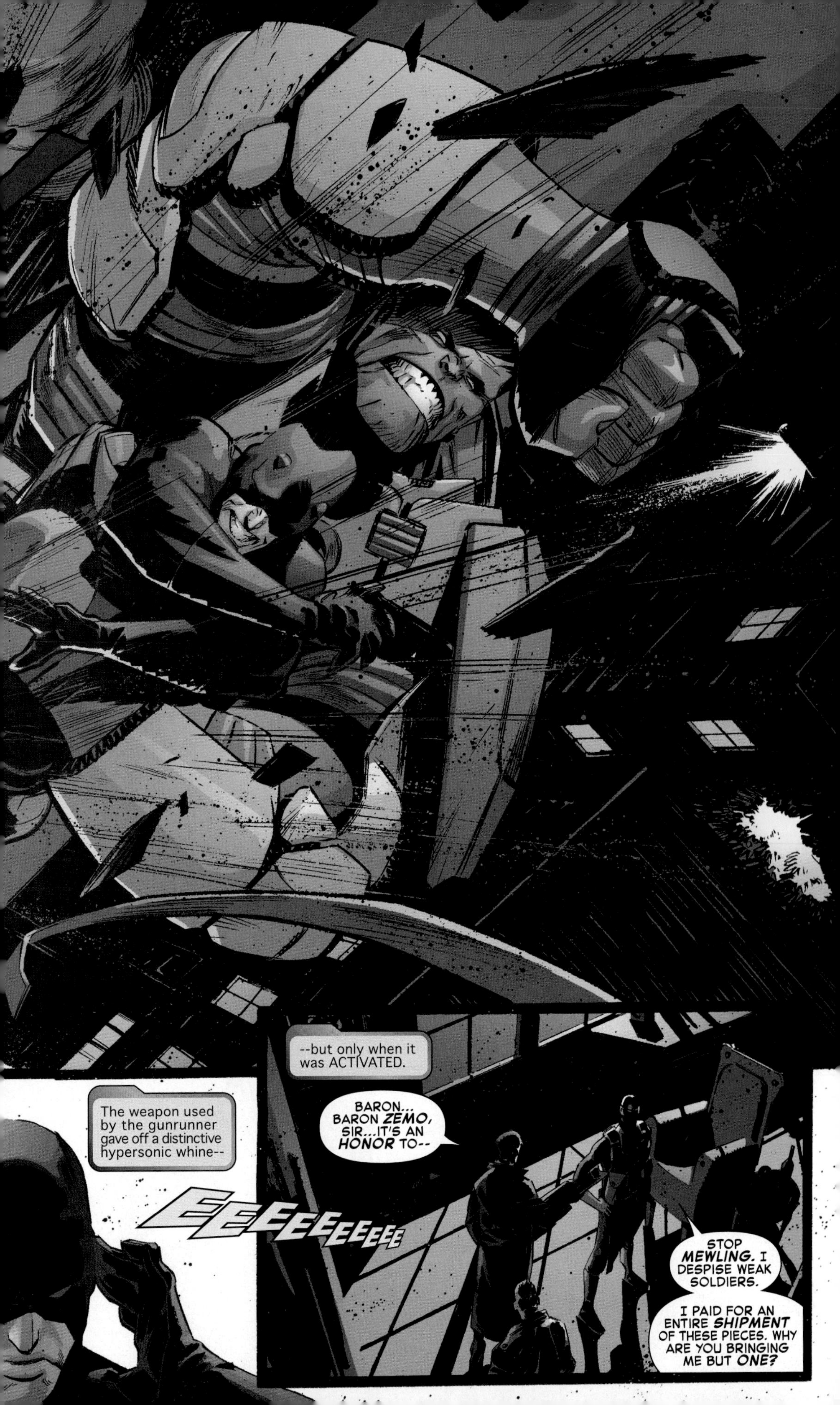

The weapon used by the gunrunner gave off a distinctive hypersonic whine--
EEEEEEEEEEE
--but only when it was ACTIVATED.
BARON... BARON ZEMO, SIR...IT'S AN HONOR TO--
STOP MEWLING. I DESPISE WEAK SOLDIERS.
I PAID FOR AN ENTIRE SHIPMENT OF THESE PIECES. WHY ARE YOU BRINGING ME BUT ONE?

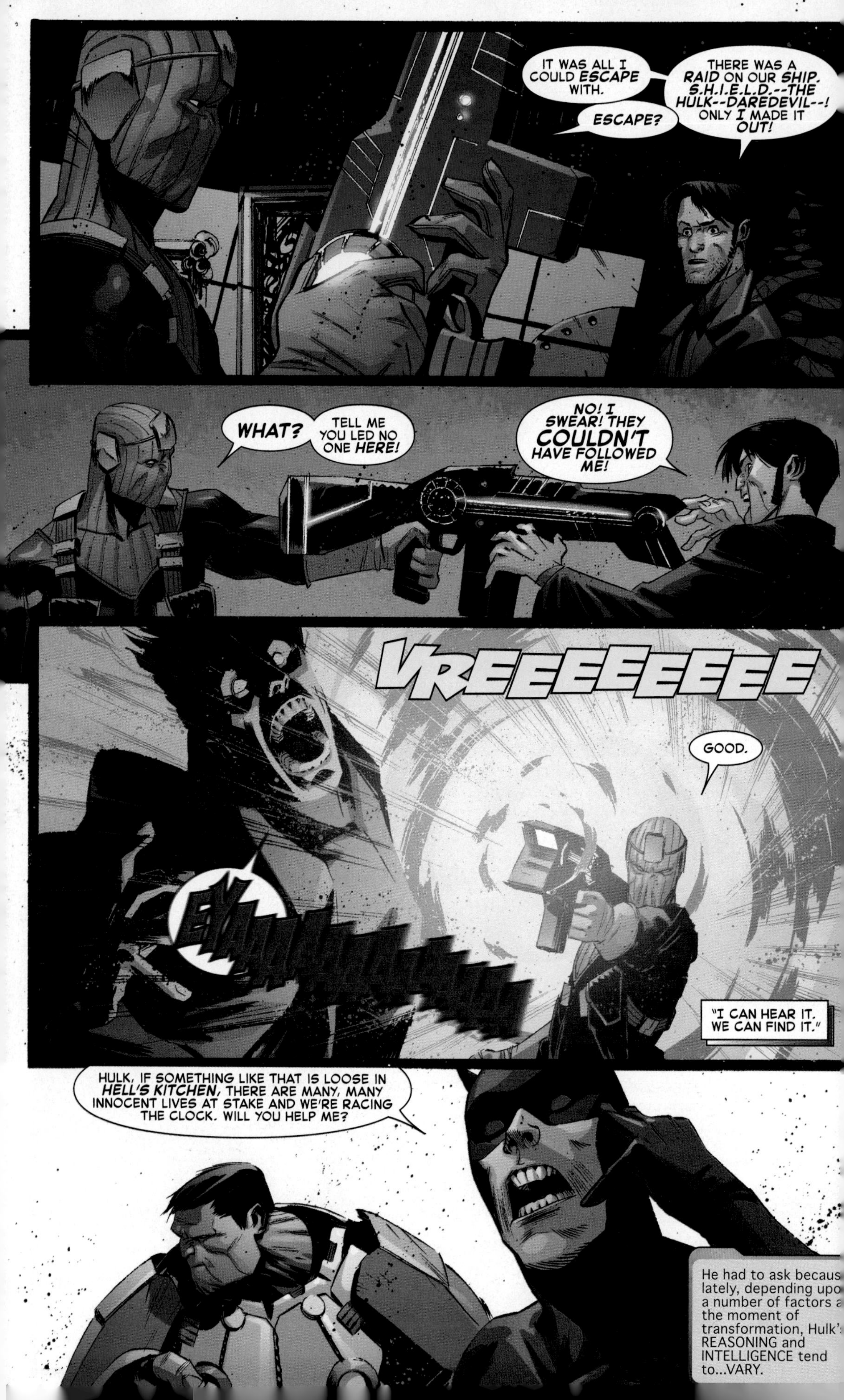

IT WAS ALL I COULD ESCAPE WITH.
THERE WAS A RAID ON OUR SHIP. S.H.I.E.L.D.--THE HULK--DAREDEVIL--! ONLY I MADE IT OUT!
ESCAPE?
WHAT?
TELL ME YOU LED NO ONE HERE!
NO! I SWEAR! THEY COULDN'T HAVE FOLLOWED ME!
VREEEEEEEE
GOOD.
"I CAN HEAR IT. WE CAN FIND IT."
HULK, IF SOMETHING LIKE THAT IS LOOSE IN HELL'S KITCHEN, THERE ARE MANY, MANY INNOCENT LIVES AT STAKE AND WE'RE RACING THE CLOCK. WILL YOU HELP ME?
He had to ask becaus lately, depending upo a number of factors a the moment of transformation, Hulk' REASONING and INTELLIGENCE tend to...VARY.

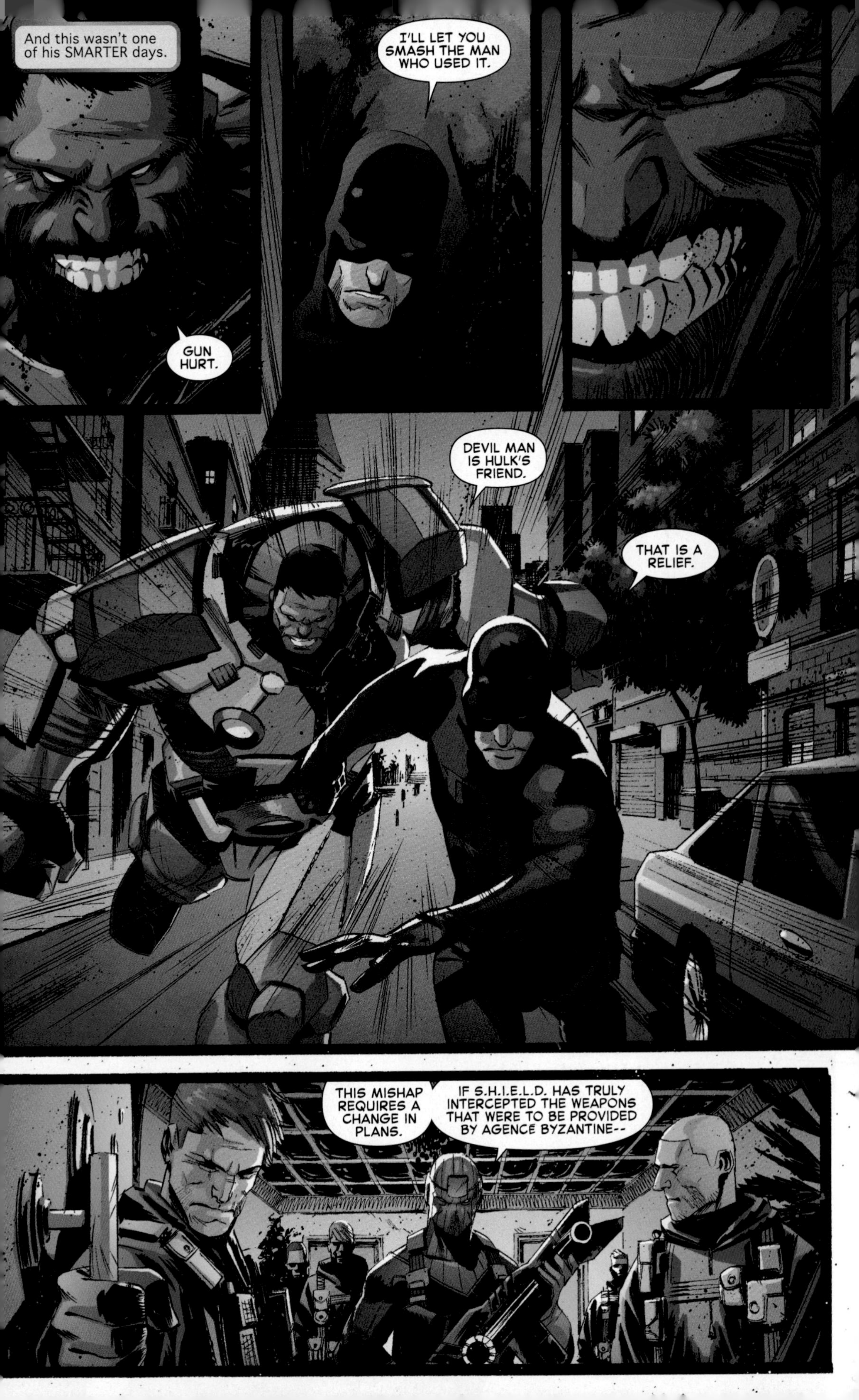
And this wasn't one of his SMARTER days.
GUN HURT.
I'LL LET YOU SMASH THE MAN WHO USED IT.
DEVIL MAN IS HULK'S FRIEND.
THAT IS A RELIEF.
THIS MISHAP REQUIRES A CHANGE IN PLANS.
IF S.H.I.E.L.D. HAS TRULY INTERCEPTED THE WEAPONS THAT WERE TO BE PROVIDED BY AGENCE BYZANTINE--

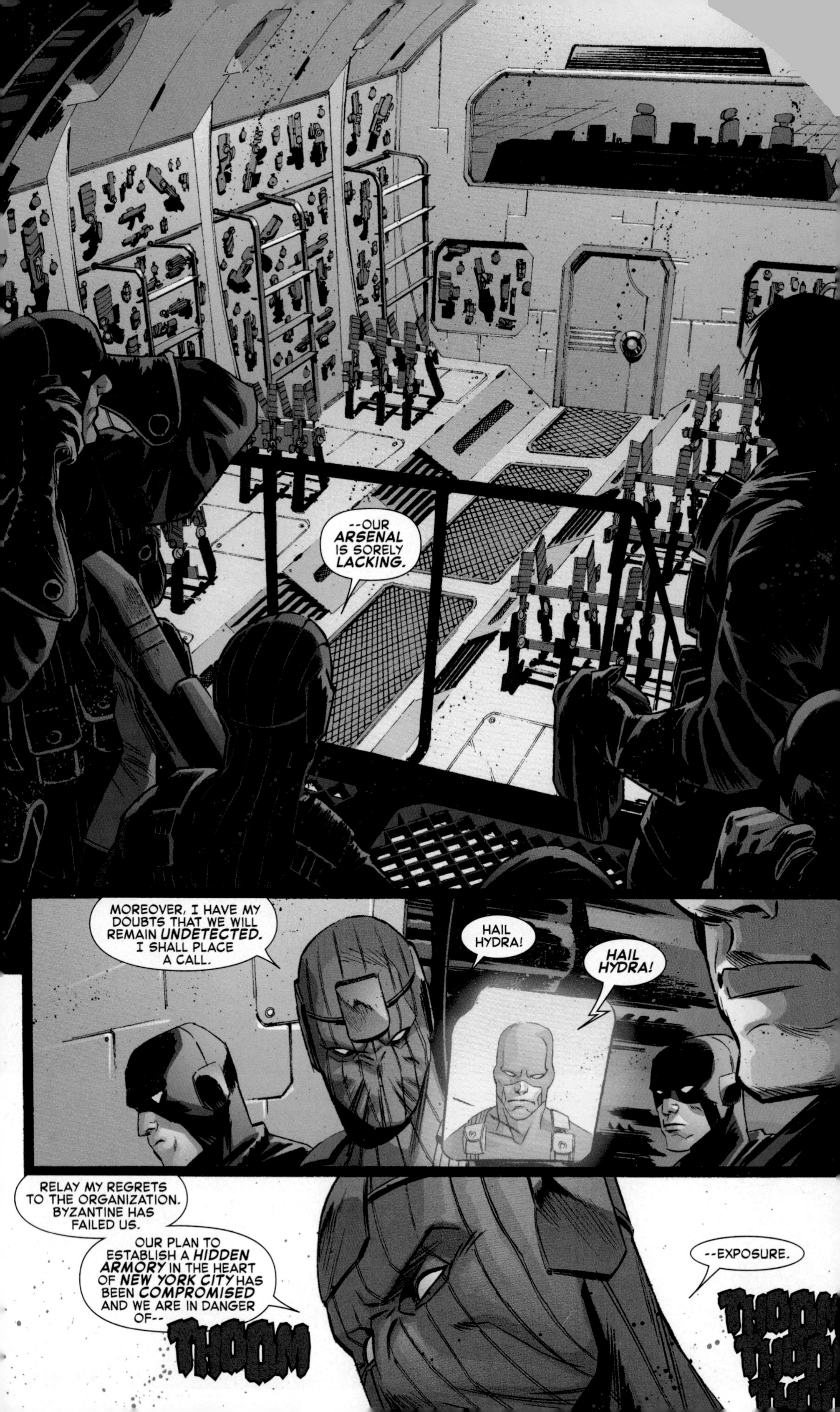
--OUR ARSENAL IS SORELY LACKING.
MOREOVER, I HAVE MY DOUBTS THAT WE WILL REMAIN UNDETECTED. I SHALL PLACE A CALL.
HAIL HYDRA!
HAIL HYDRA!
RELAY MY REGRETS TO THE ORGANIZATION. BYZANTINE HAS FAILED US.
OUR PLAN TO ESTABLISH A HIDDEN ARMORY IN THE HEART OF NEW YORK CITY HAS BEEN COMPROMISED AND WE ARE IN DANGER OF--
THOOM
--EXPOSURE.

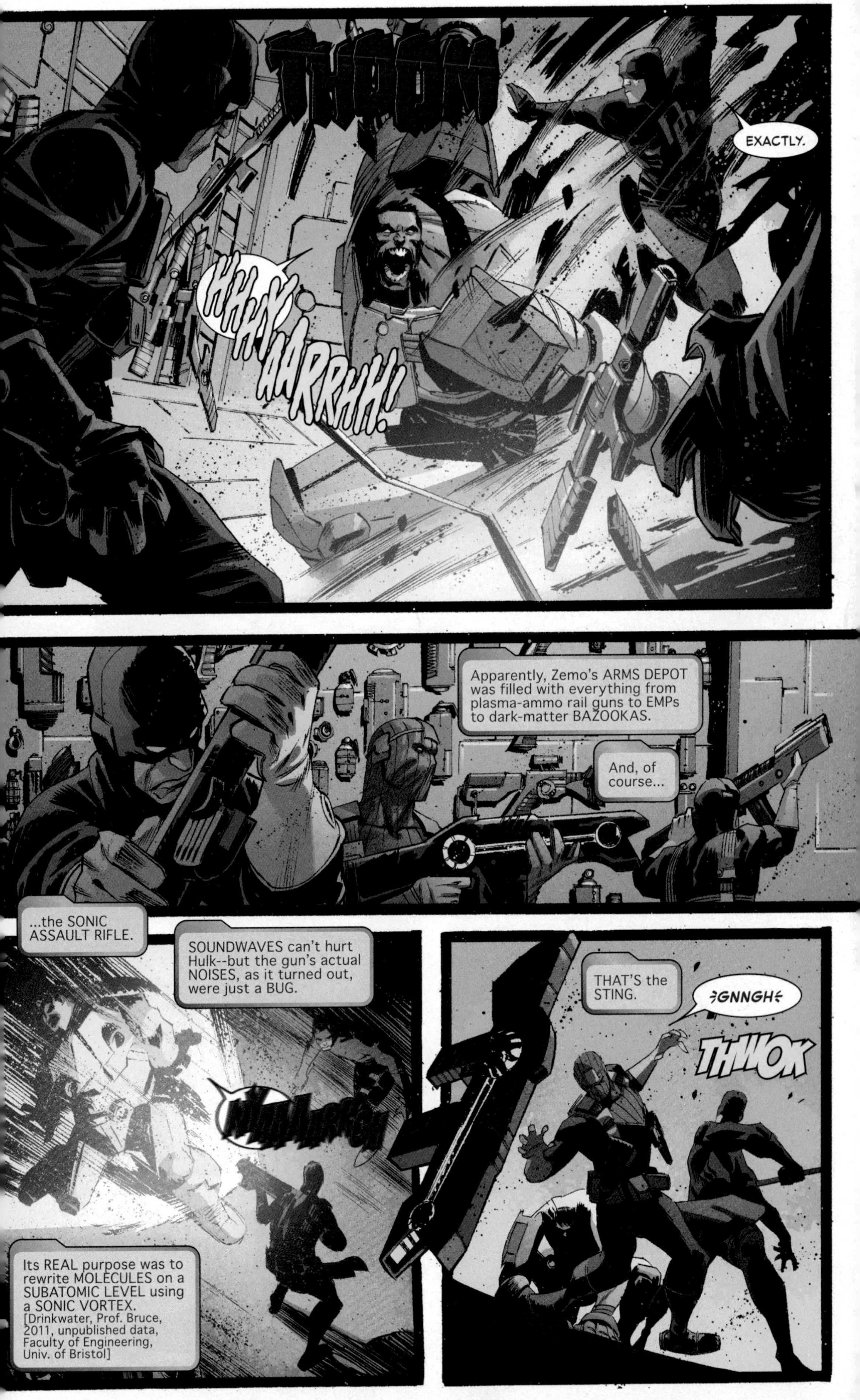
THOOM
EXACTLY.
HHHYAARRHH!
Apparently, Zemo's ARMS DEPOT was filled with everything from plasma-ammo rail guns to EMPs to dark-matter BAZOOKAS.
And, of course...
...the SONIC ASSAULT RIFLE.
SOUNDWAVES can't hurt Hulk--but the gun's actual NOISES, as it turned out, were just a BUG.
Its REAL purpose was to rewrite MOLECULES on a SUBATOMIC LEVEL using a SONIC VORTEX. [Drinkwater, Prof. Bruce, 2011, unpublished data, Faculty of Engineering, Univ. of Bristol]
THAT'S the STING.
GNNGH
THWOK

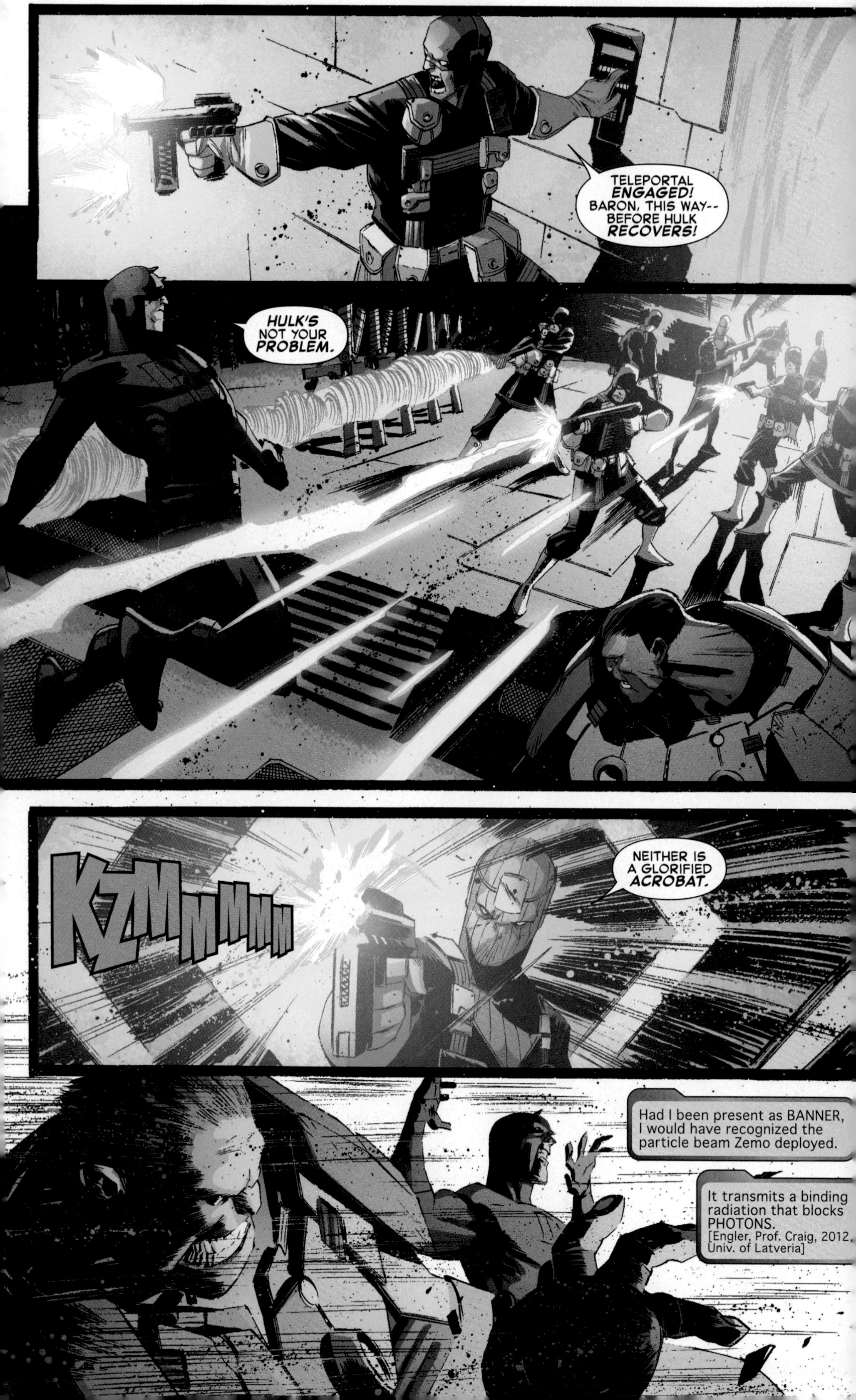
TELEPORTAL ENGAGED! BARON, THIS WAY-- BEFORE HULK RECOVERS!
HULK'S NOT YOUR PROBLEM.
KZMMMMMM
NEITHER IS A GLORIFIED ACROBAT.
Had I been present as BANNER, I would have recognized the particle beam Zemo deployed.
It transmits a binding radiation that blocks PHOTONS. [Engler, Prof. Craig, 2012, Univ. of Latveria]

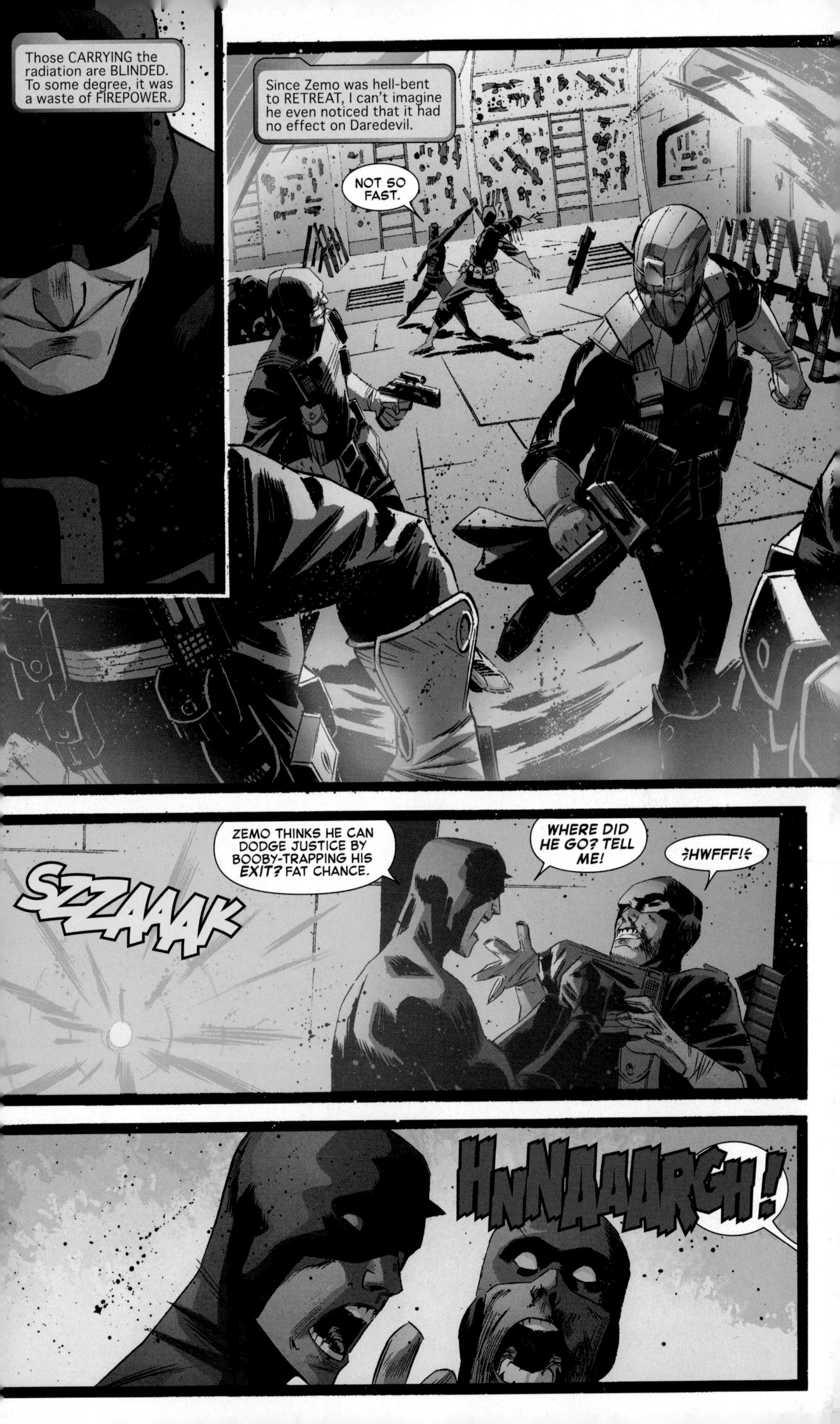
Those CARRYING the radiation are BLINDED. To some degree, it was a waste of FIREPOWER.
Since Zemo was hell-bent to RETREAT, I can't imagine he even noticed that it had no effect on Daredevil.
NOT SO FAST.
SZZAAAK
ZEMO THINKS HE CAN DODGE JUSTICE BY BOOBY-TRAPPING HIS EXIT? FAT CHANCE.
WHERE DID HE GO? TELL ME!
HWFFF!
HnNAAARGH!

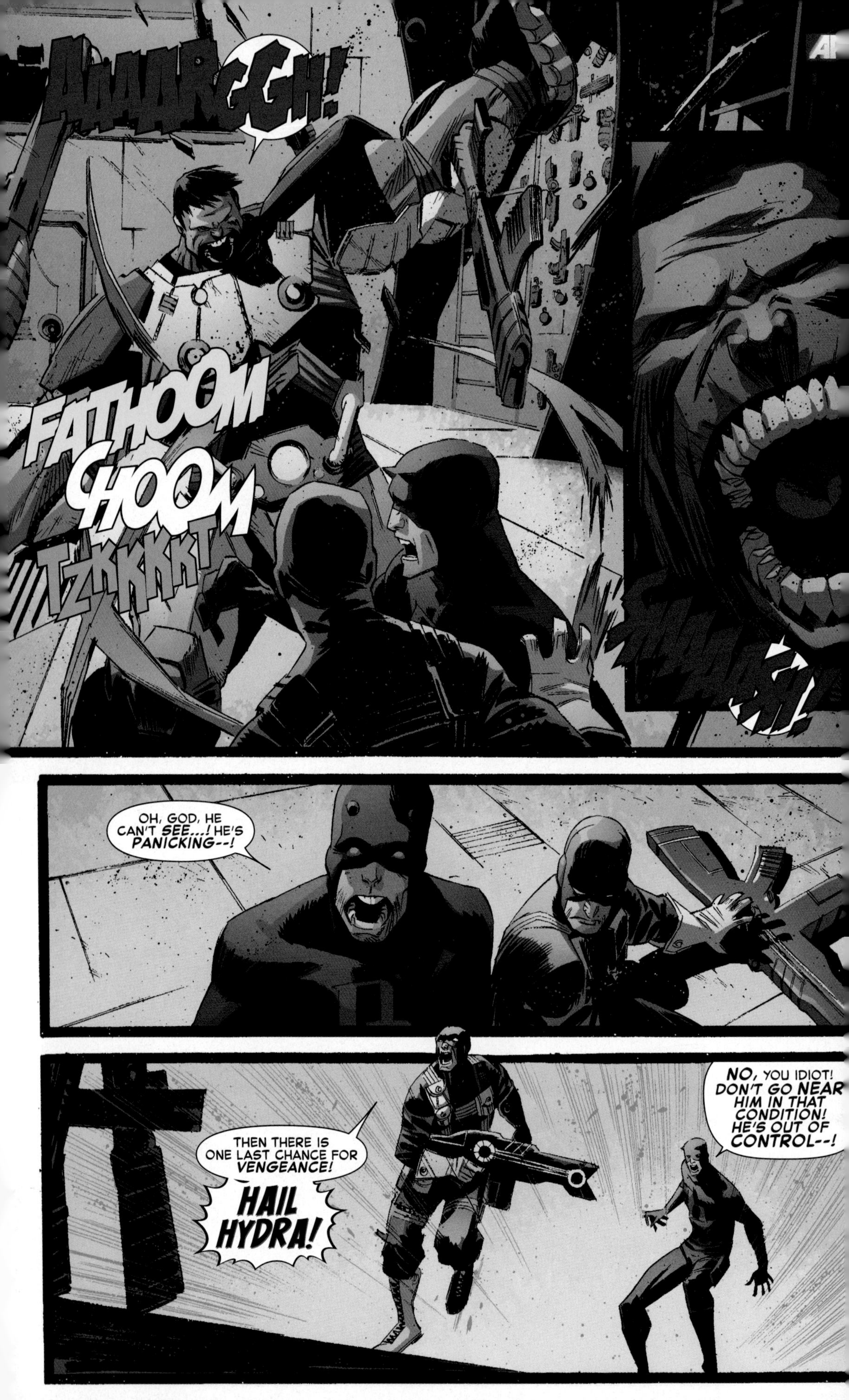
AAAARGGH!
FATHOOM
CHOOM
TZKKKT
OH, GOD, HE CAN'T SEE...! HE'S PANICKING--!
THEN THERE IS ONE LAST CHANCE FOR VENGEANCE!
HAIL HYDRA!
NO, YOU IDIOT! DON'T GO NEAR HIM IN THAT CONDITION! HE'S OUT OF CONTROL--!

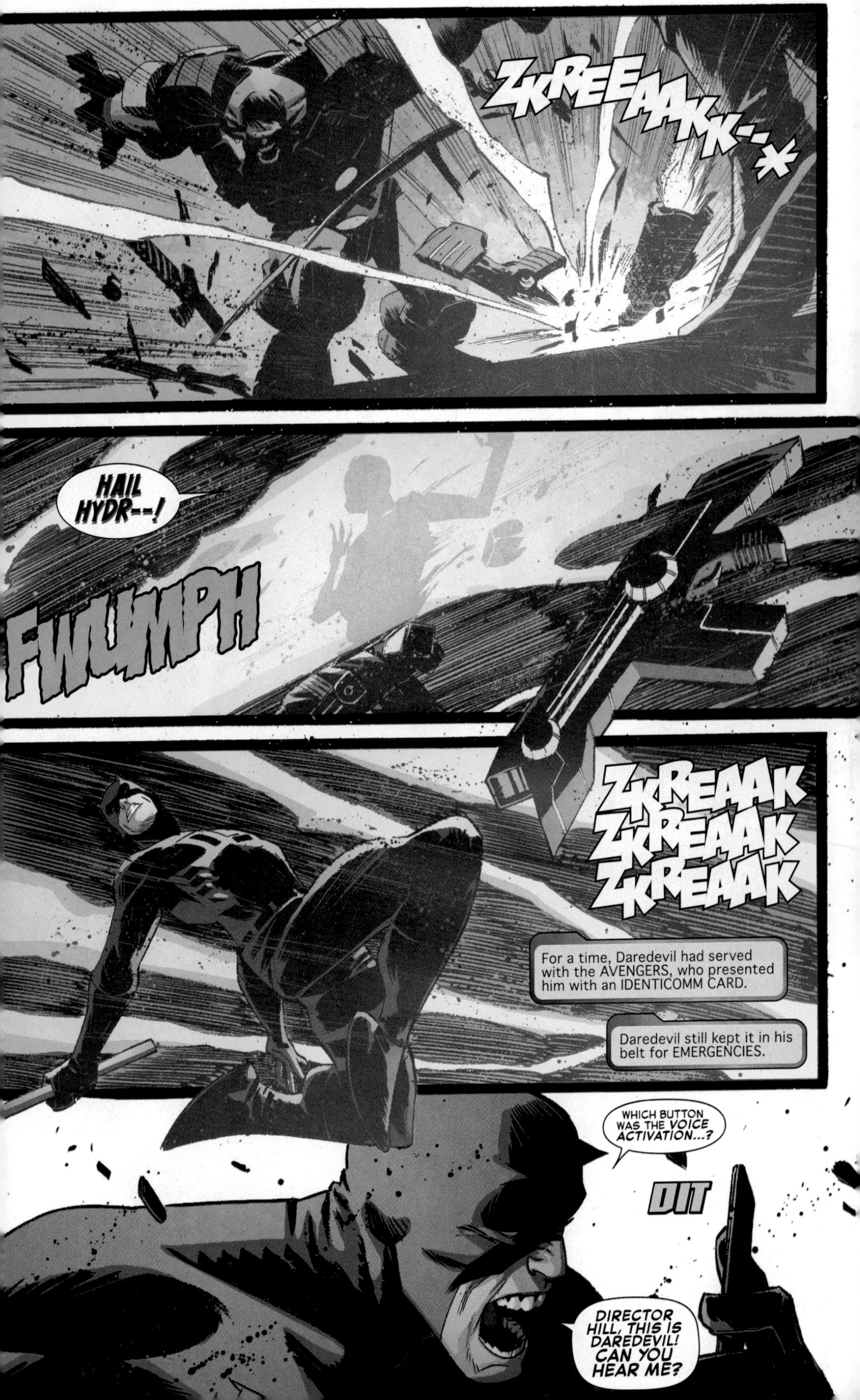
ZKREEAAKK--*
HAIL HYDR--!
FWUMPH
ZKREAAK ZKREAAK ZKREAAK
For a time, Daredevil had served with the AVENGERS, who presented him with an IDENTICOMM CARD.
Daredevil still kept it in his belt for EMERGENCIES.
WHICH BUTTON WAS THE VOICE ACTIVATION...?
DIT
DIRECTOR HILL, THIS IS DAREDEVIL! CAN YOU HEAR ME?

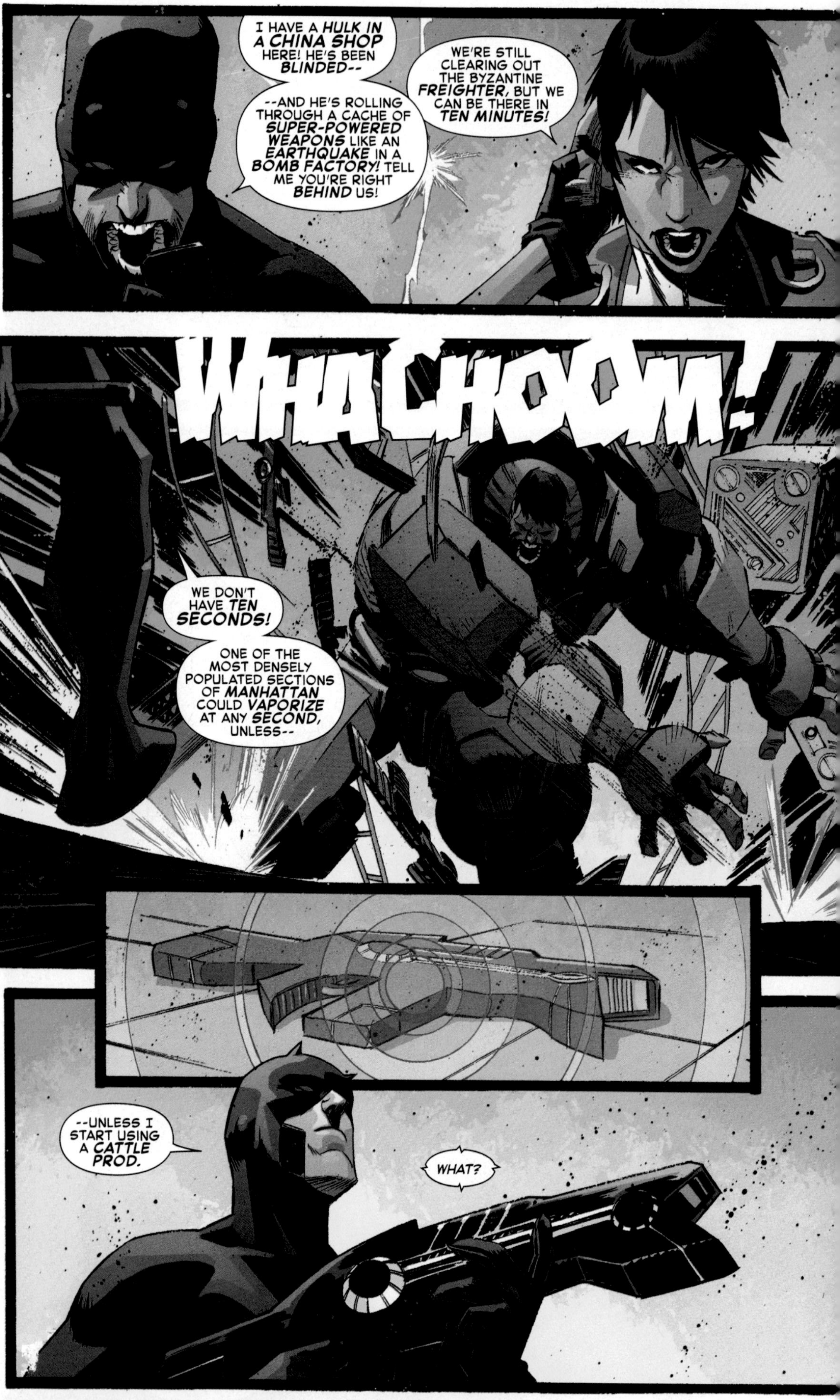

I HAVE A HULK IN A CHINA SHOP HERE! HE'S BEEN BLINDED--
--AND HE'S ROLLING THROUGH A CACHE OF SUPER-POWERED WEAPONS LIKE AN EARTHQUAKE IN A BOMB FACTORY! TELL ME YOU'RE RIGHT BEHIND US!
WE'RE STILL CLEARING OUT THE BYZANTINE FREIGHTER, BUT WE CAN BE THERE IN TEN MINUTES!
WHACHOOM!
WE DON'T HAVE TEN SECONDS!
ONE OF THE MOST DENSELY POPULATED SECTIONS OF MANHATTAN COULD VAPORIZE AT ANY SECOND, UNLESS--
--UNLESS I START USING A CATTLE PROD.
WHAT?

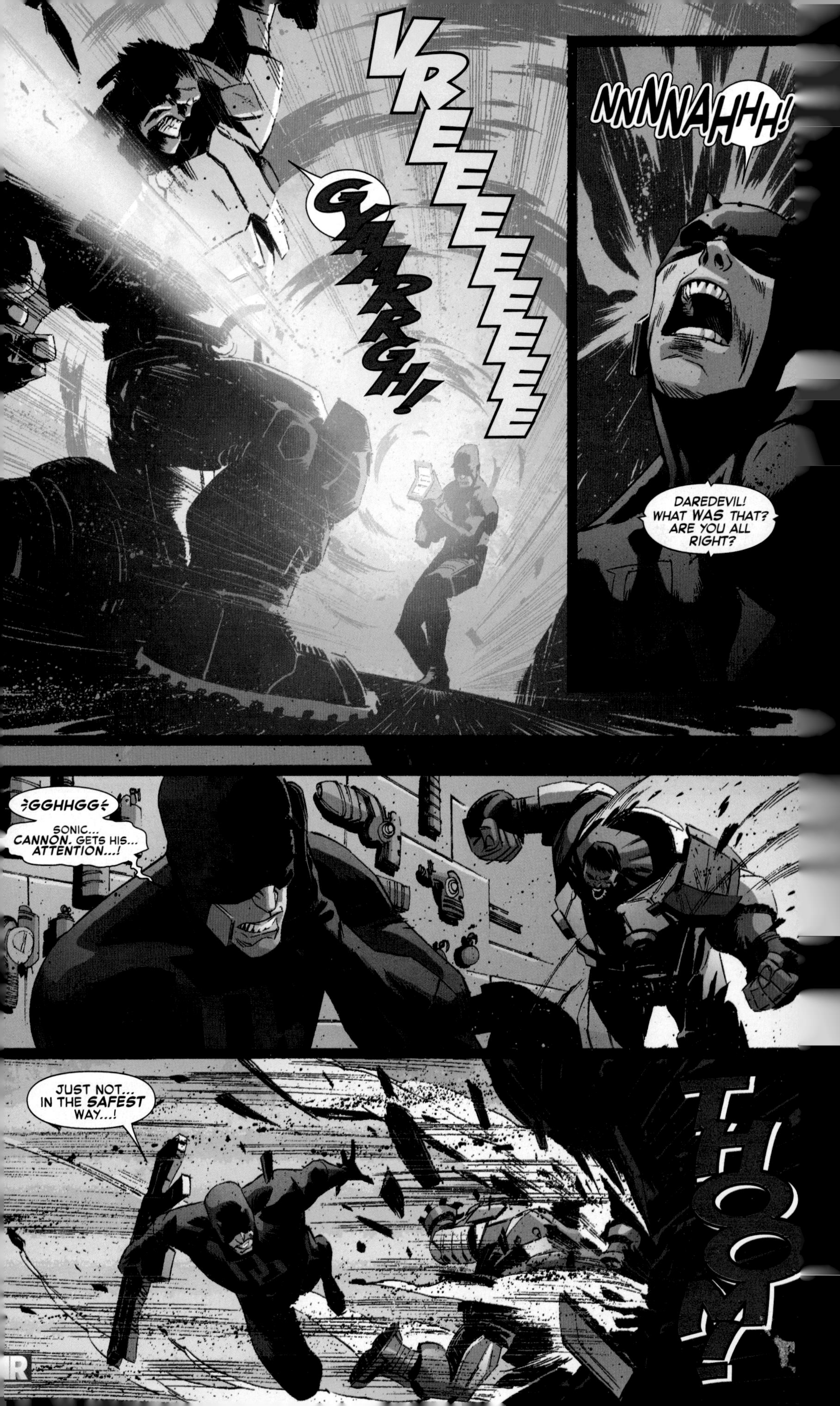
VREEEEEEEEEEE
GWARRGH!
NNNNAHHH!
DAREDEVIL! WHAT WAS THAT? ARE YOU ALL RIGHT?
GGHHGG
SONIC... CANNON. GETS HIS... ATTENTION...!
JUST NOT... IN THE SAFEST WAY...!
THOOM!

GREEN ALERT! I REPEAT, GREEN ALERT! PATCH BANNER'S LAB RATS INTO THIS LINE NOW!

VETERI, ARE YOU THERE?

He was. All the assistants were. And they are QUICK STUDIES.

OPTIONS!

THERE'S RESEARCH ON USING ULTRASOUND AS A MOOD STABILIZER IN THE 60 KILOHERTZ RANGE! THAT MIGHT CALM HULK! DAREDEVIL, CAN YOU SEE SETTINGS ON THIS WEAPON?

THERE'S WHAT SEEMS TO BE AN ADJUSTMENT DIAL, BUT I...

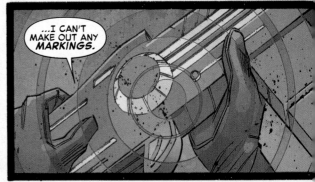

...I CAN'T MAKE OUT ANY MARKINGS.

I'LL HAVE TO DO THIS BY EAR.

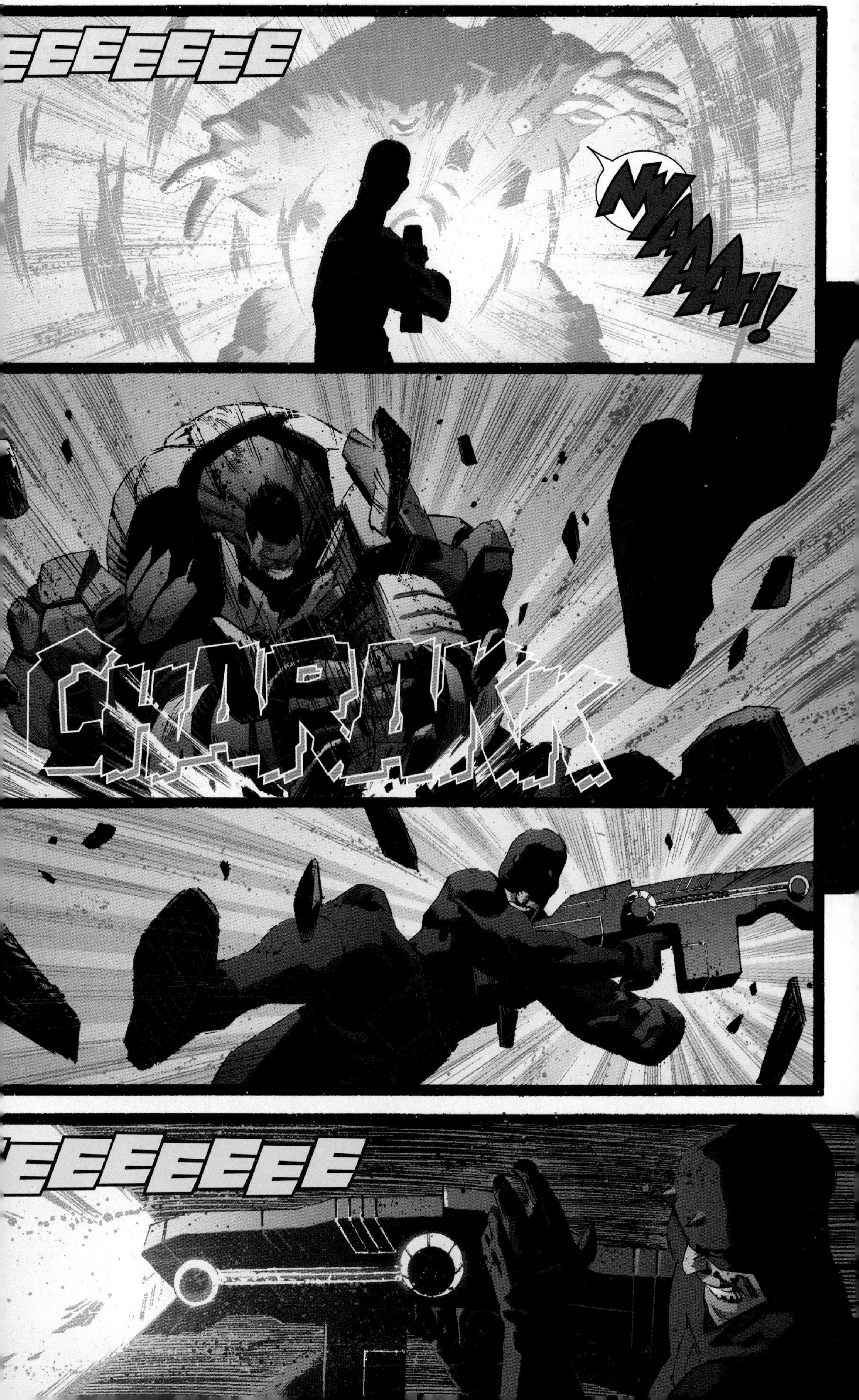
EEEEEEE
NYAAAAH!
CHUNK
EEEEEEE

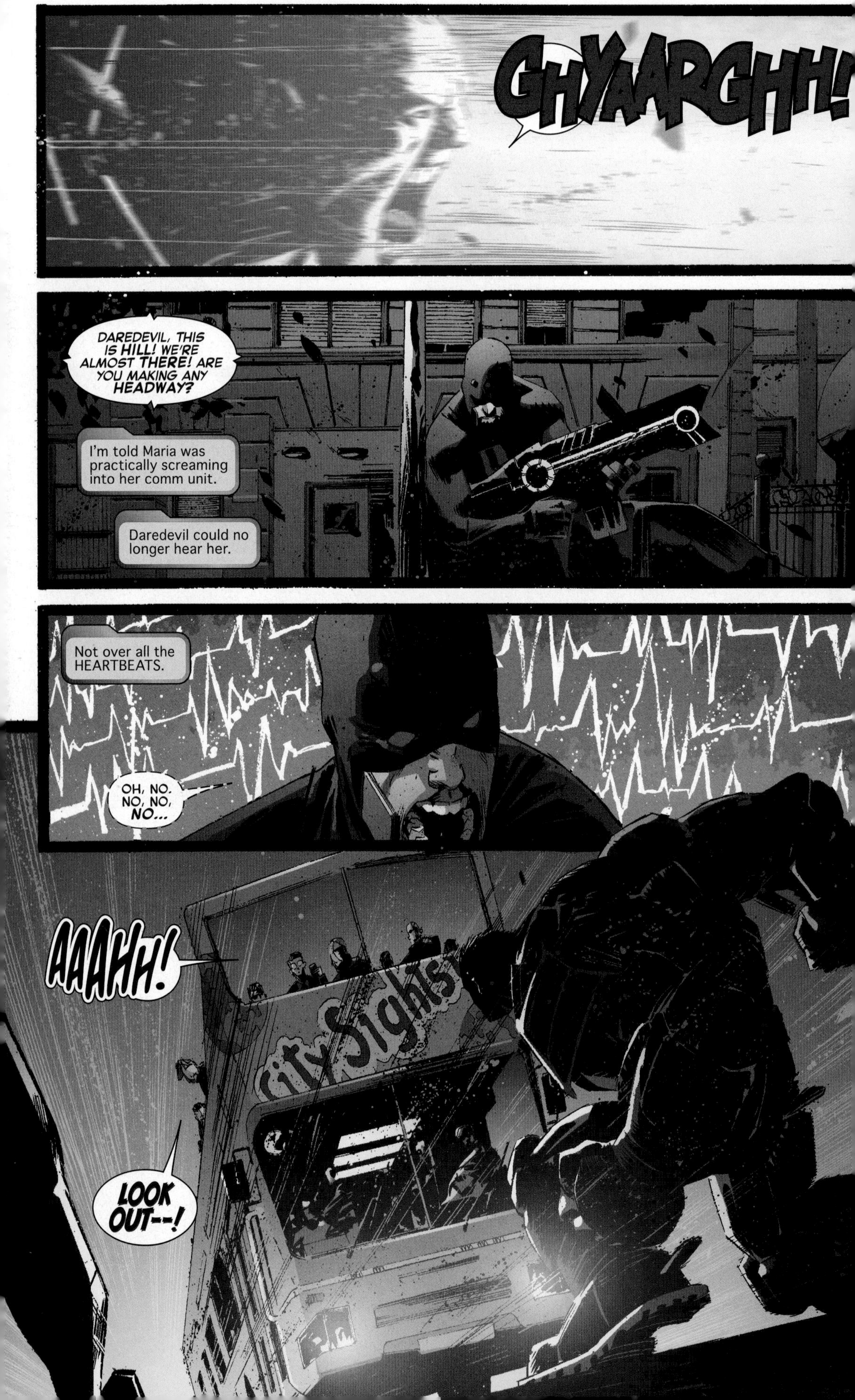
GHYAARGHH!
DAREDEVIL, THIS IS HILL! WE'RE ALMOST THERE! ARE YOU MAKING ANY HEADWAY?
I'm told Maria was practically screaming into her comm unit.
Daredevil could no longer hear her.
Not over all the HEARTBEATS.
OH, NO. NO, NO, NO...
AAAHH!
LOOK OUT--!
City Sights

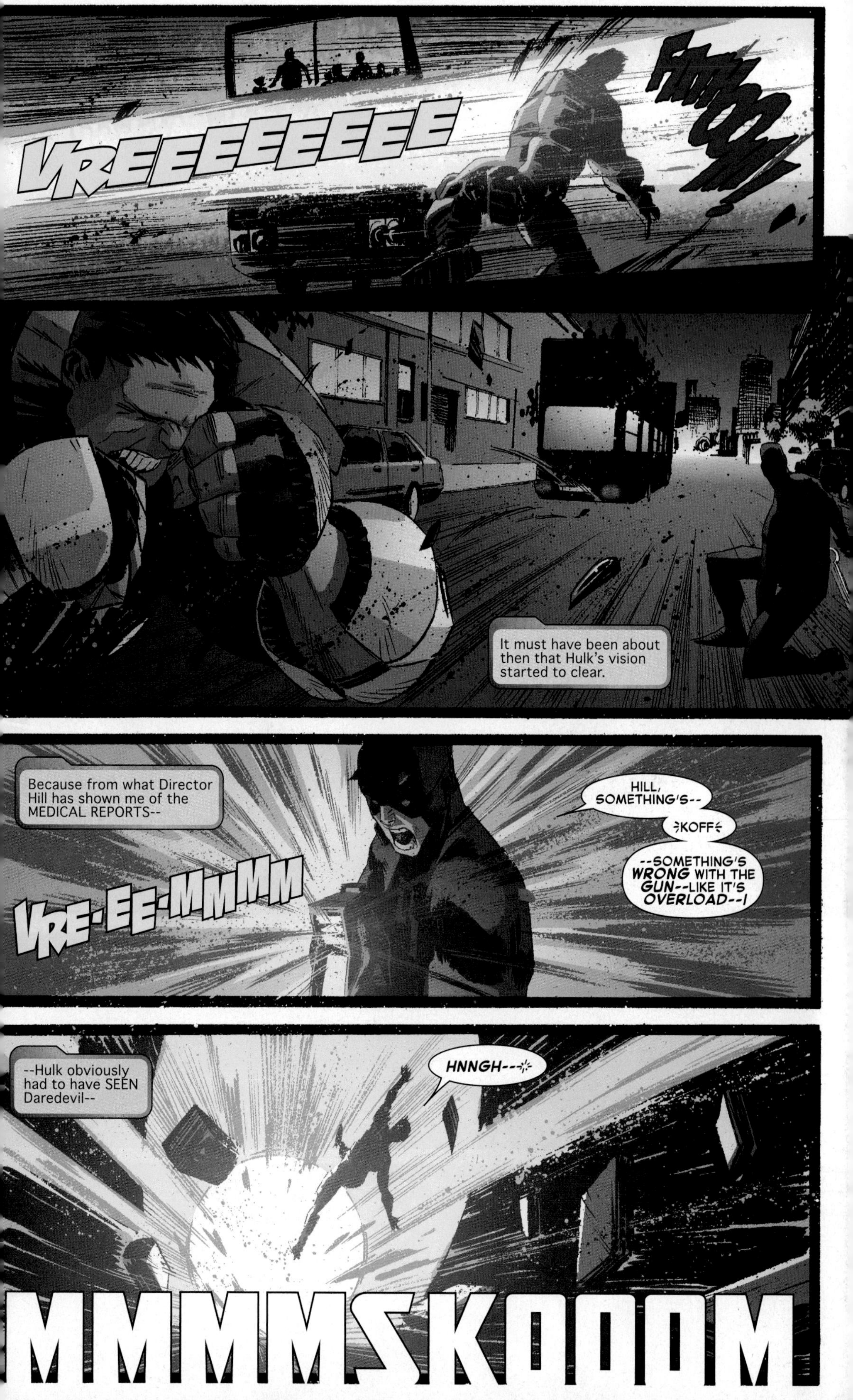

VREEEEEEEEE
FWOOM!
It must have been about then that Hulk's vision started to clear.
Because from what Director Hill has shown me of the MEDICAL REPORTS--
HILL, SOMETHING'S--
KOFF
--SOMETHING'S WRONG WITH THE GUN--LIKE IT'S OVERLOAD--I
VRE-EE-MMMM
--Hulk obviously had to have SEEN Daredevil--
HNNGH--
MMMMSKOOOM

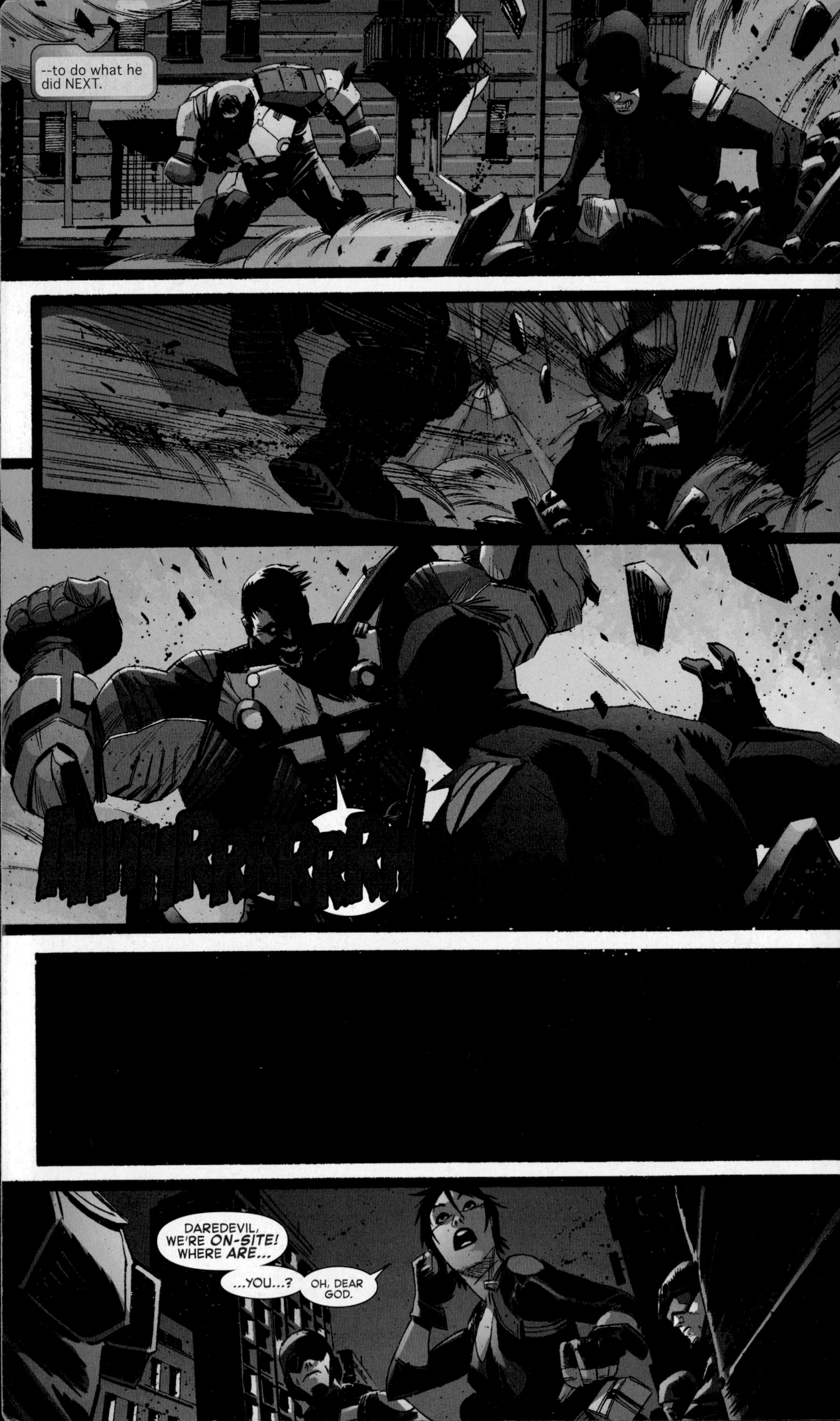
--to do what he did NEXT.
DAREDEVIL, WE'RE ON-SITE! WHERE ARE...
...YOU...?
OH, DEAR GOD.

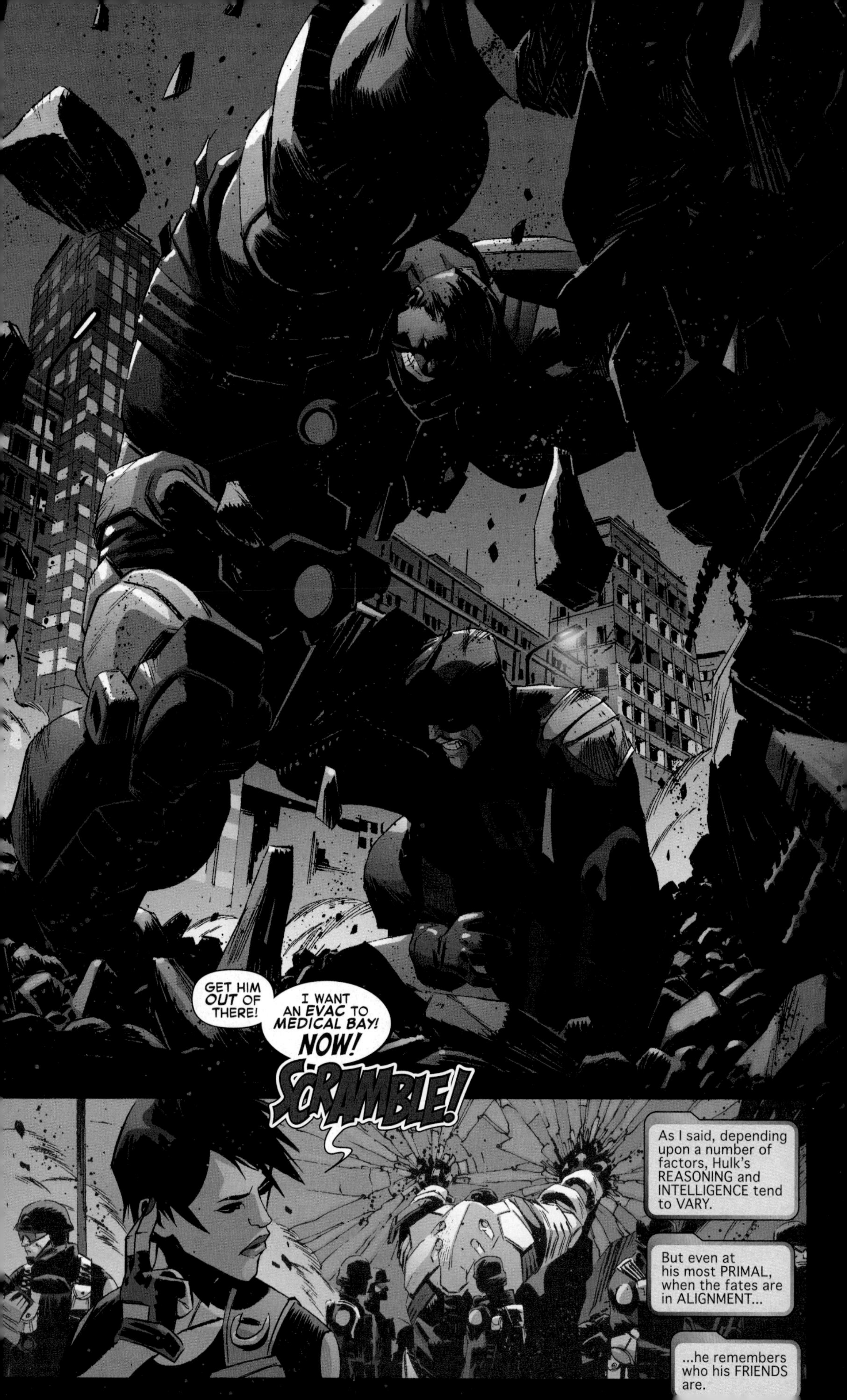
GET HIM OUT OF THERE!
I WANT AN EVAC TO MEDICAL BAY! NOW!
SCRAMBLE!
As I said, depending upon a number of factors, Hulk's REASONING and INTELLIGENCE tend to VARY.
But even at his most PRIMAL, when the fates are in ALIGNMENT...
...he remembers who his FRIENDS are.

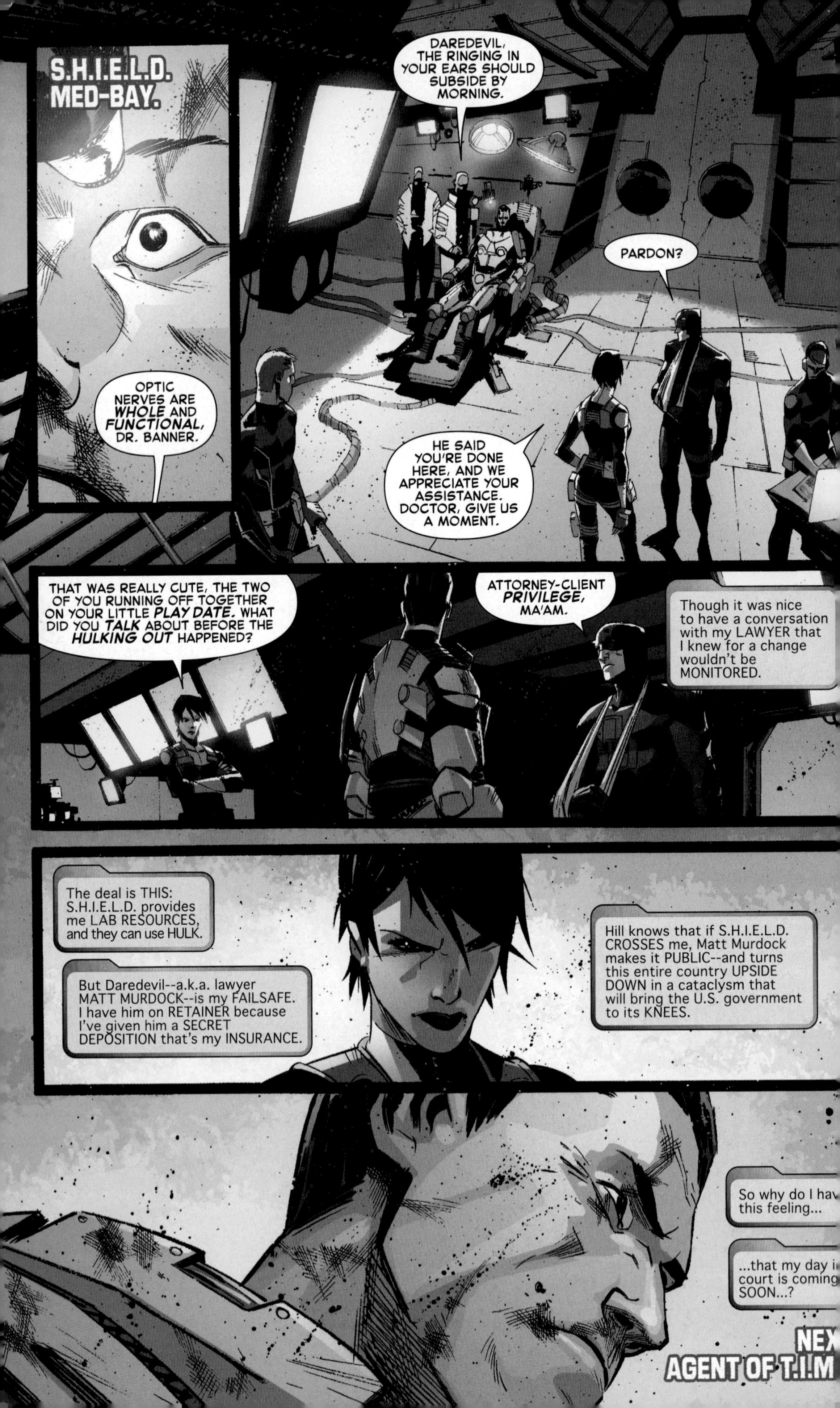
S.H.I.E.L.D. MED-BAY.
OPTIC NERVES ARE WHOLE AND FUNCTIONAL, DR. BANNER.
DAREDEVIL, THE RINGING IN YOUR EARS SHOULD SUBSIDE BY MORNING.
PARDON?
HE SAID YOU'RE DONE HERE, AND WE APPRECIATE YOUR ASSISTANCE. DOCTOR, GIVE US A MOMENT.
THAT WAS REALLY CUTE, THE TWO OF YOU RUNNING OFF TOGETHER ON YOUR LITTLE PLAY DATE. WHAT DID YOU TALK ABOUT BEFORE THE HULKING OUT HAPPENED?
ATTORNEY-CLIENT PRIVILEGE, MA'AM.
Though it was nice to have a conversation with my LAWYER that I knew for a change wouldn't be MONITORED.
The deal is THIS: S.H.I.E.L.D. provides me LAB RESOURCES, and they can use HULK.
But Daredevil--a.k.a. lawyer MATT MURDOCK--is my FAILSAFE. I have him on RETAINER because I've given him a SECRET DEPOSITION that's my INSURANCE.
Hill knows that if S.H.I.E.L.D. CROSSES me, Matt Murdock makes it PUBLIC--and turns this entire country UPSIDE DOWN in a cataclysm that will bring the U.S. government to its KNEES.
So why do I hav this feeling...
...that my day i court is coming SOON...?
NEX AGENT OF T.I.M